D060475c

FOODSTYLE

FOODSTYLE

THE ART OF PRESENTING FOOD BEAUTIFULLY

MOLLY SIPLE AND IRENE SAX

LINE DRAWINGS BY RALPH MOSELEY

CROWN PUBLISHERS, INC.
NEW YORK

Copyright © 1982 by Molly Siple and Irene Sax

All rights reserved. No part of this book may be reproduced or transmitted in any form or by any means, electronic or mechanical, including photocopying, recording, or by any information storage and retrieval system, without permission in writing from the publisher.

Published by Crown Publishers, Inc., One Park Avenue, New York, New York 10016, and simultaneously in Canada by General Publishing Company Limited

Manufactured in the United States of America

Library of Congress Cataloging in Publication Data

Siple, Molly.
    Foodstyle: the art of presenting food beautifully.

    1. Food presentation.   I. Sax, Irene.   II. Title.
TX652.S544   1982   641.5   82-1397
ISBN: 0-517-543699   AACR2

Design: Abigail Sturges

10 9 8 7 6 5 4 3 2 1

FIRST EDITION

Contents

Acknowledgments

I want to thank the following people for their contributions to me and to the book, in order of their appearance in my life: my mother for sending me clippings and lying awake nights thinking about the book; my stepmother for introducing me to inspired cooking; my stepfather for outfitting my kitchen; my friends—Joie Davidow who is a natural food-stylist, Jon Naar for that first lunch, Cloud Rich who volunteered to help in the hunt for a title, Carole Hyatt because of her own successful books, Mary Grace Butler for her clipping service, Werner Erhard for showing me that people can learn from their personal experience, John Curry for giving me the highest standards of performance.

M.S.

Once I began to thank people, there would be no way to stop. No book is the accomplishment of one person, and to get to this one I was boosted and nudged and encouraged by many people. Let me thank just the first two of them, Pauline and Ben Peirez, who gave me lots of room to grow in, and their conviction that I could do anything I wanted.

I.S.

And, from both of us, our deepest gratitude and love to Nach Waxman, our editor; also to Naomi Kleinberg at Crown; and thanks to Virginia Wentworth who served as production editor and attended to literally hundreds of details.

Introduction

This is a food book that begins where cookbooks leave off.

Cookbooks tell you how to turn raw materials into finished dishes; *Foodstyle* shows you how to make those dishes look as good as they can. Cookbooks tell you how long to grill a slice of salmon; *Foodstyle* shows you that by placing the salmon on a bed of spinach you can make the plate sing with color. Cookbooks give you recipes for beef stew; this book tells you what to do when the gravy turns out a watery gray instead of the rich mahogany you'd pictured.

Foodstyle is a book of technique. It tells you five ways to slice a tomato and ten ways to braid a roll. How to arrange cold cuts on a platter. How to cut a sandwich—a dozen new ways. It is for the accomplished cook, to whom cooking is already an aesthetic experience, who hopes, by learning about presentation (the technical name for our subject), to expand the pleasures of the palate to new adventures for the eye.

Foodstyle is divided into five parts.

Part 1, BASIC PRINCIPLES, consists of approximately a dozen essays on the theory of foodstyling. These treat the fundamentals of presentation, including such subjects as arrangement, color, garnishing and the design of visual focal points. They tell you not where to put the parsley but how to use a garnish; not what goes with green beans but what goes with green. These principles are meant to provide you with the basis for your use of—

Part 2, FOODSTYLING. This section constitutes the core of the book. It consists of a long set of entries on familiar foods, alphabetically arranged, from anchovies to zucchini. For each there is a discussion of how the food looks at its best, how it is kept looking that way, how to preserve its appearance in cooking, how to garnish it, how to select what goes with it, what to serve it in and how to arrange it. This is a quick reference section. The reader should be able to turn to it half an hour before supper to learn what looks good with broccoli, how to arrange a platter of chicken breasts or what to sprinkle on top of the soup.

We should point out here that although FOODSTYLING does constitute the bulk of this volume, it is our hope that, in due course, as you absorb the principles in Part 1, you will come to see the material in Part 2 as examples of foodstyling rather than as prescriptions and will, in fact, be able to minimize your use of these entries. It is our thought that once your consciousness has been raised and you begin to see with educated eyes what you put on a plate, you will be liberated to make your own design decisions, more creative and personal than any you could get from this or from any other book.

Part 3, TABLE STYLING, consists of entries on the basics of arranging the table—from doing a correct place setting to selecting proper glassware to folding napkins to using such special elements as centerpieces, candle-holders and trays.

Part 4, INTERNATIONAL TABLES, provides through individual articles information on styling a table for the major international cuisines—Italian, Indian, Mexican, Chinese and others. The idea is to provide elementary information on the usual ingredients that make an authentic ethnic table.

Part 5, HOLIDAY TABLES, consists of pieces on special table arrangements and service for Easter, Halloween, Thanksgiving and Christmas.

Is foodstyling a lot of trouble? That's the surprise: it turns out to be no trouble at all. Cutting a lemon with elegance takes little more effort than hacking it in half. Adding cherry tomatoes and black olives to broiled sole is next to no work.

It is ultimately a matter of training yourself to notice how things look. Once you put sliced tomato salad on a black plate, you'll never put it on white again. Once you've served a fine cut of meat breathtakingly garnished, you'll never again be satisfied with putting out a roast to fend for itself. That's what this book is all about, and once you become aware of foodstyling, you will find yourself making good design choices automatically, creating order and beauty in everything you cook.

1

BASIC PRINCIPLES

This section is about the principles of foodstyling. How do you arrange food on a plate? How do you put a food with another that will enhance its color? Where do you put the garnish, when do you use a glaze?

Don't, please, skip over it in your haste to read about cutting sandwiches or decorating cakes. Once you have these principles firmly fixed in your mind, you won't really need the second section at all. Your own eye will be sharpened and your own techniques improved. And then, if you're given the job of slicing the tomatoes for supper, you'll know without asking what color plate to choose, what slices to make, how to lay them on the plate and what to use for a garnish.

Arrangement

The world is full of patterns: the slanted backs of books on a bookshelf, the curve of a golfer's arm at the end of his swing, the tension between the little pom-poms on a cheerleader's shoes and the big pom-poms in her hands. Artists see these patterns all the time. Most of us ignore them.

But if we are to become true foodstylists, we have to become sensitive to the patterns around us and adapt them to our presentation of food. We call this technique arrangement, by which we mean the orderly and pleasing grouping of food on a plate, a bowl or a platter.

The first step is to begin to look, really look. Raise your consciousness to the designs around you. Luckily, there aren't so many patterns in the world that one is reserved for embroidery and another for layer cakes. Keep your eyes open, and you'll notice that the same patterns appear everywhere: on tiles, in fabrics, as well as in the vegetables grouped around a Thanksgiving turkey.

(Many of them exist in poetry and music as well. An *abab* rhyme scheme—june/boy/moon/joy—is first cousin to a border arrangement of olive/radish/olive/radish!)

The next step is to use these patterns very consciously in your kitchen. Never just put the supper on the plate. Think, "I have a lamb chop, a baked potato and frozen peas. How do I arrange them on the plate?" At first it will be an effort just to remember to ask the question. But soon you'll find that merely asking the question puts you halfway to the answer.

First we are going to describe some linear, one-dimensional motifs, the kind that appear in strings of beads, chains and borders. Then we move on to two-dimensional compositions. You use these when you arrange foods on the two-dimensional canvas of a plate or platter. And then we will see that three-dimensional motifs, those found in piles and mounds of food, are usually extensions of the two-dimensional plans.

One-Dimensional Designs

Begin with borders. Each one uses only one, two or three elements. They could just as well be do re mi or June boy sky. But in this book, we think of them as a tomato wedge, a sprig of watercress and half a hard-boiled egg. Once you've learned how to make patterns, you'll find that you can do them anywhere and with anything.

aaaaa. The first pattern is a simple *aaa,* an unvarying linear chain. It's a string of popcorn for the Christmas tree, a border of watercress sprigs or the circle of duchesse potato puffs surrounding a planked steak.

abab. The next—and infinitely more interesting—pattern is *abab:* tomato/watercress/tomato/watercress. This simple rhythmic alternation is much used in folk art. Think of a pleated skirt (zig/zag/

1

2

2

zig/zag) or the in-and-out ruffle around a piecrust. *(Fig. 1)*

aaaab aaaab. Extend one of the elements, and you have the next pattern. It's a string of beads with one gold bead after every eight or ten jade beads. Or it's a border of watercress leaves interrupted every three inches by a cherry tomato. *(Fig. 2)*

aba aba. Now change the sequence, adding an empty space like a musical rest. This is a more sophisticated design than the earlier ones, because it includes what artists call negative space. On the edge of a platter that holds a roast turkey, put down groupings of tomato/watercress/tomato, with spaces between the groupings. *(Fig. 3)*

abaCaba. Now, in place of the pause, put in a third element, and notice how the new element gains importance by this design. You now have an unbroken border around your turkey of tomato/watercress/tomato/EGG/tomato/watercress/tomato. *(Fig. 4)*

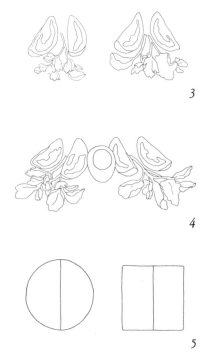

3

4

5

You can vary and extend these patterns in many ways. The simple *abab* might be broken up into *ab*(pause)*ab*. Or it could be extended into *abcabc* or even *abcdabcd*. But psychologists have discovered that we can only take in a series of five elements at a glance. After that, our vision, searching for order, breaks up the long chain into clusters. We perceive a series of six numbers as three plus three. We read the seven digits of a telephone number (MU 7-1234) as a group of three (MU7) and a group of four (1234). Your social security number, which has nine digits, is broken into three groups of three, two and four numbers, in the hopes that it will be easier to remember.

Two-Dimensional Design: Arranging a Plate

So far we have been arranging lines, stringing beads on a thread. Once we take one of the lines and use it to make a border around a scoop of ice cream, or to divide the sliced tomatoes from the sliced cucumbers, we have moved from one-dimensional to two-dimensional design. We have moved from lines to planes.

Two-part divisions. The simplest division of a plane is in two equal parts. That's a pizza that's half mushroom and half pepperoni, a sandwich cut in two, up and down or on the diagonal, or a cupcake iced half in chocolate and half in vanilla. *(Fig. 5)*

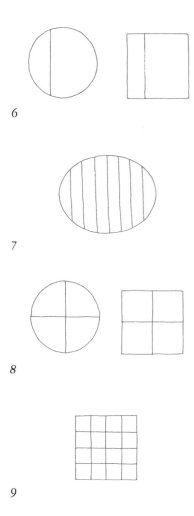

6

7

8

9

10

Move the dividing line to one side of the plane, and you have two unequal parts. Cover two thirds of the plate with scrambled eggs and the remaining third with ham. Cover three quarters of a Danish open-faced sandwich with smoked salmon and the remaining quarter with cream cheese. *(Fig. 6)*

Multiple divisions. When you add more lines to the plate, you have stripes. Make a stripe of melon slices down the center of an oval serving plate, and arrange stripes of strawberries and banana ovals in lines parallel to it. Draw thin lines of white icing over the top of a chocolate cake. Put a fish fillet in the center of a dinner plate, with potatoes on one side and green beans on the other. *(Fig. 7)*

Now cross the first lines. When you take a plane that was divided into two parts and cross the first line with a second, you have a plane cut into quarters. The obvious example is a sandwich cut into four quarters. What about a cold-cut platter with quarters of ham, Swiss cheese, salami and sliced chicken? *(Fig. 8)*

When you cross a striped pattern with a second set of stripes, you have a checkerboard arrangement. This is often used by caterers in laying out sandwiches or canapés on a platter. It's what you get when you draw one set of lines on a sheet cake, and then draw a second set perpendicular to the first. *(Fig. 9)*

Radiating design. Think about the four-part division of the plane again. Instead of focusing on the spaces, focus on the lines this time. If you add more lines coming out from the central point, you will create a radiating pattern, one in which the elements are arranged like the spokes of a wheel or the petals of a daisy. *(Fig. 10)*

The most obvious example of radiating design are the cuts that we make in a layer cake. But the next time you're in a bakery or deli, notice just how common this pattern is in food design. It's the most hackneyed way of arranging cold cuts on a platter, in lines coming from a central focal point. It's the petallike slashes in the center of a piecrust and the lines of pepperoni on a pizza.

There's a way to vary radiating compositions. Place half a hard-boiled egg in the center of a plate. Place four sprigs of watercress at the compass points around the egg. Then place four tomato wedges a bit farther out from the center and between the cress. Finally, add four slices of cucumber, again farther out, and this time in line with the cress. A design such as this can continue indefinitely. *(Fig. 11)*

11

You can add interest by moving the center of the radiating design to one side of the plate. Suppose you're serving poached eggs on English muffins, with ham and asparagus spears. To create an off-center radiating pattern, you would set the egg on the muffin to one side of the plate. On the open space, you lay three asparagus spears extending from the egg yolk, and crumple mounds of ham between them. *(Fig. 12)*

Concentric design. Another familiar design in commercial foodstyling is a concentric design, a central focus surrounded by enlarging circles. It's a bull's-eye. You decorate a pizza with gradually enlarging rings of pepperoni and anchovy circles. You pipe rings of meringue on top of a lemon pie. You put a pineapple in the middle of a fruit tray and arrange circles of fruit around it. *(Fig. 13)*

12

You can do an off-center bull's-eye, too. Go back to that egg on its English muffin, with the ham and asparagus on the side. Put the egg in the muffin to one side of the plate. Surround it with a ring of crumpled ham, and make a circle of asparagus, cut into 1-inch lengths, around the ham. *(Fig. 14)*

Medallion. A medallion is a simplification of the bull's-eye design. The Japanese influence has made people look at a plate as a frame for a single decorative element placed in its center. Think of the very complicated French designs—flowers made with vegetables and capers—that are set into aspic on the back of a ham, and you will know what a medallion is like. A flower cutout on the top of a poached egg en gelée is another medallion.

13

This is a style that often uses designs derived from nature, such as a branch (a main stem with smaller stems branching off of it) and a shell. But it uses more abstract forms as well, always surrounding them with lots of empty plate.

Put a chicken breast covered with white sauce in the center of a dinner plate. Trace a line of capers on the chicken. Put watercress at one end of the breast and a series of overlapping tomato circles at the other end. That's very chic.

Less so is a dish of cherry gelatin decorated with a flower made of four green grape halves for petals and a bit of plum skin for the stem. But it's a medallion, too.

14

5

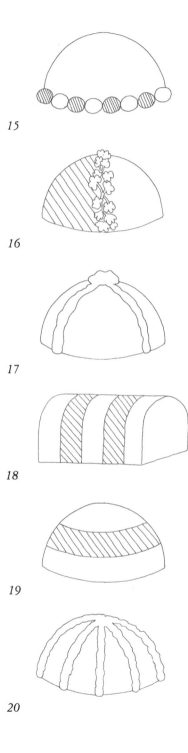

15

16

17

18

19

20

Three-Dimensional Design

Food doesn't come in only one and two dimensions. Most often, it comes in heaps and mounds. Even flat foods, such as sandwiches, are arranged to give the effect of height when we stand some of the sections on end or stick them through with toothpicks capped with cherry tomatoes. Most of the time, you use the same ideas on mounds of food as on flat foods.

Borders. Suppose you have a scoop of chicken salad, a gelatin mold or a dish of ice cream. You can make a simple *aaa* border around the edge by having lettuce stick out from under the chicken salad or making a ring of mandarin orange sections around the mold. Or you can create more complicated borders: clusters of green and purple grapes at the base of the mold *(aba aba)* or pink and white mints arranged around the dish of ice cream *(ababab)*. *(Fig. 15)*

Two- and four-part divisions. To arrange a mound in a two-part division, make a pile that is half chicken salad and half egg salad, and lay a line of parsley sprigs over the dividing line. To make a four-part division, turn an ice-cream bombe out of its domelike mold and pipe whipped cream in four lines down its sides, with a finial of whipped cream at the top. You can even make stripes on a three-dimensional food. The lines of canned apricot on the back of a ham, for example, or stripes of tomato sauce, black olives and chopped basil on a meat loaf. *(Figs. 16, 17, 18)*

Concentric design. Three-dimensional foods are well suited to concentric designs. Make circles of sieved egg and others of chopped scallion greens that start at the top of a mound of ham salad. *(Fig. 19)*

Radiating design. Arrange the same chopped egg and scallions like spokes on an umbrella on the mound of egg salad. *(Fig. 20)*

Three-dimensional designs often need a finishing touch, a cap at the top to hold the whole thing together. This is the cherry on the whipped cream or the finial of fruit on the peak of the gelatin mold. Cross strips of pimiento or tongue on top of a scoop of egg salad. Cover the surface of a gelatin mold with thin lemon half-slices in a concentric design. Then put a lemon twist at the very top of the mold. *(Fig. 21)*

On oval and egg shapes, make the same patterns as you did on round shapes. First locate the visual center of weight. In an oval, it will be halfway down the plate or the meat loaf. But in an egg-shaped food, such as a ham or an eggplant, it will be toward the wider end. That's where you start the radiating spokes of cloves on the surface of the ham. *(Fig. 22)*

Try to keep your eye fresh and your touch varied. If your impulse is always to frame food with a border, try changing and doing a bull's-eye instead.

Think about pattern every time you arrange a sandwich on a plate or put fruit into a bowl. Make order everywhere.

Au gratin. *See* GLAZING

Carving

The ability to carve is essential for the presentation of meat. Badly carved meat has to be masked with sauce, hidden underneath better pieces, served with apologies. Well-carved meat can stand proudly on its own.

Carving used to be the prerogative of the man of the house. Now it is generally done by whoever does the cooking.

To learn to carve, you should have an acquaintance with anatomy, a set of good knives and a piece of meat that has been allowed to rest for 20 minutes out of the oven so that it becomes firm. It helps if you can watch the work of a skillful carver. Failing that, careful attention to a book on the subject will do. Some useful texts are *The Art of Carving* by the editors of *House and Garden* and *Carving and Boning Like an Expert* by Oreste Carnevali. And don't overlook the help offered in such general cookbooks as *The Joy of Cooking, The Fannie Farmer Cookbook* and James Beard's *Theory and Practice of Good Cooking.*

Chaudfroid. *See* GLAZING

21

22

Color

Good food has good color: brilliant green spinach, scarlet beef, the ivory of a newly peeled banana. The food industry, aware of our response to the color of food, takes advantage of it. They dye our oranges orange, our cherries red. They paint black stripes on hamburgers to make them look as though they were cooked over coals. When they manufacture processed foods, they spend more time and money in getting the right color than the right flavor.

Maintaining Color

All cooks know about the connection between eye and appetite. They try to preserve the color of healthy food and to restore it when it is lost. Apples, bananas and pears turn brown when they're exposed to air, but the cook knows how to prevent this by squeezing lemon juice over the cut fruit.

Some metals react badly with the acid in food. Aluminum is a notorious discolorer of tomatoes and spinach. The knowledgeable cook uses a stainless-steel or enameled-steel pot when making tomato sauce.

The scarlet color of red cabbage fades in heat unless an acid, such as vinegar, is added. From that fact we get sweet-and-sour cabbage.

Chlorophyll, the green coloring in plants, turns yellow-brown in an acid solution. You've seen it happen when you squeezed lemon over broccoli. When a green vegetable is boiled, its cell walls burst, releasing acid juices that turn it pale and sickly looking.

In the 1930s it was common practice to add baking soda to vegetable cooking water in order to neutralize the acid and retain the green color. Now we know that the best way to retain the strong natural color of vegetables is to cook them only to the point when they are precisely done.

Adding Color

The practice of adding color to food is questionable, on the grounds of aesthetics, health and flavor. Visually, it's the same kind of aesthetic that dyes a white carnation blue by sticking its stem into inky water. As far as health is concerned, food dyes are now among the most common and potentially the most troublesome of food additives. Red dye no. 4 may well be the tip of the iceberg as far as toxicity is concerned, and doctors are beginning to suspect that many people are allergic to all food additives.

But there are occasions when you must dye food an unnatural color—when, for example, you want to put green icing on a cookie, and chopped parsely just doesn't seem right. Then buy vegetable coloring, which is completely flavorless. Coloring is used mainly on baked goods, especially icings. Used with caution, one drop at a time, vegetable dyes allow us to create pastel tints for birthday and holiday baking.

There is a more legitimate kind of color fakery—legitimate because the color boost comes with an appropriate boost in flavor.

There are times when we buy the freshest food available and cook it as well as we can, but something goes wrong and it turns gray and uninteresting. Then it's perfectly legitimate to restore or intensify the color by natural means.

We encourage the formation of a rich brown crust on roasts and fowl by basting them with pan drippings. We add hearty mahogany color to stews with the addition of a little caramelized sugar to the gravy. We help breads and pastries form brown crusts by glazing them with butter, beaten egg or sugar.

Boiled beef is boiled beef. Boiled lamb is worse. But both turn a rich dark brown when we fry onions so that the sugar in the onion caramelizes and turns brown, then add the onions to the pot.

We intensify reds by adding beet juice, red wine or strawberry or cranberry juice, depending on the flavor that is wanted. Think of red-colored pasta, made so by the addition of tomato paste or grated beets.

We add green color with chopped parsley, watercress or spinach. Again, think of spinach or basil pasta.

And we can turn rice orange by cooking it in tomato sauce, turmeric or saffron water.

9

Enhancing Food Color

These are tricks that intensify the true colors of food. We can enhance the apparent color of the food by placing it in the right setting. This is done by using other foods or plates of contrasting color.

Supermarket tomatoes of a dubious red will look as though they're bursting with health when they're served on a bed of dark green arugula. Strawberries seem to pop with health when you put them on a white or black plate.

This is the result both of contrast and of color law. Contrast is easy to understand. In optics texts, they show you two gray circles: one against a white background, the other against a black background. Although both grays are the same, the circle on the black background looks lighter because of the contrast.

The same effect occurs when we place a bright cherry on a mound of whipped cream, when we set a black olive cutout on a poached chicken breast, making it seem light and clear, or put a hard-boiled egg slice on pale pink salmon to make it a darker red.

Let's get back to the less-than-perfect tomato that came to life on a bed of arugula. It would have looked dismal on pale iceberg lettuce. But it wasn't only the light-dark contrast that made it look brighter. It was also one of the basic principles of color harmony, known to art students as the law of simultaneous contrast. This states that colors standing opposite one another in the color wheel lend brilliance and purity to one another. You're familiar with this phenomenon from the party game in which you stare hard at a color and then at white paper, on which you see an afterimage in the complement of the first color.

Look at a simplified color circle, the same one you had on your kindergarten wall. There are three primary colors—red, yellow and blue—and three secondary colors—orange, green and purple. When you juxtapose two colors that are opposite each other on the circle, each will seem to be more intense than when it stands alone. It's true not only for our supermarket tomato, but also for the less common pairs of purple and yellow (grapes and yellow plums, eggplant and summer squash) and blue and orange (blueberries and orange sections). *(Fig. 23)*

There are other color harmonies you should know about. They

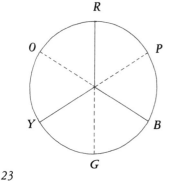

23

10

are the analogous and monochromatic combinations. If you want to create a subtle effect, put a color with another tone of the same color or with one that's next to it on the color wheel. When you mix oranges and lemons in a white bowl, you're choosing colors that are analogous—next to one another on the circle. When you make a stir-fry of broccoli, celery and scallions, or a mixed green salad, you're using monochromatic harmony, selecting tones and values of the same color.

Always suit the scheme to the character of the food. A Mexican dish of green peppers stuffed with corn and red beans is appropriately intense in color and seasoning. A breakfast tray of poached eggs, toast and milky coffee is a cool, monochromatic composition that eases you gently into the day.

All omelets are bright yellow. You can fill one with a highly seasoned ratatouille or with Italian sausage, and set it on a purple plate. But if the omelet is seasoned with nothing more fiery than a sprinkling of fines herbes or some Gruyère cheese, try garnishing it coolly with sprigs of green parsley (next door to yellow on the color circle) and putting it on a white plate.

Keep your eyes open. Think about color. Notice for example, how much of the food we eat is green, red or brown, how little is purple or blue. Notice that most garnishes are dark—parsley, olives, tomatoes—and serve to brighten the food with which they are set.

Foods Listed by Color

This list was made, with no apologies, solely on the basis of color. There is no suggestion that the foods go together in taste or texture or style. But if you have arranged a plate and think that it needs a touch of red, or of yellow, you could turn to the appropriate list and choose—if it's a salad—radishes or yellow squash, or—if it's a fruit plate—cherries or pineapples.

Red

apple	cherry
blood orange	currant
Bosc pear	pink grapefruit

Red (cont.)

plums	tomato
pomegranate	
raspberry	caviar
rhubarb	crabs
strawberry	lobster
watermelon	red snapper
beet	salmon
Italian onion	shrimp
radish	
red lentils	red-rind cheese: Gouda, Edam,
red leaf lettuce	Fontina
red pepper	

Orange

apricot	Persian melon
cantaloupe	persimmon
clementine	pumpkin
Crenshaw melon	tangerine
kumquat	acorn squash
mango	carrot
nectarine	sweet potatoes
orange	
papaya	Cheddar cheese
peach	

Yellow

apple	turnips: rutabaga
banana	wax bean
Bartlett pear	yellow pepper
Comice pear	yellow squash
grapefruit	yellow tomato
lemon	
mango	butter
pineapple	cheese
corn	

Green

Anjou pear	fig
apple	gooseberries

avocado
greengage plums
honeydew
kiwi
lime
watermelon
winter melon

pistachio nuts
artichoke
asparagus
basil
broccoli
Brussels sprouts
cabbage
celery
cucumber

grapes

fennel
greens for salad: Boston, romaine,
    iceberg, escarole, etc.
green pepper
leeks
olive
parsley
peas
pea pods
scallion
spinach
string beans
watercress
zucchini

Brown

coconut
kiwi
Seckel pear

chocolate
croutons

meat
nuts
barley
fried onions
lentils
wheat berries

Black (purple-black)

blackberry
blueberry
fig
grapes
prune
prune plums
raisins

black beans
eggplant
olive
truffle

caviar
mussels

Purple-scarlet

boysenberry
cranberry
fig
grape

plum
beet
cabbage
red onion

White *(fruit interiors)*

apple	celeriac
banana	dried white bean
casaba melon	endive
coconut	mushroom
pear	onion
lichee	parsnip
	potato
fish fillets	rice
scallops	scallion bulbs
bamboo shoots	turnip
bean sprouts	water chestnut
cauliflower	white radish

Equipment

We've made a list of the equipment we reached for most often as we tested ideas for this book. Since food decorating grows naturally from one's regular cooking, it really shouldn't require equipment of its own. But there are certain items you shouldn't be without.

Some are essential. You cannot slice a tomato attractively without a sharp knife.

Others are convenient, but have functions that can be performed adequately, if not so efficiently, with a good knife. Do you *need* an apple corer? It's hard to say.

Then there are pieces of equipment that you probably can do without most of the time, but will be grateful for when you have certain very special tasks to do. Aspic cutters and melon ballers fall into this category.

And finally, there are those everyday gadgets that you're likely to forget just because they are so common. Such as a sharp pair of scissors for cutting stencils or snipping parsley.

1. *Knives.* Good knives, kept perfectly sharp. At the least, you must have a paring knife, a serrated knife for bread and tomatoes, a chef's knife for general cutting and a long straight carving knife. And

a. *grapefruit knife*

b. *lemon zester*

c. *lemon stripper*

d. *butter curler*

e. *fluted oval melon baller*

f. *round melon baller*

g. *fluted knife*

h. *aspic cutter*

i. *aspic cutter*

j. *individual gelatin mold*

24

because we mean it when we say sharp, you'll also have to have a good sharpening steel or ceramic bar and remember to use it.

2. *Other cutters.* Most cost very little, and they can make all the difference. We don't suggest that you buy all the gadgets on the market—the egg-slicers and radish-flower makers—whose job can be done as easily with a paring knife. But you might want to think about these:

a. *lemon zester.* It strips tiny slivers from the outer skin of the peel.

b. *lemon stripper.* It makes ¼-inch widths of peel, just right for a twist in a glass of soda water.

c. *lemon peeler.* Or potato peeler. Or swivel peeler. Or whatever you call the scraping tool that is the most reached-for gadget in our kitchen drawer.

d. *cookie cutters.* They do a better job than a glass, because they have sharp cutting edges and come in more interesting shapes.

e. *aspic or truffle cutters.* They're like little cookie cutters, and you use them when you decorate with olive, pimiento, egg white.

f. *fluting knife.* You can live without one, but it makes a nice waffled slice of beet, turnip or carrot.

g. *V cutter.* Just what it sounds like. It gives a nice zigzag finish to melon or lemon halves.

h. *butter curler.* Unnecessary, but nothing else does quite the same job.

i. *mandoline.* Makes better-shaped slices than a food processor can do. Good for cutting vegetables into julienne strips. You can also do it with a knife. We grant that the mandoline isn't cheap, but it's a solid piece of equipment with a respectable culinary pedigree.

j. *pastry wheel.* Good to have for pizza, too.

k. *scissors.* Use them for snipping parsley, trimming the edges of piecrusts, cutting gashes in the top of unrisen bread, and for cutting out stencils and patterns. Kitchen shears should have stainless-steel blades. They have an uncanny way of emigrating from the kitchen drawer to the desk.

3. *Equipment for shaping.* You can use things that you have already in the kitchen, such as mixing bowls, tin cans and teacups.

a. But you should collect an assortment of *molds* for gelatin, ice cream and butter. They range from ring molds to realistic lamb and bunny molds for Easter ices.

b. In this category, we also place *ice-cream scoops.* They come in various sizes and in three shapes: round, oval and conical. Buy two sizes. Use them for potatoes, tuna salad and rice as well as for ice cream.

c. And don't forget *melon ballers.* Have them in different sizes. We suggest the ¾-inch and the 1¼-inch ballers. Buy an oval and a fluted one as well. Use the ballers for cooked beets, carrots and turnips as well as for melon.

4. *Others.* This is the grab bag.

a. *ruler.* For decorating cakes, placing elements in a mold, checking to see if you've rolled the pastry large enough, making a straight edge. As with scissors, rulers have a way of straying from the kitchen drawer.

b. *brushes.* You don't need expensive pastry brushes. Buy cheap ones from the five-and-ten, and be prepared to discard them when they get clotted with fat and egg glaze.

c. *a florist's frog.* For centerpieces. Once you have one, you'll use it a lot.

d. *wire.* Or plastic bag twist-ties. For tying up large arrangements of fruit and vegetables and attaching ribbons.

e. *toothpicks.* Also for securing: pinning the pineapple slices to the ham, folding the bologna pinwheel. And for skewering, too, which brings us to

f. *skewers.* We like the 4-inch bamboo skewers that can be bought in oriental food stores. They're good for hors d'oeuvres and for decorations. But you should also have 5-inch metal skewers used for trussing fowl and 10-inch metal skewers for dinner-sized portions of shish kebab.

g. *pastry tube and tips.* If you don't have a set, you won't miss it. Once you have it, you'll use it all the time. But buy a good one, because a cheap, inadequate tube will make a mess and frustrate all your artistic efforts.

h. *parchment paper and doilies.* The parchment paper is for lining cake pans and making stencils. The doilies are ready-made stencils.

i. *wax paper and aluminum foil.*

Flambé

Aside from getting rid of the taste of pure alcohol—which you can do as well by long, slow cooking—flambéing adds little to the taste of a dish. It is, however, a very dramatic and effective style of presentation. Few foods are flambéed in private. It's most often done at the last minute, and in front of the guests.

To avoid misfires, remember to have the food and spirits warm (not boiling, though, or the alcohol will evaporate before you have a chance to ignite it). Pour on the warm brandy or rum. Touch a match to it, and duck. Blue flames should shoot up quite effectively. You don't have to quench them. When the alcohol has been consumed by fire, the flames will disappear.

Be careful in your choice of serving dish. Copper and stainless-steel pans are both reflective and fireproof. A china or crystal platter might just crack.

Focal Points

A focal point is a logical way to organize a design. It's the visual touch that everything else leads to, the first thing you see when you look at a composition. It's the fireplace in the living room, the rose window on the front of the cathedral, even, we regret to say, the caterer's china doll with her skirt made of radish roses.

It's good to be able to think of a focal point when you need something that will pull together the composition of a plate or platter. All the better if it can be made with things you have on hand in the kitchen. There are, of course, suggestions throughout the book. Here are a few specific ones.

1. Some beautiful fresh produce. The trick is to have more than one vegetable, and to fill in with greens. For example, on a platter of cold cuts, make a focal point of shiny peppers—long green Italian and slim hot red peppers—rising out of a hedge of parsley. On a cake plate, two pears, one standing up and one lying on its side. Or a green pear flanked with two small Seckel pears and lots of mint around them.

2. Something skewered. The base is an apple or potato half, placed cut-side down and masked with greenery. Then stick many skewers into it. Thread small leaves of romaine or leaf lettuce onto 4-inch bamboo skewers and among them, stick skewers holding green olives, tomatoes and pickles.

3. A collection of onion flowers. Take one large red onion and two small white ones. Cut them into several wedges nearly all the way through, and soak them in cold water for an hour to open them out. Place the onion flowers on a platter of smoked fish.

4. An unusual flower holder. Choose a small white head of cauliflower. Spread the flowerets apart, keeping the cauliflower intact, and stick the stems of flowers between them, using the vegetable as a florist's frog. You have to use brilliant, flashy flowers—not roses and baby's breath, but African daisies and zinnias—and, of course, you should not hide the cauliflower completely under too many blossoms. For another flower holder, cut the top off a cantaloupe, not straight across but in deep V-shaped cuts. Scoop out the seeds and stick hearty

stalks of zinnias into the flesh in the bottom of the melon. The juice will keep the flowers fresh.

5. A woodland scene. For the center of a platter of canapés, arrange mushrooms, parsley and dill in a flat basket. *(Fig. 25)*

6. An unusual holder for sauce. Half a coconut decorated with palm fronds on a platter of cut fruit, or a big seashell on a platter of cold shrimp and vegetables.

7. A piece of tableware used in an unaccustomed way. A white cream pitcher filled with cherry tomatoes, a vase holding stalks of spaghetti, a wine goblet filled with olives or a sugar bowl containing a bouquet of wild flowers.

8. A vegetable treated in an unusual way. A single huge artichoke, stuffed the way they do it in New Orleans, with bread stuffing between the leaves. The trick is to turn the vegetable upside down after you trim it, pressing it flat to open up the leaves. Turn it upright, and open the leaves a bit more to make room for the stuffing. Spoon stuffing into the spaces between the opened leaves, then tie a string around the artichoke. Drizzle with olive oil, top with a lemon slice and bake until the vegetable is somewhat soft. Let cool, remove the string and place in the center of a platter of cold meat.

25

Garnishes

This book is about how food looks, and not about how to garnish it. We wrote it, in a way, to get away from the notion that to improve the look of a plate all you have to do is add a sprig of parsley, a maraschino cherry or a handful of potato chips. The visual appeal of a plate is made of many elements: the food itself, and the care with which it is cooked, the combination of foods and their arrangement on the plate, the interaction of the food with the color and material of the dishes, napkins and table setting. But one of these elements is unquestionably the garnish.

In classic French cooking, garnishes are side dishes. There is a whole vocabulary of them, recognized instantly by professional chefs. A dish dressed "a la financière," for example, is accompanied by veal quenelles, cockscombs, kidneys, mushrooms, shredded truffles, olives and crayfish. (The financier, clearly, wants to know that he's getting his money's worth.) A dish served "a la strasbourgeoise" comes with sauerkraut, salt pork and slices of foie gras. Such a garnish would probably cost more, take more work and skill, than your whole supper. And it's not at all what we have in mind.

In recent years, a second school of garnishing has begun to emerge in Western consciousness. This is *mukimono,* the Japanese art of carving fruits and vegetables. When *mukimono* is at its most realistic, it produces little chicks and frogs that are an uneasy blend of catererese and Disney. But when it is more abstract, it produces startling designs that go well with Western foods. Many of the garnishes used in the nouvelle cuisine are derived from Japanese garnishes.

We developed certain principles as we experimented with different garnishes in the course of working on the book. A garnish must be *edible.* It must be *substantial.* And it must be *complementary* to the food it goes with.

Edible because anything else is shamefully wasteful in a family kitchen.

Substantial, because we discovered that multiple garnishes simply work better than single ones. We're so accustomed to seeing a single olive, a pimiento strip or a wedge of hard-boiled egg that we hardly notice them anymore. But when the olive is combined with cherry tomatoes, the pimiento strip with scallions or the egg wedge with sprays of dill, then we begin to notice.

It's better to use a slice of egg, a carrot stick and parsley all together than to use any one of them alone. Better to take that pimiento strip, cross it with another pimiento strip and put a slice of green olive at the crossing. This applies even to parsley. Mixed Italian and ordinary parsley looks better than either of them by itself.

And the garnish has to complement the food. There has to be a reason for it being there. It can add taste, such as the darkly glazed onions and potatoes that surround a roast. It can add color, such as the red pepper and black olives that are arranged in a chain on a bowl of white potato salad. It can add texture, such as the bush of prickly alfalfa sprouts on a sandwich plate. It can add scale, as on a large platter for a buffet table.

American parsley

26   *Italian parsley*

20

Most particularly, a garnish defines and complements the style of the food. Shriveled black olives look peasantlike and Mediterranean, while stuffed green olives look like an American picnic. Sprouts and nuts look like health food. A molded cone of white rice is elegant and classic. An abstract design carved in green cucumber skin or white turnip looks like new-wave cooking, and would not complement a great dish of the bourgeoise cuisine, a beef bourguignonne or a blanquette de veau.

Throughout the book, the garnishes are signaled by their own logo, a tiny sprig of parsley. Some sections, such as croutons, are all garnish. But because garnishes have to be edible, and are made of real food, they are most often buried in sections that first treat food itself. This should be helpful when you have a few asparagus spears or mushrooms or a single slice of ham: not enough to be served in itself, but just enough to adorn another food.

26

Chinese parsley (coriander)

Glazing

A glaze is a coating that makes the surface of food look good. It adds flavor, color and shine, and it creates a uniform background for decorations. Glazes come savory or sweet, hot or cold, and are applied before or after the food is cooked. Most of them get their effect either from the action of heat on sugar or from the reflective property of aspics.

The quintessential glaze is icing, covering a layer cake. In addition to complicated cooked frostings, we brush finished baked goods with simple mixtures of milk, fruit juice, melted chocolate, liqueurs and sugar. Baked fruit tarts are brushed with melted red currant or apricot jam. Cream puffs and jelly apples are coated with caramel, which is nothing but cooked sugar.

Breads and rolls are brushed with glazes before they are cooked to darken and harden their crusts. Most of these glazes have sugar in them, since it is the melting of the sugar that produces both the brown color and the shine. Even when there is no apparent sugar, it is there, nonetheless, in lactose in the milk. Before they are baked, rolls and coffee cakes are glazed with plain sugar, with beaten whole eggs or egg whites with sugar, with mixtures of egg and milk.

21

The same sugar glazes work on savory foods. Thus, we cover a ham with brown sugar and mustard so that the melting of the sugar will produce a glossy brown surface. When we sauté vegetables such as turnips in butter and add a little sugar to the sauté pan, it is once again the sugar that darkens the surface of the vegetables. Often, no sugar is added because there is enough already in the carrots or onions to become caramelized in the cooking.

After being cooked and chilled, cold savory foods are glazed with aspic, a gelatinous liquid that sets when it is cooled. The aspic is used alone or is mixed into mayonnaise to make an opaque coating suitable for decorating. Both plain aspics and mayonnaises collées mask the surfaces of cold hard-boiled eggs, cooked cooled fish, ham and chicken.

An aspic glaze is also used in the preparation of chaudfroids, which are dishes that look as though they were meant to be served hot, but are served cold instead. Cold poached chicken breasts in aspic are chaudfroids; chicken chunks in mayonnaise are not. The preparation is frequently done with chicken, ham and fish. The food is first covered with a white, brown or pink sauce containing a jelling agent. Then decorations are applied: these are among the most decorated dishes in the French cuisine. Finally, a coating of aspic goes over everything.

For examples of designs on chaudfroids dishes, you should look into the *Larousse Gastronomique* and Jacques Pepin's *La Technique*. Most designs are based on flower shapes. The most elegant are made with truffles, pâté, tongue and leaves of tarragon, but others are done with stems and leaves of blanched scallions, chives and leeks, and flowers made of blanched carrots, red peppers or ham, and shapes cut with pickles, olives, hard-boiled eggs and cucumbers.

We also say that food is glazed when we place it under the broiler to make a brown surface. Asparagus au gratin is glazed when the buttery crumbs on it turn brown in the heat. *Au gratin* means, literally, "the burnt part," but actually it's a finishing step that improves the appearance of many foods. The name has come to describe any sauced food that is covered with a layer of crumbs and some fat, such as butter, oil or cheese. It is then placed in the oven or under the broiler until the top is nicely browned. Familiar foods served au gratin are macaroni-and-cheese, fish and chicken in cream sauce, and vegetables covered with butter and crumbs.

And, finally, we also say that food is glazed when we apply any sort of thickened sauce that clings to its surface. Thus, cornstarch-thickened sweet-and-sour sauce, spooned over sliced tongue, is a glaze on the tongue.

Molds—Aspics, Gelatins, Mousses

Every kitchen should have at least two molds: one ring mold and one pudding mold, either melon-shaped or fluted. They are used to shape sweet gelatin desserts, such as commercial gelatins, homemade coffee, chocolate and wine jellies and Bavarian creams. They are used for sweet and savory cold mousses, such as chocolate mousse and shrimp mousse. And they are used to make aspics, such as tomato aspic, tongue in aspic or eggs en gelée.

Choose metal molds, because they chill fast and well. Tin may change the color of acid mixtures and should be avoided. But there are many aluminum, stainless-steel and ceramic molds available.

A Well-Shaped Mold

To ensure a mold with a clearly defined shape, allow enough time for it to set—at least four hours. Overnight is even better. Use boiling water to dissolve the gelatin completely. Avoid fresh pineapple, mango, papaya and figs, which contain enzymes that prevent gelatin from setting. (Canned pineapple is harmless.)

To assist later unmolding, brush the inside of your mold before you pour in the gelatin. Use a tasteless oil for opaque mixtures, cold water for clear mixtures.

The moment of truth comes when you turn it out. Dip the mold into warm water up to the level of the gelatin for fifteen seconds. Count them: *one* Mississippi, *two* Mississippi and so forth. Insert a paring knife around the edges between gelatin and mold. Clap a plate over the top and invert. Give it a rough shake, as though you were shaking down a thermometer. If nothing happens, shake again.

We guarantee that the first time you try this, nothing will

27

28

happen. Don't despair. Stick the mold back into the warm water, this time for ten seconds. *One* Mississippi, *two* Mississippi . . . invert and shake again. The gelatin will plop out onto the plate.

Decorating a Mold

There are three ways to decorate a molded food. You can decorate the bottom and sides of the mold, so that when you turn it out, the decorations will be on the top. If you have transparent gelatin or aspic, you can decorate in layers within the mold. Or you can turn out an undecorated mold and apply decoration to its surface.

In any case, try to make a design that corresponds to the shape of the mold. Look at its inside, rather than its outside, to judge the shape. Then locate a geometric form in the lines of the mold. Try to echo that form, first outlining and then punctuating. For example, you can outline the ridges on a ring mold with blanched strips of scallion, and then punctuate the pattern with flowers cut from radishes and carrots. You can cover the surface of a melon-shaped mold with an armor of thinly sliced orange or cucumber half circles that copy the shape of the mold. *(Figs. 27, 28)*

Decorating the Bottom of the Mold

The mold should be ice cold and the gelatin syrupy. It has to be at the proper consistency to hold the decorations. Wait until it has cooled to a syrup that is a little thicker than unbeaten egg whites or heavy cream.

While it cools, lay out your design on a countertop. Do a pattern in olive bits, cucumber skin, pimiento, carrots, tarragon leaves.

When the gelatin is right, spoon some of it into the mold and slide it all over the inner surface by tilting the mold. You may want to use a paintbrush to help you make an even coat of gelatin. Then place the decorations in this thin layer, using your fingers or a tweezer. Spoon a little more gelatin on the sides, covering the decorations. To make sure that they remain in place, put the mold into the refrigerator.

24

When this first layer is firmly set, pour in the rest of the liquid gelatin. To prevent the layers from separating, you are supposed to do this at the moment when the aspic already in the mold is firm, but its surface is still a little tacky. If that moment has passed you by, reheat a little of the second batch, spoon and tilt it over the firm surface to soften it, and then add the rest of the mixture. Chill well.

Decorations Layered Inside the Mold

When you add fruit and vegetables to the body of a transparent mold, you create a design in depth. You have to think not only of how they will look from the outside, but also how they will appear in each slice.

You can put a decoration into a mold either by creating a definite layer or by simply stirring it in. To make a layer, follow the instructions for decorating the bottom of the mold, but make the layer of gelatin much thicker. Pour in an inch of gelatin. Let it set. Then arrange a sunburst of canned peach slices on it. Another inch of gelatin and a second sunburst, this time of pear slices. More gelatin to the top of the mold.

Be inventive. In a cylindrical mold, make a design inspired by the layered arrangements in jars of Italian pickled vegetables. Make a layer of pimiento stars in tomato aspic, then of quartered black olives, then of capers, then of sliced stuffed green olives and finally one of sliced hard-boiled eggs.

Or make a Victorian design by pouring 2 inches of gelatin into the bottom of the mold, letting it set, and then drawing curly designs all over it with mayonnaise squeezed through an icing tube. Let it set in the freezer for 5 minutes before you pour in the rest of the gelatin, and you'll have a suspended linear design, like that on Venetian glass. (Fig. 29)

And, of course, you can just stir fruits and vegetables into the mold and let them settle where they will. Remember, different fruits have different weights. If you stir them into liquid gelatin, some will drop to the bottom, while others will float on the top. According to *The Joy of Cooking*—and they should know, if anyone does—apple cubes, banana slices, grapefruit and pear slices, strawberry halves, broken nutmeats and marshmallows will all float. Fresh orange slices,

29

25

grapes, cooked prunes, canned apricots, cherries, peaches, pears, pineapple, plums and raspberries will all sink.

This technique does not create as orderly an appearance as the layered technique, by which you can, for example, set a design in the thick gelatin in the center of a mold of a flower made with petals of melon slices and a strawberry center. Or of a sprig of dill that looks like a flower stalk with blossom-cut vegetables surrounding it.

But it gives an attractive, chockful look: a lime mold bursting with honeydew balls, or a ruby-red fruit mold full of different fruits.

Decorating the Surface of the Mold

Finally, you can make a plain gelatin shape, turn it out onto a plate and decorate it after it is unmolded. You do this by painting or spooning on a coating of liquid gelatin just at the place where you want to add the decorations. Then cover them with more gelatin. (Don't use the same decorations on the outside of the mold as you have folded into the inside, however, or the inner food will look dull and dead in contrast.)

This is a good technique to use with opaque mixtures, with strawberry Bavarian cream and cold ham mousse. On the cream, place a ring of blueberries around a whole strawberry. On the pinkish ham mousse, place fans made of sliced gherkins around a central ring of sliced hard-boiled egg.

Sauces

Sauces are thickened liquids that we add to food to enhance its flavor, improve its looks and, sometimes, to stretch an expensive ingredient. Most are based on a few "mother sauces," as the French call them.

Some are thickened with flour, such as white cream sauce and brown gravy. Some are thickened with egg, such as hollandaise and mayonnaise. Others are thickened with cornstarch, such as barbecue and sweet-and-sour sauces. Others, like tomato sauce, are thickened by reduction, by being boiled down. There are dessert sauces in all these categories: egg-thickened custard and zabaglione, fruit purees, melted jam, chocolate and caramel sauces.

A sauce should be just thick enough to flow from a spoon. It should be smooth, well-flavored and of a good color. Many sauces acquire a final shine with the addition of a bit of butter. But any cookbook can tell you how to make sauces. What the foodstylist wants to know is how to use them. How do you add sauce to a plate of food?

Sauces once were used to cloak food. But with the new aesthetic that came in with nouvelle cuisine and the Japanese influence, they became a background rather than a cover for food. We now often add the food to a sauce, rather than adding sauce to a food.

Take a plate and fill the bottom right up to the shoulder with a thin layer of sauce. If the sauce is hot, then the plate had better be hot, too, or you'll get a slick of congealed fat. For a dessert, spill a thin pool of sauce into the bottom of a wine goblet or in a shallow bowl.

Then put the food on top of the sauce. Garnish it. In this way, the food is framed and set off by the color of the sauce. Its natural shape and texture are plain to see, and the flavors mix readily enough once knife and fork go to work.

You can use some of the sauce as the garnish. Drip streamers of sauce over the food, spilling chocolate sauce over the pear. Or dip part of the food into the sauce: cold cooked shrimp half-coated with mustard-curry sauce. Or place a band of sauce across the food to tie it into a visual bundle, laying stalks of asparagus over hollandaise sauce, and then crossing the asparagus with stripes of the hollandaise.

For example:

A background of pale green cream sauce colored and flavored with parsley and dill. Over it, a slice of pink poached salmon with a thin lime slice for a garnish.

A pool of pureed raspberries in a wineglass and, over it, a whole poached pear garnished with mint leaves.

Duck breasts and figs lying on a golden-brown orange sauce.

A cheese-covered veal cutlet lying over, not under, tomato sauce.

A monochromatic plate made with strawberry sauce on the plate, and a red-poached pear in the center.

If you are exceptionally ambitious, you could try a trick from the haute cuisine, a plate with two background colors rather than one.

The food goes on the line where the two sauces meet. It's easiest to use it with cool dessert sauces. Try a plate covered half with strawberry sauce and half with crème Anglaise, with a slice of pound cake over them and three sugar-dipped berries on the cake. Or half chocolate sauce, half caramel sauce, with a scoop of coffee ice cream over them and a sprinkling of nuts over all.

Skewered Foods

A skewer lets you hold things together in the order you choose. It is both a piece of cooking equipment and an aid to garnishing. We string pieces of lamb and vegetables on a skewer for grilling, and also make skewers of marshmallows and jelly beans for a child's birthday cake.

Cooking on skewers is the oldest method of grilling, descending from the hunk of raw meat stuck on the end of a twig. It has a rich cuisine in Middle Eastern kebabs, Indian koftas, Syrian chalazons and Moroccan brochettes.

For skewering meat, vegetables and other foods that will be subjected to high heat, most people prefer slim metal rods. There are also useful bamboo skewers sold in oriental supply houses that are around 4 inches long. If you soak them in water, they won't blaze up even under the broiler; they can also be used for skewering decorative foods that are not subjected to heat. Not useful for broiling, but the most common skewers for garnishing, are ordinary toothpicks. After all, even two olives in a martini glass make a skewered arrangement.

When you arrange a skewer for broiling, choose foods that cook in the same amount of time. One way to deal with long-cooking meat and quick-cooking vegetables is to put them on separate skewers. To cook green peppers and turnip cubes on the same skewer, parboil the turnips so that they will be nicely charred but cooked through in the same time as the peppers. To slow down the cooking of fragile foods such as chicken livers or prunes, wrap them in bacon and pierce the bacon with the skewer.

28

Arrangement

If they aren't arranged with absolute control, skewers just look messy. Think of them as having a linear pattern. Do a grilled skewer on an *abab* pattern, alternating chunks of lamb and chicken. Or do a garnish skewer in the same pattern. For a glass of lemonade, alternate strawberries and grapes on a toothpick.

It's helpful to make up an alphabetical plan on paper, then assign a food to each letter. Add a cap to the end of the series. Use a vertical slice of mushroom, half a canned apricot, a carved radish. Just something to show that it's over. You will achieve order magically.

Any of the plans we describe can, of course, be used equally well on grilled meat skewers, steamed vegetable skewers and uncooked garnish skewers.

Grilled Skewers

Begin by making a skewer in a mirror order—*abcbdadbcba*—with the same elements reading in from each end. Use cubes of meat ▨ , squares of red pepper ⌓ , rings of yellow squash pierced through the skin ⊙ , and chunks of zucchini ◖ .

Vegetable Skewers

For vegetable skewers, use the 8-inch bamboo skewers from Japanese cooking. Leave the vegetables raw for a skewered salad. To cook vegetables, just steam them and then put them on the barbecue for a few seconds, long enough to develop a nicely charred surface but not long enough to incinerate them.

This composition relies on the repetition of one element, watercress threaded through its stem so that its leaves flop vertically. You can go on adding different vegetables so long as you tie them

29

together with watercress. The plot is *abcbdb.* . . . Our skewer has zucchini ( ) , watercress , black olive, , cherry tomato ( ) , and, at the end, a mushroom, sliced vertically .

31

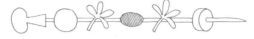

Try another vegetable skewer with an *abcabc* plan. Use cauliflower , red pepper wedges and scallion tassels .

32

Fruit Skewers

Do a fruit skewer on an *ababcacb* plan. Use arcs of pear) , peach) , and red cherries . Garnish with a sprig of mint and use a pineapple wedge for a cap .

33

For another fruit skewer, spear strawberries ( ) , canned pineapple chunks , green grapes flopped to the side , in an *abac* pattern, with a cap made of half a canned apricot, its hollow filled with a whole strawberry .

34

Using Skewers

Cooked skewers of kebabs and vegetables are served on large platters, surrounded by bunches and bunches of parsley. Individual meat skewers go on dinner plates, the meat on beds of rice.

Vegetable skewers on 4-inch bamboo rods go on a dinner plate alongside the fish or meat. Lots of them can be stuck into a potato half in a bowl of salad (the potato, of course, well hidden by the greens).

Fruit skewers go on the plate alongside a dessert.

Olive and pickle skewers lie alongside an omelet or a bowl of soup. Bacon and cheese skewers accompany a quiche Lorraine. And candy skewers are stuck into the tops of cupcakes at a child's party.

Stencils

Stenciled food works when it is prepared very casually or when it is clearly an arts-and-crafts project.

By casual, we mean a dusting of powdered sugar through the holes of a paper doily, so that a slightly blurred snowflake appears on a chocolate cake.

And by arts and crafts, we mean all the projects you do with the children at holiday time. You cut a star out of a piece of folded construction paper. Then you place the paper over a frosted cupcake or a sandwich and you paint through the open space with liquid food coloring.

The design should be frankly naïf. First come gingerbread men and Christmas trees. A Pennsylvania Dutch-style outline would be fine. Or the first letter of a child's name. *(Fig. 35)*

What to stencil with? Powdered sugar is good, as are cocoa and coconut. Use colored sugar, chocolate shot or varicolored sprinkles. For best results with sugar, pass the sifter back and forth over the stencil. If you overload the sifter, the outlines will become blurred. Stencil cookie-cutter cookies before you bake them. This won't work as well with drop cookies. It's hard to control the design because they spread out and distort in the baking.

Use a stencil on the top of an unbaked piecrust: a cherry in red sugar on a cherry pie, or an apple in green sugar on an apple pie.

Stencil the white icing of a cupcake or an individual cake square.

To decorate sandwiches made with white bread, paint over the stencil with a brush dipped in liquid food coloring. It will make a hit at children's parties.

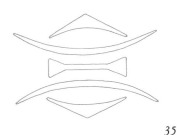

35

31

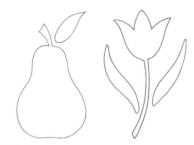

36

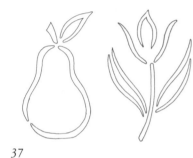

37

38

If you want to make your own stencil, you can do it by drawing on a sheet of paper the outline of any shape, say a pear or a flower, that you wish to use. Cut the shape out of the paper and then apply color through the opening that remains. Or take the shape that you have actually cut out and apply color around it, leaving the area beneath the shape uncolored. *(Fig. 36)*

Another way to design a stencil is to draw the shape you want as a double line and cut out the space between the lines. Leave a few points uncut to hold the central form in place. When you stencil through this, you will get colored areas outlining the design. *(Fig. 37)*

Finally, don't discount the usefulness of the edge of a sheet of cardboard. To make canapés that are half caviar and half chopped egg white, start by laying a piece of cardboard diagonally across the toast. This allows you to spread on the caviar and leave a neat line at the edge. Then on goes the egg.

You can use the same technique to get a curve by tracing an arc on the cardboard against the edge of a saucer, then cutting and using the template to make two-part patterns joined in an arc. *(Fig. 38)*

2
FOODSTYLING

Amandine. *See* NUTS

Anchovies

A good item for the emergency cupboard. Anchovies add a dark accent and a salty, piquant taste to bland foods. Cross them over deviled eggs, lay them in parallel lines on heavily buttered canapés and Scandinavian open sandwiches. Place them, rolled, on cream cheese canapés. If you find the salty flavor overwhelming, a half-hour soak in cold water or milk will lessen the bite.

Italians serve an hors d'oeuvre of red peppers and anchovies, in which the fish's color brings out the red and its saltiness picks up the bland oily taste.

Anchovy paste was much in use in the thirties and forties, the golden days of cocktail parties. It is made by crushing the fish with many times its weight in sweet butter, adding lemon juice and chopped parsley, then piping the mixture onto melba rounds.

Apples

Apples are round, with shiny red, yellow or green skins. For cooking, we buy them tart and firm, choosing varieties such as Granny Smiths, Northern Spies, Cortlands. For eating, we buy Yellow and Red

Delicious, McIntosh, Winesaps or whatever local variety we are lucky enough to find on the market. The apple season used to be autumn and early winter, and apples sold at other times of the year were mushy and tasteless. Now we get ripe apples from the Southwest, South America and Australia all year round.

Raw Apples

Once you cut into an apple, the air will discolor its white flesh. You can retard the browning by rubbing the cut surfaces with lemon, orange or pineapple juice, or by dipping the fruit into acidulated water made by adding 1 tablespoon vinegar or 3 tablespoons lemon juice to a quart of water.

We seldom get a raw apple for dessert: certainly less often than melon, strawberries or grapes. But in fact a single apple makes a refreshing ending to a meal.

In Europe, they know how to peel their apples at the table by removing the peel in one long curved strip. Then they eat the fruit with a knife and fork. Most Americans haven't learned the technique.

If you want to serve a whole apple for dessert, set it on two lemon leaves on a dessert plate. The florist will give you the leaves. Add a triangle of hard cheese and two walnut halves, or else a chunk of candied ginger and two dates. If the apple has a stem, you can tie a narrow plaid ribbon around it. If it has none (more likely with modern picking machines), stick florist's wire into the place where the stem should be, and loop the ribbon through it. A white pottery bowl or basket piled high with ribboned apples makes a nice centerpiece.

For an individual serving, cut an apple into very thin wedges, as though you were making a tarte tatin. Dip them in acidulated water, and arrange them in a pinwheel on a dessert plate. Or cut the apple into rings, remove the cores, dip the rings in lemon-water and make a comet shape on the plate, with the largest rings at one end and the smallest at the other. With either arrangement, add cheese, dates, chocolate or nuts.

Make a salad of cold cooked beets, onions and unpeeled Golden Delicious or Granny Smith apples. The combination of the yellow or green apple skin with the bleeding beet red is brilliant.

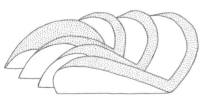

39

Cut an apple into quarters. Take a quarter and, using the two edges as a guide, make two cuts in the peel ⅜ of an inch in from the cut sides. Repeat until the apple is a nest of resting V slices. Then shingle the slices for a fruit-platter garnish. *(Fig. 39)*

Baked Apples

40

Baked apples are basically ugly. They're dumpy, shapeless and neither red nor brown but something pale in between the two.

It helps to choose a variety of apple that will hold its shape when it's cooked, such as a Cortland or Greening. Take out the core and peel away some of the skin around the stem to make a pattern. Try a scalloped edge, or cut shallow zigzag points. Do a Pennsylvania Dutch apple by removing the skin in a pattern of scallops and ovals. Cut ½-inch vertical dashes all over the skin. When the apple is baked, the tiny flaps will curl back. *(Figs. 40–42)*

41

Color and season baked apples by basting them with water in which you have dissolved "red hots": fiery little cinnamon candies. Or use maple syrup, apricot jam, marmalade or honey to make a glaze.

Fill the center of a baked apple with stewed apricots and blanched almonds or with prunes and walnuts.

42

Slice a baked apple into quarters, nearly through to the base. A serrated knife will let you cut through the tough skin without mashing the apple. Open it like a flower, put it on a flat dessert plate and fill the center with whipped cream cheese and chopped nuts, or with sour cream and dates.

Serve baked apples in clear glass bowls or on glass plates. Red glass bowls give them a wonderful rosy hue.

Core and bake tiny lady apples, and use them as a garnish for ham or goose.

Candy Apples

On Halloween, pierce the stem ends of firm raw apples with popsicle sticks, first whittling one end of each stick to a point so it will go in easily. Dip the apples into melted caramel, dark chocolate or a sugar syrup tinted red. Before the glaze hardens, press on a jack-o'-lantern face made with nuts, sunflower seeds or M&M's. Dip the top of the apple into chopped nuts. Stand the sticks upright in a florist's frog to let the apple glaze dry neatly.

Applesauce

Applesauce turns pink when you add cranberry sauce, grape jam or pureed strawberries to it. Mix in red horseradish, and you get a similar color, but a radically different taste. Hot or cold, this goes with pork or pot roast and is very nice with potato pancakes.

To garnish plain applesauce, spoon some sour cream or yogurt in the center, then sprinkle with cinnamon or grated orange rind. Add texture with raisins, blueberries, chopped nuts, granola or cookie crumbs.

Warm applesauce, cold ice cream and cookie crumbs register in the mouth amazingly like apple pie a la mode, and make an easy family dessert. Spoon the applesauce in a small bowl, add a scoop of ice cream, chocolate or vanilla, and sprinkle all over with the crumbs.

On a platter of potato pancakes, serve applesauce and sour cream in hollowed-out baked potato shells.

Apricots

The second best thing about apricots is the color. (The best thing, of course, is the taste.) Fully ripe apricots are plump, golden pink and have a distinctive sweet flavor with a faint citrus undertaste.

Unfortunately, apricots are usually picked before they are ripe and arrive at local markets pale, tart and crunchy. Pale yellow apricots never really ripen. They just soften and develop a shriveled skin. Many people prefer to use preserved apricots, just as many people prefer to use canned tomatoes rather than tasteless hard tomatoes.

Canned apricots have a beautiful, somewhat unreal color, and are packed in an overly sweet syrup. But dried apricots are quite good, and when they have been reconstituted by soaking in water, they have the best flavor of any save the truly ripe fresh fruit.

(They may look funny. All dried fruit tends to darken when it's allowed to dry naturally. It turns purple-brown, like grapes turning

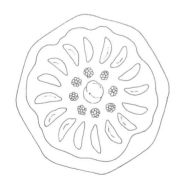

43

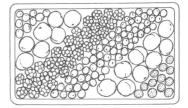

into raisins. We accept black raisins, but we want rosy-pink apricots. That's why commercial processors use sulfur fumes to bleach the apricots as they dry, and why supermarket apricots are a cheerful orange shade.

The apricots you buy in health-food stores are shriveled and brown because health-food people think using sulfur is unsafe. Most nutritionists say that even though sulfur is indeed a toxic substance, it appears naturally in many foods such as eggs, and that it isn't harmful in small quantities.)

Serve whole raw apricots on a dessert plate with two lemon leaves that you get from the florist. Accompany them with slabs of dark chocolate, with a handful of almonds or with leaf-shaped chocolate almond cookies.

Choose a dark plate to set off the color of cooked or canned apricot halves. Make a white background by spreading a thin puddle of zabaglione on a plate. Set an apricot half in the center and surround it with raspberries, strawberries or blueberries. Slice a second apricot in wedges and make a border around the outside. *(Fig. 43)*

For a platter of fruit, choose a long serving plate and place across it stripes of apricot halves, red berries, blue berries and green grapes, or other fruit combinations. *(Fig. 44)*

Use canned or poached apricots instead of peaches for a Melba, combining the fruit with vanilla ice cream and pureed raspberries. Or cover a white plate with dark chocolate sauce. On it, put a scoop of raspberry sherbet, and surround that with apricot slices.

Buy dried apricot leather. Then cut long strips 1½ inches wide and roll them up into rosebuds, keeping one side tight while the other flares out. Use these to garnish a ham or pork roast or duck.

Artichokes

Globe artichokes are big, firm and green, and look a little bit like flowers. If they have brown spots on them, don't worry: those are frost marks, which don't affect the taste at all. An artichoke is eaten leaf by leaf, after which the bottom is eaten with a knife and fork. It's a food that takes a lot of handling, both at the table and before it even gets there.

45

46

Preparation

Any general cookbook will give you instructions on how to prepare an artichoke for cooking. The object is to remove all the sharp and unpleasant bits: the prickly top, the leaf tips and the spiky "choke" in the center. First you cut off the top, then the tip of each leaf, and finally you spread open the leaves, pull out the tender violet blossom in the center and scrape out the choke with a teaspoon. *(Fig 45)*

If you're careful, you can preserve that tender blossom. Set it aside while you scrape out the choke and stuff the artichoke. Then invert the purplish flower on top of the stuffing. *(Fig. 46)*

To keep the color bright green, rub all cut surfaces with a cut lemon. Or cook the vegetable in water spiked with lemon juice or vinegar. And don't overcook.

To vary the look a little, cut the leaf tips off in a V rather than straight across. And no matter how you present it, remember to slice off the stem evenly so that the artichoke will stand up firmly.

Tableware

Unlike other vegetables, artichokes are always served as a separate course. Put them on clear glass plates on bright cloths or mats, so that they seem to float over the background.

There are pottery artichoke plates with indentations for the vegetables and hollows for the discarded leaves. If you don't use these special plates (and many are quite unappealing), you have to provide bowls for the uneaten parts of the leaves and small pots for butter or dunking sauce. Of course, the center of the artichoke makes a natural container for thick sauces like hollandaise, mayonnaise or sour cream with red caviar. If you're serving melted butter with lemon or cold vinaigrette, you'd better use a small bowl at each place setting.

Parts of Artichokes

The tiny artichokes that come in jars with oil and vinegar are called artichoke hearts, but they aren't. They're baby artichokes, softened by being marinated. Real artichoke hearts are the bottoms of the vegetable, the part that's left when you've eaten all the leaves and taken away the choke. They often show up on complicated platters, holding mushrooms or sausage or simply as one of a vegetable arrangement.

In nouvelle cuisine, you may see artichoke leaves in salads. At a rather grand party, we saw cooked artichoke leaves taking the place of crackers or potato chips around a bowl of dip. They radiated out from the bowl in a sunburst, looking like petals on a great flat flower.

Stuffings

Artichokes may be served unstuffed, stuffed in the core or (a New Orleans custom) stuffed between the leaves, so that they look like huge, opulent cabbage roses.

Hot stuffings go into hot artichokes, cold stuffings into cold. Think of the color contrast. Make up a red bean salad or a crab and pea salad to go into a cold artichoke. Prepare olive-flecked Spanish rice or yellow shrimp curry to go in a hot artichoke.

(It's easy to stuff them when you remove them from the cooking water and drain them upside down, with the leaves spread out. For instructions on stuffing, then cooking, raw artichokes, see also FOCAL POINTS, page 18.)

And small raw artichokes make natural candleholders for a summer table. Cut off the bottoms so that they will stand upright. Scoop out the centers and wedge a votive candle into each one. Scatter them here and there on a picnic table.

Asparagus

Fresh asparagus is crisp, intensely flavored and, above all, seasonal. It's best and cheapest for a few weeks in the spring. Canned asparagus is pale, soft, sweet and available all year round. You either like it or you don't. If you do, it makes an adequate salad vegetable all year round, but is really too soft to eat hot. Frozen asparagus is an adequate substitute for fresh. Its flavor is reasonable, and its color, if you don't overcook, is excellent, if a bit garish.

Break off the stem of fresh asparagus at the point where you can.

You don't have to cut off the white end of the stem. Instead, hold it in one hand and grab with the other, figuring that it will snap off at the point where it becomes tender. Tiny spring asparagus don't need peeling, while thicker and later ones do.

Preserve the brilliant green color by not overcooking the vegetable. (It can even be eaten raw.) You get the best color when you stir-fry it in oil. Otherwise, boil in an inch of water in a skillet or steam upright in a tall pot.

The simplest way to serve asparagus is to stack it in parallel lines on a serving dish. Don't have all the ends lined up evenly, however. Push the bottom layer westward and the top layer eastward, so that there is a great display of blossom at one end of the dish. Use the same technique when you place five stalks of asparagus on an individual plate for a first course or to one side of a dinner plate. *(Fig. 47)*

Cross the parallel lines of the stalks with a garnish. Drizzle hollandaise sauce over them. Lay on parallel strips of ham, of smoked salmon or sliced pimiento. You can do multicolored stripes, too, making a line of chopped pimiento, another of chopped black olives and a third of minced egg white.

Chopped hard-boiled egg, used alone or mixed with bright parsley, is a traditional garnish for asparagus. Sprinkle it across the stalks, or roll the tips of still-wet asparagus in chopped egg.

The favored way of eating asparagus in the Netherlands, as a matter of fact, is to serve it on a pool of melted butter, accompanied by half a hard-boiled egg. The Dutch mash the egg and butter together, then wipe the asparagus through the succulent mess.

That's not the end of our egg suggestions. Try serving asparagus at breakfast, alongside a lightly coddled egg in an eggcup. You open the egg, then dip the asparagus into the yolk before each bite.

If hot asparagus is to be covered with a cheese sauce, reserve four of the stalks. Blanket the rest with the sauce and slant the reserved asparagus down the length of the dish in parallel lines. If your serving platter is round, arrange the reserved stalks in spokes with a tuft of parsley or watercress in the center.

One spring we saw a round tray of lightly cooked asparagus arranged in a circle, the stalks pointing outward and the blossom ends bent up around a small glass bowl of melted butter. There must have

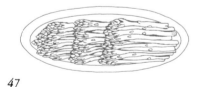

47

48

40

been three dozen asparagus on the plate. It looked like one hundred, and it looked sensational. *(Fig. 48)*

You can use asparagus as a garnish, too, to add a strong linear punch to composed salads. For example, lay a tomato slice to one side of a salad plate. Arrange three asparagus tips so that they radiate out from its center. Then drizzle mayonnaise over them in an arc that echoes the curve of the tomato, and tuck watercress leaves under the edges of the tomato. *(Fig. 49)*

Or use four bright-green asparagus on top of a bowl of Salade Niçoise or chef's salad. The base is the salad, with all the ingredients chopped up in it. Then on top, lay four asparagus pointing to the four compass points, with a tuft of parsley or some cherry tomatoes and black olives in the center.

Avocado

These tropical pears are medium to dark green and have smooth or bumpy skins. Like bananas, they are picked before they are ripe, and finish the process in transit and in our kitchens.

Choose a firm, green-skinned avocado. The fruit is ripe when the flesh yields to the touch, but you can buy it unripe and let it develop for one to two days at home. Stowing it in a paper bag will hasten the process. Keeping it in the refrigerator will slow it down without harming the quality of the fruit. If you cut into an avocado and find that the flesh is brown, it has become overripe and should be thrown away.

Once it is cut and peeled, the flesh of the avocado discolors quickly. You can prevent this by cutting it just before you serve it and by rubbing the cut surfaces with a lemon or orange. If you use only half the avocado, rub the cut flesh with lemon and cover it tightly with plastic wrap. Tradition asserts that the stone left in place prevents discoloration. This clearly helps an avocado half, since the stone keeps the air away from part of it; the claim, however, is that a stone stuck into pureed avocado will keep it from discoloring as well. In fact, the lemon juice we add to guacamole serves that purpose.

The simplest presentation is to cut the avocado in half lengthwise, so that the pear shape is evident. Slice a little from the

50

5r

·52

bottom so that it stands steady, and set it on a bed of sprouts or lettuce leaves to keep it from sliding all over the plate.

Remove the pit. You can enlarge the cavity to make room for more stuffing, but a smaller cavity makes the stuffing spill out and look opulent. It's a good trick when you're using something expensive, like lobster or crab meat salad.

Fill the pear with something pink. Like all the green-fleshed fruits, such as honeydew, grapes and figs, avocado looks good with food in the pink-to-scarlet family. We serve it with shrimp, tomatoes, strawberries. Try ham salad. Anything with russian dressing. Raspberries. Strawberry sherbet and blueberries. *(Fig. 50)*

If the stuffing isn't pink, add a radish flower, and hook two shrimp over the edge of the fruit.

Fill the hole with a scoop of salad, and stick an orange slice on end into it. Surround it with watercress.

You can also halve, core and peel the avocado. Peeling is problematic: it has to be done at just the right point of ripeness if the peel is to come away easily without damaging the flesh.

Slice half an avocado horizontally, and then reassemble the slices, facedown, for an individual serving. Spoon vinaigrette over the pear to keep it from discoloring, and then sprinkle it with chopped hard-boiled egg. Surround with radishes and dark greenery. *(Fig. 51)*

Arrange lengthwise slices of avocado in a fan or pinwheel, with a circle of tomato wedges and orange or grapefruit segments at the place where they join. *(Fig. 52)*

Combine avocado slices with sweet red pepper rings and lemon wedges or with yellow cheese and tomato wedges and use as garnishes for chicken.

To surround guacamole: tomato wedges and dark greens.

To serve with chili: a salad of avocado, corn and sweet red pepper.

Bacon

These days we use bacon less as food than garnish. It's expensive, full of preservatives, high in fat. But it tastes wonderful, and luckily, a little goes a long way.

42

To preserve bacon's appearance, cook it slowly. Start it in a cold skillet or broiler rack and heat it gently to keep it from curling.

Bend two strips into V-shapes and hook them to one another to form an X. If you cook them this way, they will stay together, and you can place the X on top of a fried egg or an open-faced cheese sandwich. *(Fig. 53)*

53

Twist bacon strips into tight spirals. Put them on a broiler rack, with metal skewers holding down the ends of the bacon so that they won't unwind. Cross two or three of these on a plate with silver-dollar pancakes between the legs of the X. *(Fig. 54)*

Thread a spiral or ripple of bacon onto a bamboo skewer. The skewer lets you turn the bacon easily under the broiler. When it's done, stick a wedge of pineapple or a cherry tomato and bit of watercress onto one end of the skewer. Lay a phalanx of these spears alongside a mass of scrambled eggs on a breakfast buffet.

54

Use bacon to wrap around and drape over other foods. For hot snacks before a meal, wrap chicken livers and water chestnuts, or prunes soaked in port or pear chunks with Cheddar cheese. Wrap a frankfurter in bacon. Lay bacon strips or latticework over baked beans, meat loaf or meat pies.

Cooked, drained and crumbled, bacon becomes a garnish, a kind of brown parsley. For spinach salad, of course, but try it on egg salad or potato salad as well.

Imitation bacon bits are made of soy protein and are probably better for your arteries than the real thing. But they are ersatz and have chemicals added to them that the pig never thought of.

Baked Alaska

Decorate the meringue on a baked Alaska with the back of a soup spoon. For a brick-shaped dessert, one made with horizontal slices of pound cake and a quart of ice cream, draw S curves down the length and up the sides of the meringue. Spoon teaspoonfuls of meringue around the top and down each corner. Swirl these blobs with a toothpick.

It doesn't have to be a last-minute effort. You can construct a baked Alaska days ahead of time and then freeze it. Put the unwrapped cake in the freezer. When it's hard, wrap it in aluminum foil.

Begin to preheat the broiler when you sit down to dinner. After the main course, clear the table, pour more wine for everyone and remove the foil-wrapped package from the freezer. Take off the foil and slide the cake under the broiler. Cook it for about 3 minutes, checking to be sure that the meringue doesn't burn. Garnish with cherries or berries and mint. Pour on flaming brandy when you're ready to carry it into the dining room.

You can also make baked Alaskas in hollow orange or lemon shells filled with ice cream. Carry the meringue down, covering all the ice cream. Then swirl the meringue to a peak, using the back of a teaspoon.

Bananas

Because of the jingle, we all know that bananas are best when they are flecked with brown and have a golden hue; that they are, in fact, one of those fruits, like mangoes, that taste best when they look worst. Buy firm yellow bananas, then let them ripen at home.

We've also learned that we must never put bananas in the refrigerator. That's not altogether true. If you're stuck with too many bananas and not enough people to eat them, you can put them in the refrigerator. The skin will turn a ghastly brown, but the ripening process will slow down, and the bananas, once peeled, will be quite edible.

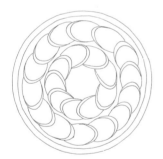

Like apples and avocados, bananas discolor and soften when the inner flesh is exposed to the air. Citrus juices keep them white for a while, but the effect doesn't last, and they turn brown and mushy. Add bananas to fruit compotes just before you serve them, and cut bananas for dessert after you've eaten the main course.

55

We're used to slicing them straight across in chunks, but there are several ways to slice a banana.

Make plain circles, slicing straight across. Mix thick chunks with sour cream or yogurt. Cut thin disks and float them on lemonade or fruit punch.

56

Make ovals by cutting the slices at a slant. Stick an oval slice on end into chocolate pudding or fruit sherbet just before you serve it. Cover a dessert plate with strawberry puree and arrange a sunburst of banana ovals on it, with a dab of sour cream in the center. Or use the ovals on the dark icing of a layer cake. Make concentric overlapping circles of oval banana slices, one going clockwise and the other counterclockwise. Lay down the outer circle first, and then arrange the inner circle leaning against it. Put three canned apricot halves in the center of the cake and paint the bananas with melted apricot jam. Or put mandarin oranges in the center and glaze the bananas with orange marmalade. *(Fig. 55)*

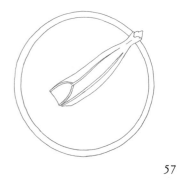

57

Make triangular chunks of banana, creating substantial mouthfuls to combine with grapes and apple chunks. Slice straight down, then on the diagonal, and repeat these two cuts down the length of the fruit. Sprinkle with coconut and serve with curries. *(Fig. 56)*

Cut the banana in half lengthwise for a banana split. Serve it with raspberry sherbet and garnish with mint leaves. This is the way to cut bananas for broiling or baking.

Or cut it in half lengthwise and then again crosswise, making quarters: another good cut for baked or broiled bananas.

58

But if, like most people, you usually serve a banana raw, out of hand, emerging from its own wrapping like some exotic flower, you might remember that for a child's appetite you can cut the fruit in half and peel back the skin from the cut edge. If he's hungry he can always ask for the second half.

A prettier, adult version of this is to cut off the bottom end of the banana in a V. Then split the skin in four places and peel back the skin to form a flower. *(Figs. 57, 58)*

Beans, Dried

Although dried beans are among the world's oldest foods, it has taken the health-food movement and the price of beef to make them popular in America. Except for a few old favorites such as chili con carne and Boston baked beans, we are only now learning to cook these protein-packed legumes.

There is a wide variety of dried beans on the market, as well as several kinds of canned beans. They range in color from black to ivory white, with stopovers at red, brown and green. To the initiate, each variety has its own flavor, but to the new bean-eater, they all taste rather bland and benefit greatly from the addition of regional seasonings.

Bean Salads

What could be more prosaic than bottled three-bean salad? Improve it by adding chopped pimiento to the mix. Pour it on a bed of shredded iceberg lettuce and place a star of hard-boiled egg wedges and watercress in the center.

Next step up: make your own dried bean salad by mixing cooked beans with vinaigrette sauce. The visual trick is to use three different colors of beans, in white, red and brown. Cook them separately, because they take varying times to cook and may bleed their colors. Season them individually with oil and vinegar. Then mix them all together, or arrange them in a pattern in a bowl or on a plate. If you use a pancake turner or a pot lid as a barrier, you can keep the areas distinct. To a bowl holding three wedges of different-colored beans, add chopped sweet red pepper on top of the dividing lines and a circle of hard-boiled egg and parsley in the center.

Make a striped platter of bean salad. Try a white bean salad made with chopped sweet red pepper and lots of parsley, for example, arranged on a platter in stripes alternating with stripes of cold cooked green beans. Garnish with lemon wedges and shiny black olives.

This combination makes a good first-course salad on individual salad plates. Make a circle of white beans. Surround it with the green beans and, in the center, place a pinwheel of olives and lemon.

More ideas for cold bean salads. Put red or pink beans on a bed of spinach and garnish with chopped egg white mixed with parsley.

Stuff a tomato with pale lima beans, and surround it with cold asparagus.

Spoon salads of different-colored beans into spikes of endive, and arrange them on a plate in a fan or wheel pattern.

Cooked Beans

When beans are cooked and served hot, they often lose their shape. No shape, plus bland taste: obviously, something crisp and organizing is needed in the container or the garnish. Cooked beans look best when they are given form by their containers and set off with garnishes of crisp, brightly colored vegetables.

Serve refried black beans on beds of shredded iceberg lettuce, and garnish with grated yellow cheese and radish flowers. Garnish black beans with thin orange slices, alone or with slices of avocado.

It's not authentic, but both the looks and the usable protein in chili are augmented when you stir in some bright yellow corn. Garnish red beans with avocado or with crisp cucumber twists.

Float thin lemon slices or knots made of lemon rind on top of black bean soup.

Serve cooked beans in sweet red pepper shells or in hollowed-out zucchini. Mix brown lentils with cooked white or brown rice.

Garnish pale green dried beans with lemon wedges and dark green parsley.

We've never had baked beans that looked better than the kind they used to serve in the Automat. They were baked in individual earthenware crocks and came out bubbling hot under a lid of bacon strips. It's still a good way to serve baked beans, and it will keep them from running into the hot dogs and coleslaw.

Bean Sprouts

Suddenly, there are many varieties of bean sprouts in our markets: white mung bean sprouts, soy sprouts and alfalfa sprouts as delicate as angel's hair. Whether they are as nutritious as is claimed, they are a good alternative to lettuce as a way of adding texture to a plate.

To prolong their usefulness, cover them with water when you bring them home, and store them in the refrigerator. The water should be changed every day. Treated this way, they should be good for a few days, but no more than a week. To use, just drain them and pat them dry. In the Orient, vegetables are never served raw because

of the type of fertilizer used in their cultivation. That means that it's not truly authentic to use raw bean sprouts in a Chinese or Japanese meal. (Although it's perfectly safe to serve Western-grown sprouts raw.) Pour boiling water over them in a strainer, or put them in a pot of water, bring it to a boil, and then drain immediately and douse the sprouts with cold water so that they retain their crispness.

Use the sprouts for a base. Cover a small plate with a nest of alfalfa sprouts and arrange raw carrots, broccoli and sweet red pepper on it.

Cover another plate with a mattress of sprouts and on it, arrange cold hors d'oeuvres. Try some mozzarella and tomatoes drizzled with oil, a slice of pâté and an egg en gelée.

Add sprouts to a salad, making a clump of raw alfalfa sprouts in the center of a bowl of greens. Or serve them as a salad by themselves, garnished with radish and orange slices or with thinly sliced scallion greens. *(Fig. 59)*

Use the sprouts to break up the geometric severity of a sandwich or pâté plate. Next to the bread, place a tuft of sprouts holding, perhaps, three gherkins.

Use cooked sprouts as a quasi-pasta, infinitely low in calories, with sautéed mushrooms or tomato sauce.

Beets

Beets have a good strong color. They're the original vegetable coloring, staining everything in sight anything from pale pink to dark red. Making a virtue of inevitability, people have used them to color Easter eggs, to tint applesauce pink and to make horseradish—even pasta—red.

Never peel beets or cut off the stems before you cook them. You can cut off most of the greens, leaving 1 inch in place. Peeled or stemmed beets let most of their color, as well as their nutrients, bleed out into the cooking water.

They can be baked just like potatoes, then peeled and sliced. And they're one of the few vegetables that are really as good canned as they are fresh.

Cooked or raw, beets are another of those root vegetables, such as turnips and potatoes, that are easy to cut and carve. You can make them into any shape you like.

Leave small beets whole, or cut them in half. Carve them into olive-shaped balls. Slice large beets into disks. Cut the disks into julienne strips, and the strips into cubes. You can vary any of these cuts by using a wavy knife, producing rippled slices and strips.

Put raw beets through the shredding disk of a food processor and add to a salad. Carve a whole raw or cooked beet into a beet rose, just as you would a radish rose. Or make a beet tulip and use it as a container for red-cabbage slaw.

Because of the bleeding color, it's hard to combine beets with other foods. Either you keep them apart, or you use the quality to your advantage.

To keep them apart, arrange a barrier. Make a composed salad of shredded beets and shredded carrots. Put them side by side on a serving plate, and separate them with a hedge of parsley or lime sections.

But if you want to use the color, mix diced cooked beets with Golden Delicious apples or with steamed yellow squash. The relentless red color combined with the yellow skins of the other foods provides a vivid Technicolor effect. The Russians make a winter salad of beets, mixed vegetables and dill pickles, and let it all turn bright red. In New England, red-flannel hash is intentionally red from the addition of leftover beets.

Combine scarlet beets with red-orange food. Fill a tangerine shell with chopped pickled beets. Make a chrysanthemum from an orange shell (see page 182), and heap it high with raw shredded beets.

Green is the complement to red. Garnish beets with dark watercress and parsley. Serve whole small beets on a bed of lightly sautéed beet greens, an especially beautiful combination when the stems are lightly touched with red. Mix small cubes of cooked beets with bright green frozen peas for a better, brighter mixture than peas-and-carrots.

White food can be a problem with beets because the color will stain them. Dark foods, on the other hand, are splendid. Carve a cup from a single large beet, and fill it with shiny black olives. Set it on a base of endive to make a central focus on a platter of cold sliced meat.

Berries

Berries are special. Unfortunately, the growers are devaluing their own product, for we now have strawberries year-round. And often, in midwinter, they taste remarkably like absorbent cotton.

The other side of this new availability of strawberries is that many berries that were once common have now disappeared from all but local farmstands. In the spring we have blueberries, although it is hard to find wild huckleberries. Raspberries are there in the spring at exorbitant prices, in midwinter at three times that price. You have to look farther for blackberries, loganberries, boysenberries, gooseberries and currants to use in cooking. A whole generation is growing up for whom "berries" means only strawberries and blueberries.

Buy berries in season or buy them frozen. They should have bright color, firm consistency and, if you're lucky, a sweet wild fragrance. If you can, look below the top level in the berry box to be sure that you aren't getting rotten produce. Then store them, unwashed, in the refrigerator.

Serve berries in oversized wineglasses or in low glass bowls. Whole strawberries can go on flat plates or in soup bowls. And all red berries are special on black plates.

Serve mixed berries in honeydew melon halves or scooped-out oranges, lemons and tangerines. Put whole, washed berries in baskets lined with lemon leaves or ferns.

Whenever you top berries with whipped cream, crème fraîche or zabaglione, remember to reserve one or two to put on top of the cream. It makes a big difference, looks special but uncontrived.

Strawberries

Strawberries-and-cream begins with a ½-inch pool of cream in a wide soup plate. The berries emerge from the cream like islands in a lake.

Do a very orderly plate of a circle of berries cut in half, facedown, with all the points outward, and a mint-garnished whole berry in the center. Around the first ring, do another with the halves facing up. (*Fig. 60*)

Midwinter strawberries taste blah but can be used as garnishes. Use one where you would expect a maraschino cherry: on a hot fudge sundae, on a grapefruit half or in a glass of lemonade.

Salvage out-of-season strawberries by dipping them in melted chocolate, cooling them in the refrigerator. Pass a plate of these with dessert, or use one chocolate-dipped berry to the side of a bowl of plain, undipped berries.

61

Dip whole strawberries in beaten egg white and then in granulated sugar. Arrange the frosted fruit on a bed of leaves. *(Fig. 61)*

Place strawberry halves on half-slices of orange to use as a garnish around duck or chicken. *(Fig. 62)*

Make three slices down to the stem of a large strawberry without severing it. The parts will open up into a blossom, which you can put on top of a scoop of ice cream.

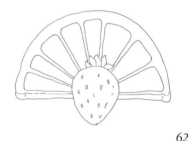

Cut a large strawberry into quarters, and arrange the petals in the center of a dish of pudding or on whipped cream. *(Fig. 63)*

62

Blueberries

Of all the berries, only blueberries, so far, are both seasonable and somewhat reasonable in price. They can be used opulently. Three boxes of blueberries stretch a box of raspberries a long way without compromising the quality of the more expensive fruit.

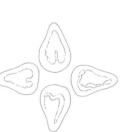

Now that strawberries are never out of season, they have become the omnipresent fruit garnish, the equivalent of parsley. To shock the eye, use blueberries instead when they're in season. The dark-blue color makes a sharp contrast with nearly all other fruits. Think of them with honeydew, with peaches, with bananas.

63

Raspberries

Be careful when you wash them. It is possible to lose most of a pint of raspberries by rinsing them in a colander under running water. The little nubbins break off and drain away, and there you are, having spent a fortune for what is left.

Raspberries have become too expensive to use any way but plain, like caviar. They're lovely with cream, heavenly with crème fraîche.

You can stretch them with blueberries or with pale green grapes. It's something like stretching the wild rice with white.

Pureed frozen raspberries make a gloriously colored sauce. Just give them a whirl in the blender. (Add an equal amount of frozen strawberries and no one will know the difference.) This makes an elegant dessert sauce with poached pears or peaches or with ice cream. One package makes enough for six servings over ice cream. Two packages will cover six dessert plates, on which you will place a wedge of fudge cake and a spoonful of whipped cream.

Beverages, Cold

We mean tall drinks, recreational drinks—the kind you serve to company and want to look special.

Start with the container. Choose beautifully shaped glasses, such as brandy snifters, red-wine goblets and tall slender iced-tea glasses. Experiment a little, and use them to serve drinks that they weren't designed for. Put orange juice in a champagne flute, chocolate milk and whipped cream in a wine goblet, a yogurt shake in an iced-tea glass.

(There are extremes, of course. Once in Italy we had vodka served in test tubes. There was a leaf-lined bowl of crushed ice. Each slim test tube had been pushed down in the ice. The fact that you couldn't put it down once you took it up meant that you were forced to drink the vodka all in a gulp, as the Russians do.)

There's also the whole rum-by-the-pool school of using fruit shells as containers for drinks. You've seen pineapples filled with fruity rum punch, and watermelons filled with crushed ice and vodka, with each guest provided with his own straw. (The alcohol, we assume, supplies the hygiene.) You can copy the idea for individual servings by emptying orange shells and filling them with crushed ice, then pouring in some vodka punch and adding a straw.

Ice as Decoration

The most obvious decorations for tall drinks are the ice cubes.

Freeze seedless grapes, blueberries or strawberries, and use them instead of ice to chill glasses of lemonade or iced tea.

52

Puree strawberries in the blender. Pour the mixture into an ice-cube tray, freeze it and drop the cubes into lemonade.

Make cubes of grape juice, cranberry juice or sweetened iced tea. Colored cubes look particularly good when they're served in champagne flutes. Try iced-coffee cubes floating in milky cold coffee.

For a children's party, fill an ice bucket with fruit-juice cubes, and let them help themselves.

Make ice cubes with water, and place a decoration in each one before it freezes. A small strawberry, a blueberry, mint leaves, a lemon curl, a mandarin orange section are all good.

Then there's the trick of freezing a bottle of vodka or aquavit in a block of ice. You cut off the top of a two-quart plastic-coated milk carton. Fill it with water. Set the bottle of vodka inside and surround it with flowers or—at holiday time—holly leaves and pine branches. Let it freeze solid, and peel off the carton.

Fruit Garnishes

Garnish tall drinks with fruit except, of course, for Bloody Marys, which take stalks of celery, carrot sticks or skewers of black olives and radishes. With a citrus peeler, remove all the rind from a lime in one long piece, and stick one end into the Bloody Mary, letting the other end hang down and curl on the plate.

Hook a thin slice of lemon-dipped apple over the edge of a glass of apple juice.

Drop a cluster of frozen grapes into iced tea. Use frozen green grapes in a glass of purple grape juice.

For lemonade, cut two very thin lemon slices. Pin them together with a toothpick, catching a spray of mint between them.

Cut a long curl of grapefruit rind and let it float, suspended, in a glass of orangeade.

In apple cider, put a cinnamon stick or a wedge of lemon stuck with a clove.

For the lemon wedge that you hook over the edge of a glass, cut half the rind away, leaving it attached, and curl it back alongside the fruit.

Dip a fruit garnish in egg white and sugar and stick it on a swizzler or on the edge of the glass. Try this with strawberries or with pineapple sections.

Mash fruit and spoon it into the bottom of a glass of club soda and white wine. Remember the Russian practice of serving raspberry preserves in glasses of hot tea.

Or the fruit can be skewered and laid alongside the glass on the saucer. Using toothpicks or short bamboo skewers, follow a simple *aba* scheme: strawberry/mint leaf/strawberry or cantaloupe/honeydew/cantaloupe.

Don't forget the trick of frosting the rim of the glass. Dip the rim into lightly beaten egg white or lemon juice and then into sugar. Let it dry. With Bloody Marys and Margaritas, use salt instead of sugar. The Italians dip the edges of coffee cups into anisette and sugar, and you get to munch on licorice-flavored sugar as you drink your coffee.

Punch

No one *owns* a punch bowl. Everybody borrows one. If your friend with the punch bowl isn't available the next time you give a large party, serve the punch from tall pitchers into wineglasses—not, however, into tall glasses, since punch mixtures are usually both highly alcoholic and disarmingly delicious and fruit-flavored.

You can devise your own punch bowl, using a large ceramic bowl, a pickling crock or a watermelon half.

Float fruit on the punch. Or make a wreath-shaped block of ice in a ring mold. Fill the mold halfway with water and stick it in the freezer. When it's very cold, add mint leaves and grapes. Fill with more water and put it back to finish freezing.

Biscuits

Biscuits are a good example of the way a familiar food can be varied and improved by changing nothing but its shape.

Roll biscuit dough into its usual ¼–½-inch-thick sheet. Then cut it into traditional circles with a biscuit cutter or a glass, or into

54

diamonds with a sharp knife. Or slice off biscuit fingers ½ inch wide and 3 inches long. For a fancy lunch, cut with a cookie cutter in an uncomplicated shape: a crescent or a scallopped circle.

Roll the dough into 6-inch circles, and cut each circle into six wedges. The biscuits will resemble English scones or griddle cakes.

Roll out two thin layers of biscuit dough. Spread one with strawberry jam or chopped ham salad, and cover the filling with the second sheet of dough. Then cut the sandwiches into squares or diamonds before you bake them.

Roll out the dough very very thin. Sprinkle it with cinnamon sugar, and roll it up into a jelly roll. Slice the roll into ½-inch-thick pieces and bake.

All of the versions of rolled biscuits can be glazed with a wash of milk or of beaten egg before they are baked.

Bread

Home-baked bread and rolls should be splendidly shaped and glazed: not perfect, not like machine-made bread, but smooth and symmetrical nonetheless.

Once the mysteries of yeast baking have been mastered, and you know the feel of well-kneaded bread, the look of dough that has doubled in bulk and the sound a fully baked loaf makes when you tap it, then it's time to pay attention to the look of the loaf. To a large extent, a loaf of bread is shaped, slashed and glazed in order to improve its crust. But these techniques have developed into a form of decoration all their own.

There are two basic forms of shaping. The first is done in a pan, either in a traditional loaf pan or in such variations as a brioche mold or a coffee can. The second method of shaping is free-form. This includes traditional round loaves, long baguettes, braids and double braids, but it has also developed into a minor form of sculpture among people who make daisies and animals out of bread dough.

Slashing protects the basic shape of the loaf by preventing it from simply cracking open randomly as it expands. Professional bakers have developed patterns of slashing that are now part of the look of a loaf.

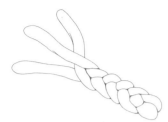

64

65

Glazing bread is simpler than glazing sweet cakes, being mostly directed toward creating a darker or a harder crust than unglazed dough would form.

Shaping

To shape bread for a loaf pan, pat it between your palms until you form an oval lump long enough to touch the ends of the pan. The buttered interior of the bread pan will help the bread to rise.

There are other ways of shaping loaves. You can make two spherical lumps of dough and place them, touching, in a bread pan. They will cleave together when they bake.

Some bakers roll out a thick sheet of dough with a rolling pin, then roll it up and put it into the pan, seam side down. Others roll the dough, then fold in the sides, patting it into shape with their palms, and keeping the seam on the bottom of the pan.

To shape a loaf for a brioche mold or a coffee can, just make a roughly circular ball of dough, and place it in the container, with the smooth surface down.

To shape free-form dough takes skill, since only the force of the crust itself works to preserve the shape. One help is a basket that the French call a *banneton*. It's a shallow wicker bowl that they use to impress a shape on a rising round loaf. You can do the same in a buttered metal or glass bowl, and then turn it out onto the baking sheet.

You can also shape a round or oval loaf with your hands, gently patting and tucking the dough underneath as you turn it.

To shape a long french bread, roll out a rectangle of dough. Fold the long sides toward the center. Fold in half again lengthwise. Turning the seam down, pull and pat the dough into shape.

To shape a braid, roll a thick rectangle of dough and cut it into three strands, leaving them attached at one end. Then simply braid it, crossing the left over the center, then the right over the center, and repeating to the end. Tuck in the ends. *(Fig. 64)*

To make a double braid, cut the dough into two unequal parts. Make a large braid from the larger part, a small braid from the smaller part, and set the small braid on top of the large one to rise. *(Fig. 65)*

56

To make a false braid, pat the dough into a rather thin rectangle. Measure the width, and divide it into three panels. Cut downward-slanted slashes toward the center on each of the side panels. Then fold the strips over one another and over the center panel, starting with the top of the loaf.

Scandinavian cooks make a complicated five-strand braided bread. They roll out the dough and cut it into five equal strands, leaving them attached at one end. If the left-hand strand is always called 1, and the numbers go across from left to right, the braiding goes in a sequence of three steps that are repeated. First 2 over 3. Then 5 over 2. Then 1 over 3. Try it with yarn before you try it with bread dough. *(Figs. 66–68)*

Slashing

Slashing is done on the top of a loaf of bread after it is shaped and before it goes through its final rising before it bakes. As the bread expands, the slash opens out and forms a decorative pattern, rather than bursting any which way. You slash bread either with a very sharp knife or by snipping with shears.

Cut bread in a loaf pan either three times straight across the length, three times slanted or once down the length of the loaf.

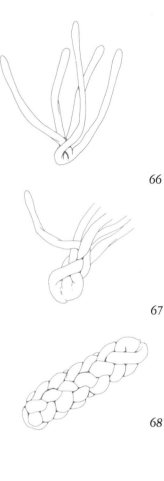

66

67

68

69

57

Cut long french bread several times on the diagonal down the length of the bread.

Cut a round loaf either in a cross or, more decoratively, in a checkerboard over the top of the mound. Or cut three parallel slashes.

Cut bread made in a ring mold in many short slashes across the width of the bread.

Braided loaves are usually not slashed, since they don't often open up in the baking.

Glazing

Bread is not usually glazed for flavor, but rather to change the look and quality of the crust. As simple an act as brushing the loaf with cold water just before it goes into the oven actually helps the bread to rise. By keeping the outer surface of the bread moist and soft, it permits the action of the yeast to proceed freely.

Common glazes are done with whole eggs or egg white. Beat an egg white with 2 tablespoons of water, and brush it onto a loaf before you bake it to encourage a dark, crisp crust. Use a wash of whole egg with a tablespoon of water, milk or cream to encourage a well-browned crust.

Any loaf can be sprinkled on the glaze with caraway, poppy or sesame seeds, with coarse salt or with well-fried onion bits.

Serving

To serve bread, line a basket with a colorful napkin. Place the sliced bread in the basket.

Put unsliced bread on a bread board, with a serrated knife nearby.

A more formal presentation is to place a single roll on each bread plate. The European way is to place a roll at every place setting, right on the table.

Special Breads

To make garlic bread, cut a long loaf of french bread nearly through in 2-inch slices. Brush garlic-flavored butter on the cut surfaces. For a more decorative look, add chopped parsley or basil to the butter.

To make melba toast, put plain bread in the toaster. When it's done, it will be quite easy to slice each piece in half through the still-soft center of the bread. Then place under the broiler, to toast the uncooked side.

Bread Crumbs

A thickener and a coating, but also a garnish.

Use as a garnish in two ways. To make a dish au gratin, sprinkle dried bread crumbs over it, dot with butter and slide the dish under the broiler until the crumbs are brown.

Crumbs are also used as garnish when they are browned in melted butter in a skillet, often with the addition of parsley, bacon bits or chopped nuts. They are then poured over such foods as asparagus or broccoli.

Breakfast Cereal

There's a simple fact about cereal: if the kid hates oatmeal, you won't get him to eat it by drawing a little clown in maple syrup on top of it. He'll just eat off the maple syrup. Period.

Forget cute. Think wholesome.

That means serving cereal in hearty earthenware or ceramic bowls in dark brown, beige or blue-and-white stripes.

It means sprinkling bowls of cold cereal with not one but two kinds of fruit, such as strawberries, blueberries, mandarin orange or banana slices. Or adding almonds, coconut or sunflower seeds to make a mock-granola.

Serve hot grits in half an orange shell, with a sprinkle of crumbled bacon on top. If you serve it in a soup bowl, then make two parallel lines on top with the bacon bits. Good with hot cornmeal mush, too.

Any hot cereal can be topped with a thin orange slice, either lying flat, standing on end or in a twist. Flank it with strawberries.

Top the cereal with a spoonful of melting preserves.

With a cluster of lingonberries or a pile of raisins.

With thin-sliced apple wedges.

With a whirl of honey, maple syrup or brown sugar.

Best of all, top cereal with a spoonful of thick whipped cream and strawberries, like belgian waffles. The cream goes on at the table, where it begins to melt instantly. You can use yogurt instead, but it's not the same, not the same at all.

Broccoli

Broccoli at its best is a brilliant emerald-green, nearly purple. Once over the hill, it becomes yellow, the stems turn woody and the whole thing begins to sprout flowers. Choose top-notch broccoli and separate the stems from the flowerets. Begin to cook the stems at least 5 minutes before you add the flowerets to the pot. And don't overcook. One minute too long in the wok or steamer, and broccoli turns gray-green and limp.

Color

Set off the strong color with white. Garnish broccoli with sieved hard-boiled egg whites or egg whites chopped with parsley.

Stir-fry it with bamboo shoots and water chestnuts.

Combine the flowerets with snowy cauliflower flowerets.

Yellow is good, too. Sprinkle with hard-boiled egg yolks or finely chopped lemon zest. Or with gremolata, an Italian seasoning made of finely chopped parsley, lemon rind and garlic.

Spoon golden hollandaise or cheese sauce over the stems. Hold out a few flowerets. Cover the vegetable with the sauce and place a cluster of flowerets on top to show what lies beneath.

Lemon sparks both the color and the taste. Reassemble the cooked flowerets in a mound. Cut several thin lemon slices through to the rind. Twist them into S curves, and stick them here and there on the mound of broccoli. Nice with orange slices, too. *(Fig. 70)*

Broccoli looks wonderful on a bright red plate.

70

Shape

In shape, it isn't one vegetable, but three. We serve broccoli whole, in flowerets or in stems.

Lay whole stalks of broccoli on a serving plate with parsleyed new potatoes or sautéed mushrooms on either side. Cross the stems with strips of pimiento or red pepper.

Use the flowerets to make a border around a mound of food. Do an unbroken chain, or cluster groups of flowerets with cherry tomatoes and black olives.

If you have used the flowerets and have only the stems left, don't despair. First, peel them. Then cut them as you would a carrot or asparagus. Slice them straight across into circles. Slant the circles to make ovals. Slice lengthwise to make julienne strips. Finally, dice the strips. Many of these cuts can be used raw in a plate of crudités; all of them go well in a stir-fry.

The final solution for broccoli is to puree it. It's easily done in a food processor, which turns it a pale, buttery green. Serve it with other purees, such as carrot, turnip or cauliflower. Don't forget to hold out a bit of the whole vegetable and place it in the center of the puree for identification.

An interesting way to use broccoli is to separate the stems from the flowerets and then puree only the stems. Use the puree as a sauce with the lightly steamed flowerets.

Brussels Sprouts

Have you ever seen a really fresh Brussels sprout? It is bright green, and it wears its leaves spread open like a miniature cabbage.

This relative of the cabbage is available all winter long. When it comes to our markets it is usually tightly closed. If you're lucky, you'll find Brussels sprouts that are bright green: they don't have to look like olive-colored lumps. Peel away the yellowed or black-spotted leaves. Then cut an X in the stem end and soak the vegetable in water for 15 minutes before you cook it to dislodge any soil that is left between the leaves.

71

Surprisingly enough, for a vegetable that is so frequently overcooked, Brussels sprouts can be eaten raw. Cut them in half vertically and serve on a plate of crudités. Or stir-fry briefly, leaving them tender and still bright green. Steam the sprouts and let them cool, and serve them with mayonnaise or vinaigrette. Or combine hot steamed sprouts with sautéed cherry tomatoes and black olives. The clue, always, is to stop the cooking before the sprouts turn pale and become overcooked.

Even though supermarket sprouts huddle tightly closed, they don't have to stay that way. After peeling off the discolored leaves, unfurl the next few leaves, using your thumb and index finger to turn them outward, re-creating the cabbage shape. Then steam briefly to develop the color. Suddenly beautiful, these make excellent garnishes. *(Fig. 71)*

A slightly fussy but colorful idea for a garnish is to hollow out the center of a cooked Brussels sprout. Fill it with parsley-dotted cream cheese, with egg salad or, best of all, with a cherry tomato.

Butter/Margarine

Whether you choose butter or margarine is a matter for your own conscience, taste and pocketbook. Many people, worried about animal fats, choose margarine. Others, who feel that margarine has too many additives, choose butter. Dieticians think we're better off with neither. But for the true voluptuary, there's nothing as good as the taste of fresh bread spread with creamy sweet butter.

Both butter and margarine come in ¼-pound sticks, in pound bricks and in tubs. In addition, butter can be bought in bulk. For fancy carving, margarine seems to be the more workable medium. A butter curler moves more evenly across its surface than that of butter, and the curl bends more easily. Whenever you do butter sculpture, however, you have to be careful with the temperature of your utensils and of the butter itself.

We have a weakness for butter served simply. We like the pretense that it comes to the table fresh from the creamery, wrapped in damp leaves. It is, of course, pure make-believe in this day of ultrapasteurization and deep-freezing.

Start with a chunk of bulk butter. If you can't get it, a carton of whipped butter will do. Turn it out onto a heavy earthenware plate, a wooden trencher or a pewter dish. But first cover the plate with freshly washed lemon leaves from the florist. The butter will look as though it comes straight from the dairy.

One very expensive restaurant in New York creates this same illusion by providing every table with a pound of bulk butter wrapped in lettuce leaves.

Serve butter as they do in France, in individual earthenware crocks. Soften the butter, press it into the crocks and refrigerate again. They go one to a place setting.

It is, in some circles, considered more elegant—and it is decidedly more thrifty—to serve butter in portions rather than in bulk. After all, he who cuts the pats controls the serving size. To cut a brick of butter into neat pats, cover a knife with wax paper or the butter wrapper. Before you slice it, you could score the stick of butter with the tines of a fork.

Shape individual butter pats in round wooden stamps carved with flowers. These are made in Scandinavia. Scald the stamp, spread softened butter into it, then push the plunger so that the decorated disk drops out into ice water.

More portion control. Use a melon baller to scoop out balls of butter. Pile them on a serving plate.

Decorate the butter balls with Scandinavian butter paddles. Place a ball between two of the striated wooden paddles and roll it around and around. This random activity makes, for some reason, a very tidy crisscross on the surface. *(Fig. 72)*

A highly specialized tool is the butter curler, a metal hook attached to a wooden handle. You scrape the sharpened side of the hook along the top of a brick of butter. Off comes a long, thin strip that curls immediately into a shell. It's not only pretty, but practical. It makes a tiny portion. And because there is so much surface area, the shell is always at the right consistency for spreading, even when it comes right from the refrigerator.

All of these small portions of butter keep best when they are put into ice water and held in the refrigerator. If your dining room is cool, they can sit on a plate on the table. If it's hot, they should be put in a

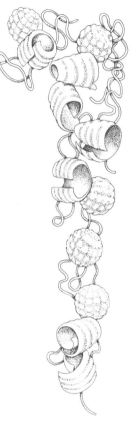

72

63

bowl that has chunks of ice in the bottom, with the ice covered by a lettuce leaf.

The least durable way of serving butter is vermicelli, made by scraping a lemon zester over a bar of butter. You keep the narrow squiggles of butter in ice water until you're ready to serve them, heaped on a leaf rinsed in cool water. If you're very speedy, you can pile a heap of butter vermicelli on a dish of hot vegetables and run to the table.

Caterers make butter flowers with softened, often tinted butter and cake-decorating tools. It's much easier to learn to make a huge butter rose. A pound of butter will make four beautiful pale-yellow roses. And don't sneer until you've seen them. They're gorgeous.

All you need is a cheese scraper. Pull it over the surface of a ¼-pound bar of cold but not frozen butter. Each scrape creates a rectangular "petal" that curls up as it's cut. The rose is built from these petals.

To make the rose in a 3½-inch ramekin, scrape off lengths of butter and stand them vertically inside the walls of the pot. The tops will fold outward slightly, but you may have to bend them to increase the flowery look. Then put other lengths inside them in ever-smaller circles, having all the petals overlap. In the very center, stand a single petal rolled up into a cylinder.

When you're done, place the ramekin in a shallow bowl of chopped ice, with a real rose leaf sticking out of the ice. Or make the flower on a flat plate covered with lemon leaves. *(Fig. 73)*

Butter Garnishes

From fine to applied art—butter is used, too, to garnish other foods. Mix softened butter with fresh parsley, basil or dill, and put a dab on steak or vegetables to melt and flavor them. Spread canapés or open-faced sandwiches with this butter. Roll the flavored butter into a cylinder and freeze it, and all you have to do is cut off a piece when you want it.

Make butter yellow by mashing it with hard-boiled egg yolks or lemon rind. Make it green with finely chopped parsley, spinach or watercress. Make red butter in the food processor or with a mortar and

73

pestle by blending butter with paprika or pimiento. For biscuits and popovers, blend butter with strawberries. For waffles and pancakes, process it with honey and cinnamon.

The great classic butter garnish is beurre noir: butter cooked to a rich dark brown and used to flavor and color white foods such as cauliflower, fish and brains.

Cabbage

Cabbage is a winter vegetable: homely, sustaining, but, alas, something less than beautiful. The most common variety is pale green, with smooth leaves, but we have also dark green, curly leafed savoy cabbage, dark red cabbage and both bok choy and Chinese celery cabbage.

Choose firm, unwilted heads. If you use only part of a head, wrap the rest in plastic wrap and store it in the refrigerator. Green cabbage is greenest in late summer, whitest in midwinter. The magenta color of red cabbage can be preserved if you add vinegar or lemon juice during the cooking. Thus, sweet-and-sour cabbage.

Cabbage is cooked shredded, in chunks and in leaves. However you cook it, the color stays brightest and the odor quietest if you undercook. To make individual stuffed cabbage leaves, blanch the leaves, cut away a wedge from the stem and roll the leaf from the cutaway edge to the tip. You can make round cabbage rolls by placing the leaf with its filling on a dish towel, and then twisting the towel tightly. Most spectacular of all is a whole stuffed cabbage, made in cheesecloth, in a string bag or, as in Julia Child's *Mastering the Art of French Cooking,* volume 2, in a bowl.

Raw cabbage, until recently, meant either sauerkraut or coleslaw. Now we have an explosion of recipes for cold marinated Chinese cabbage. But coleslaw is still probably the form in which we most frequently encounter cabbage. You can enliven its appearance by mixing red and green cabbage, or by adding shredded carrot, green or sweet red peppers or parsley to the plain cabbage.

Use coleslaw as a garnish on a sandwich platter when the lettuce supply is less than wonderful. Serve it in tomato cases or cucumber cups or hollowed green peppers.

Add shredded red cabbage to tossed green salads. Use a bed of dry shredded cabbage underneath raw marinated vegetables.

A whole red cabbage can be made into a container for dips. Hollow out the center, and put a clear glass bowl in the space. Then tuck raw vegetables among the leaves. The loose-leafed savoy cabbage is best for this purpose.

Cake Decorating

Cake decorating is a huge subject. Chefs take courses in it: beginning, intermediate and advanced. At its most specialized, it requires more technical skill than anything else in cooking. At its simplest, it's a craft anyone should be able to perform.

You won't become a pastry chef by reading this essay. No spun sugar, no roses sculpted from butter cream. But you'll learn enough of the principles to do a more than competent job without having to master complicated techniques.

You will choose a design by looking at the section on ARRANGEMENT (see pages 1–7) and applying it to the shape of your cake. Then you'll follow the design either by manipulating the frosting, by adding a contrasting color of frosting or by applying other food to the surface of the cake.

The basis of all cake decoration should be the shape of the cake and the shape of the pieces you're going to cut. It's obvious. Square and rectangular cakes are cut into squares, round cakes in wedges, loaf cakes into slices and ring-shaped cakes into wedges without points.

The decoration should reflect these serving shapes. It can be done as obviously as by making lines of contrasting icing piped out from the center to the edges of a round cake. Or it can be as offhand as placing a broken border of mints around the bottom of a ring cake, so that each cut falls halfway between the clusters. *(Figs. 74, 75)*

74

You don't have to overdo it. Just make sure that the decoration complements, rather than interferes with, the shape of a serving.

So first you choose a basic pattern: concentric, radiating, symmetrical or asymmetrical, striped or checkerboard.

If you're frosting a chocolate cake with white icing, to minimize chocolate crumbs mixing with the frosting, first glaze the cake with a

75

mixture of icing diluted with water. Then ice the cake. To achieve a neat finish on the icing, you first cover the plate with two sheets of wax paper that overlap an inch in the center. After you spread on the icing, you pull out the sheets of wax paper, and all the messy bits will come with them.

76

Now trace your design on the icing with the point of a toothpick, so that later on you won't have to worry about spacing the decoration evenly. Restaurant supply houses sell inexpensive plastic triangles and compasses to help with this job, but you can do just as well with a toothpick, a straightedge and, at most, a compass.

Once you've chosen your design and traced it on the cake, you have the choice of doing it by sculpting the icing, by putting on a contrasting color of icing or by adding other foods. None of these techniques takes any technical skill whatsoever.

Suppose you decide to do a concentric design on a round layer cake.

If you're going to manipulate the frosting, first apply it heavily all over the cake. Then put the point of a spatula or knife or the tip of a teaspoon in the center of the top of the cake. Turn the plate slowly as you drag the spatula out toward the border, creating a spiral on the top of the cake. *(Fig. 76)*

77

If you're going to add a contrasting frosting, cover the cake in white icing. Then draw on three thin bands of chocolate icing: one at the edge of the top, and two more, each an inch inside the outer ring. To finish it off, place a blob in the top center. *(Fig. 77)*

And if you're going to decorate by adding other foods, do that in rings, too. You can take your pick: nuts (halved, whole or chopped), candy (M&M's, mints, jelly beans, gumdrops, chocolate chips), candied fruit, chocolate curls, half-slices of orange or lemon, frosted grapes or berries dipped in egg white and sugar, mandarin orange sections, sprinkles, colored shot, colored sugar, coconut, raisins, dates. *(Fig. 78)*

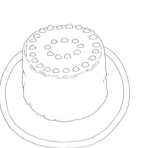

78

The food you apply should have some relation to the flavor of the cake. On a Black Forest cake, use alternating circles of candied cherries and chocolate curls. On a spice cake, use candied ginger and walnuts.

Now imagine using these three techniques with other designs, and you'll be well on your way to being a competent cake decorator.

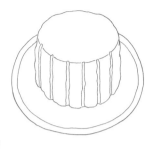

79

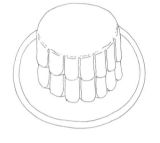

80

81

82

Sides Versus Top

Another choice is to decorate only the sides or only the top of a cake. By the techniques of sculpting, adding contrasting icing or adding other foods, you will:

Use your spatula to push vertical stripes of frosting up the thick icing of the sides of the cake. Or to sculpt columns of overlapping petals on the sides. *(Figs. 79, 80)*

Cover the sides with dark chocolate icing and the top with a raspberry glaze.

Press cookie crumbs into the icing around the sides of the cake, leaving the top icing plain.

If the top is left plain, it's a good idea to put some of the side decoration in the center. Thus, if you have a lemon cake covered with white icing, and if you've spread marmalade over the icing around the sides, place an orange flat in the center and accent with greens, or put a lemon gumdrop in the center top. *(Fig. 81)*

If you've covered the sides with a zigzag of licorice sticks to make the cake look like a drum, put three chunks of licorice on the top.

Borders

Create a border around the top by icing the top heavily, and then pushing a lot of the icing out to the edge. Cut parenthesis-shaped lines into this rope of icing. *(Fig. 82)*

Drizzle dark chocolate or bright raspberry jam around the edge of the top, and let it drip down the sides of the cake. *(Fig. 83)*

Make a border of nuts or candies around the edge. Look at the section on ARRANGEMENT (see pages 1–7) for variations in a linear chain.

Some Easy Tricks with Cakes

They're almost too simple to mention. But, in case it hadn't occurred to you:

Make a zigzag design over the top of a rectangular or loaf cake with the serrated blade of a bread knife.

68

Frost a cake with chocolate. Then lay three 1-inch-wide strips of wax paper on it. Sift on powdered sugar, and there will be chocolate stripes on the white top of the cake.

Do the same with a doily or stencil, and you'll have a snowflake on the top of the cake.

83

Frost a rectangular cake. Take a fork, and draw parallel lines down the length of the cake. Then take the fork and cross these lines, doing one set north-south and the second set east-west.

Put white frosting on a cake, holding back about ¼ cup. Color the reserved icing with melted chocolate or jam. Dip a cookie cutter into the colored frosting and press it into the sides or top of the cake.

Buy a tube of colored frosting at the supermarket. With it, make tiny flowers all over the surface of a chocolate-covered cake, so that you have a gingham design. Or make chains of flowers laid out in radiating lines on the top of the cake and down the sides. Then cut the cake so each slice gets a chain of flowers. *(Fig. 84)*

84

Ice a cake with white frosting. Melt an ounce of chocolate with about ½ teaspoon of butter. Drizzle the melted chocolate in thin parallel lines on the cake from the tip of a teaspoon. (You can also use lines drawn with tubed colored frosting.) With a dinner knife, cross the chocolate lines so that they are pulled slightly out of shape, and it looks like the icing on top of a Napoleon. *(Fig. 85)*

There are lots of other things to do with cake. There are molds that let you make Easter bunnies and lambs. There are ways to cut sheet cakes so cleverly that, with a few minutes work, you'll wind up with a cake shaped like the Statue of Liberty. And there are ways to spin sugar so that you make breathtaking replicas of roses, ferns and satin ribbons.

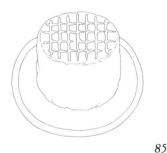

85

They're all fine, but they're not within the province of this book. We wanted to show you ways to approach a plain iced cake and, with some planning and next to no skill, make it look finished. For a fuller discussion of techniques of cake decorating, you might look into such books as *Simplified Cake Decorating* from Ateca, a major manufacturer of cake-decorating equipment; *Creative Cakes* by Stephanie Crookston, Random House, 1978; and the *Wilton Yearbook of Cake Decorating,* Wilton Enterprises (Book Division, 1603 S. Michigan Ave., Chicago, IL 60616, annual).

Canapés

In the movies of the thirties, someone was always giving a cocktail party. While the guests drank Martinis and Sidecars, the butler passed among them with a silver tray of canapés.

Now we give white wine parties, serve a whole Stilton and a basket of raw vegetables and let the guests help themselves. But on special occasions it's still a treat to have a small platter of canapés passed, not by the butler, but by the host.

A canapé is a treat to the eye, and one bite in the mouth. Make them on squares of dense-textured bread, thinly sliced rye or pumpernickel or a good white bread that is toasted. Like the miniature Danish open sandwiches that they resemble, they first must be spread with softened butter to keep the filling from soaking in.

Patterns for Canapés

Absolutely the easiest arrangement of canapés is a checkerboard made of alternating squares of bread completely covered with black caviar and pink smoked salmon. Surround the checkerboard with a line of parsley. If it's too expensive a platter, cover the bread squares with yellow cheese spread and ham salad instead.

The handsomest canapés have a bold graphic look that pays tribute to the Art Deco style of their heyday. There are thousands of possible variations. Here are five designs made from common canapé ingredients. *(Fig. 86)*

The first is a bread square divided in half parallel to its sides. It can be covered first with a square of ham, which is then half-covered with a rectangle of cheese. Or take a notecard and, holding it perpendicular to the bread, spread one side of it with red caviar and the other side with cream cheese. *(a)*

The second pattern is a bread square divided in half on the diagonal. Cover the bread entirely with dark pureed spinach. Then, use your notecard again, this time dividing the square on the diagonal. Spread finely chopped egg on one half of the bread. *(b)*

The third pattern is a triangle superimposed upon a square. The base of the triangle touches two corners of one side of the square. The

a

b

top of the triangle meets the center of the opposite side. Let the rectangular background be ham, the triangle white provolone. *(c)*

In the fourth pattern, there is a diamond superimposed on the square. To make this, cover the bread with mustard mayonnaise and set a diamond of dark sausage on top of it. *(d)*

And in the fifth pattern, there is a circle superimposed on the square. Cover the bread with a slice of ham. Then place a juice glass upside down over it. Spread the part of the ham not covered by the glass with chopped egg. Or cover the bread with red caviar and make the circle by laying a slice of hard-boiled egg on it. *(e)*

Once the basic patterns have been set, you can add a garnish or not to each canapé. In general, the modern graphic look is best served without a garnish. But you can put a dot of caper or a bit of black olive in the center of the circle of hard-boiled egg. You can lay a flat leaf of Italian parsley on the dividing line on a canapé that is half-covered with provolone and half with ham salad. Or you can add height by sticking a slice of carrot, a cube of cheese or a puff of cress upright on the canapé.

Arranging the Tray

One way to arrange the tray is to be sure that there are one or two common ingredients among all the canapés. Suppose it's something like chopped egg or red caviar. Every pattern will have one or the other on it: a garnish of red caviar, a base of chopped egg salad. Then you can put all the canapés of different designs together with their sides touching, and they will form a striking geometrical design. If your platter looks chaotic, reduce the variety of designs and ingredients.

For a more formal look, you will arrange the tray simply, leaving lots of empty space. Let the silver show, or cover it with a white linen napkin. Then make a line of five identical canapés down the center of the tray. On either side, make an *abab* chain, using two different kinds of canapé. Accent with greenery, with lemon halves or with cherry tomatoes.

c

d

e

86

71

Candied Fruit

A very beautiful, very transitory garnish for desserts, made by dipping strawberries, grapes, pineapple chunks or tangerine sections into a sugar syrup. The syrup hardens, forming a brittle, transparent crust through which you can see the color of the fruit.

Candied fruits have to be made within a few hours of serving. They are beautiful served on a white dish or laid on the saucer underneath a goblet full of sherbet or ice cream. If you want to try to make candied fruit garnishes, see *The Joy of Cooking.*

Candy

Serve it from the box, unless you're ashamed of the source. Some candies carry their own prestige. They come in tiny gold boxes with wax seals and cost enough to make you laugh at the phrase *penny candy.*

But once some of the candy has been eaten, you can't serve it from the box anymore. That's like putting out an already-cut birthday cake. You have to remove it to a plate.

Take cheaper candies out of their boxes, too, and arrange them on plates covered with paper doilies, crumpled colored tissue paper or green leaves. Arrange them in circular or radiating designs. If you have two varieties, arrange them in an alternating checkerboard pattern or in alternate circles.

Serve penny candy as though it were high quality, and it will be convincing.

Make up a tall glass jar of different candies in layers: licorice, then pastel mints, then foil-wrapped chocolate kisses.

Sparkling candy, like gumdrops and jelly beans, looks good in crystal bowls. Peppermint sticks and lollipops stand in juice glasses. Jordan almonds go in white earthenware pots de crème.

Put fudge in a basket lined with a napkin. A dark brown napkin under white fudge, a tan napkin with dark chocolate.

Serve fruit-shaped candies, such as chocolate-covered cherries, orange and lemon jelly slices and raspberry drops, in wooden berry boxes.

Garnish a plate of mints with mint leaves. Put green mints in red glass dishes for Christmas.

Combine real fruit with candy. Surround a pyramid of strawberries with chocolates.

Capers

Anchovies add a visual *dash* to food, and capers are the *dots* that go with them. They are the buds of a woody shrub, *Capparis spinosa,* that grows in southern Europe. The unopened flowers are picked, then pickled in vinegar, and we buy them in small, costly jars. Visually, capers work like asterisks: dark spots to draw the eye. For example, one caper placed on the mashed egg yolk of a deviled egg. They are part of the essential preparation of several dishes, such as steak tartare and vitello tonnato.

Carrots

Raw carrots are the one vegetable everyone likes because they are crunchy, vaguely sweet and brightly colored. These root vegetables, members of the parsley family, are sold in leafy bunches or plastic bags all year round. The best ones are deep orange in color, firm and smooth in shape. Small carrots have the best taste, but large old woody carrots have their uses, too. They can be grated in a food processor and used on top of a green salad, or they can be cut into big chunks and cooked under a roast along with the potatoes.

Health-food people prefer to eat their carrots only scrubbed, and not scraped. Most people scrape or peel them with a vegetable peeler, like the brighter color and sweeter taste that result.

To make carrot sticks, cut the vegetable in half lengthwise, then place the halves facedown on the counter for stability. Then cut into julienne strips with a paring knife. Cut across the strips, and you have cubes.

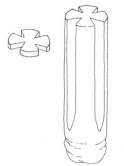

You can simply slice a carrot directly across the grain into rounds. Chinese cooks have more interesting ways of cutting them. They slice them on a slant into long, thin ovals. The thinness allows the carrot to be cooked through in the same amount of time as bamboo shoots and water chestnut slices.

The Chinese also use a technique called the roll cut to make carrot pieces with lots of surface area for the absorption of flavor. The carrot is cut on the diagonal, then given a quarter turn and cut again. Every two cuts makes a chunk. *(Fig. 87)*

Another oriental technique is to incise three or four narrow V-shaped wedges down the length of the carrot, using a paring knife or, if you like to cook Chinese, a cleaver. Then make horizontal slices, creating flat flower shapes. Serve them raw on salads, or steam them and float them on soup, or combine them with other cooked vegetables in dishes such as pasta primavera. *(Fig. 88)*

For more elaborate shapes, you can use an aspic or truffle cutter to stamp out star shapes from slices of parboiled carrot. Use these red-orange cutouts under aspics and in salads. If you use the same cutter on a thin slice of turnip, you can fill the star-shaped hole in the carrot disk with a star-shaped bit of white turnip.

Carrots and . . .

With a melon baller, scoop out rounds of parboiled carrot, and mix them with peas, or sprinkle on cooked spinach.

Because of peas-and-carrots, we know that orange carrots look good with green. Try other greens: watercress, dill, parsley and mint are all compatible with the carrot's slightly sweet taste.

Mix disks of broccoli stem with disks of carrot in a stir-fry. Stir-fry roll-cut carrots with halved Brussels sprouts.

Mix julienne-cut carrots with similarly shaped potatoes and turnips and sauté in butter all together. Place olive-shaped carrots, potatoes and turnips underneath a roast, to cook in the melting fat.

As Garnish

Take a fat old carrot and carve one of the flowers described under RADISHES (see page 214). For example, whittle the end of the carrot to

87

88

a point. Make thin petallike slices toward the point, and then twist the body of the carrot out from the "flower."

Make a carrot ribbon. Japanese chefs do them with huge, sharp cleavers; you can use a vegetable scraper. Slice a big carrot in half lengthwise, and then scrape a single wide strip from the cut surface. Pull the scraper toward you, and drop the strip into ice water, where it will curl up by itself.

These thin strips are very malleable. Thread one on a skewer. Fold one in a flat bow or into a rose. Fringe the ends or the sides of a carrot ribbon and drop it into ice water to make it curl up.

This is easier than it looks. Cut a lengthwise slit into a carrot ribbon, leaving both ends intact for at least an inch. Soak the strip in salted water to make it malleable. Then stick one end through the slit. Use as a garnish.

Less fanciful (and less work, if you have a food processor) are carrot shreds. With them, make puffs and nests of raw shredded carrot salad, with sprigs of Italian parsley tucked around them. Use them as a base for pickles and bits of cold vegetables.

If you can get tiny sweet carrots, cook them whole. Arrange bunches of three carrots with a few sprigs of greens—Italian parsley or dill—at the top to simulate carrot greens. Place this at one end of a meat platter, with the carrots pointing away from the meat.

Casseroles

In classic French cooking, a casserole is a serving dish made from rice and filled with food in a sauce. In America, of course, a casserole is both a pot—often made of earthenware—and the food that is served in it. It's the mainstay of young actors, graduate students, and people with large families—everyone who wants filling food at a low cost.

The food is a long-cooked mixture of meat, sauce and starch. Visually, it tends to be a homogenous mass, gray to brown in tint, with, at best, a crunchy top. Luckily, the pots themselves are usually well designed and brightly colored.

It would be nice if you could always suit the style of the food to the pot. If you could cook your rice pudding in a homely brown crock, your Italian macaroni and sausage mixture in bright red enameled steel. But in fact we usually choose pots that are the right size rather than the right style and it usually turns out to be all right.

Individual casseroles look best. Remember the individual pots of baked beans served at the Automat? And onion soup in its own crock? Set each one on a dessert dish, and that on a dinner plate. A very hot crock of onion soup can be set on a folded napkin nest on the dinner plate. It protects the plate and helps to keep the soup hot.

But suppose you have this big pot full of leftovers and noodles and sauce. The only place to decorate it is on its top. Put a design in place for the last few minutes of cooking. It's a simple matter, and it makes a great difference.

Use ingredients you hold back from the food—tomatoes and parsley on an Italian noodle casserole, hard-boiled egg slices on a creamy chicken a la king. Or use foods of contrasting colors—red and green pepper rings on a cheese and rice casserole or pimiento and black olives on a tuna noodle casserole.

Arrange a circle of overlapping tomato and mozzarella slices around a central puff of green Italian parsley.

Make a wheel of canned asparagus stalks around three tomato wedges over a dark cheese and spinach mixture.

Do another wheel, this one of strips of orange Cheddar, on a pale macaroni-and-cheese.

Cover the surface of the casserole with a crust. Try buttered cornflakes or bread crumbs, or a pinwheel of toast triangles. A ring of biscuits, mashed potatoes piped in a circle or spread with a knife, and shapes cut from the frozen dough found in supermarket cases are all simple standard coverings for casseroles.

Make a lattice of bacon slices on a pot of ham or beans. Cook until the bacon is crisp, then pour on a thick slick of maple syrup or honey and heat through.

Or do a lattice of bright yellow cheese. Melt it slightly, but leave enough space between the latticework so that it doesn't all run together.

Catsup

There's no right way to serve catsup. The bottle on the table has no style. But neither do we like the chubby plastic tomato that squirts catsup through its stem. Nor do we want to spoon catsup on our french fries from a cut crystal bowl. Maybe a white ceramic bowl and spoon, a mustard pot, or a small white crockery pitcher would do.

Then again, perhaps certain foods, such as catsup, Rice Krispies, Coke and tins of caviar, are meant to come to the table in their commercial containers.

Cauliflower

A head of cauliflower looks like a big ball of popcorn. Buy the whitest, creamiest cauliflower you can get, with the most tightly clenched flowerets. The yellow curds and slatternly look of overgrown cauliflower can never be set right. A few brown spots can be trimmed away without great loss, but heavily spotted cauliflower should be left behind.

It is in season most of the year. For the few months when it isn't, frozen cauliflower makes an acceptable alternative.

To retain the vegetable's white color, steam it over milk or water. Cook whole or cut into flowerets. If you add lemon to the cooking water, it helps to eliminate cauliflower's cabbagelike odor.

With Green

It looks wonderful with green. Parsley is good. Or place cooked cauliflower on a bed of dark green raw spinach, and wedge some spinach leaves here and there between the flowerets. *(Fig. 89)*

The next time you make spinach and bacon salad, substitute raw or cold cooked cauliflower for the usual mushrooms.

Broccoli is a natural companion for cauliflower, being similar in shape, very different in color. Make groupings of three pieces, using two flowerets of broccoli and one of cauliflower or the other way around.

89

77

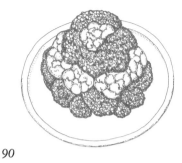

90

91

Form a mound on a florist's frog, using both broccoli and cauliflower flowerets. Intermix the green and white vegetables—use one color for the base and the other for the dome or place them in alternating rows. *(Fig. 90)*

Other green and white combinations can be made by tossing cold cooked cauliflower with snow peas, or sprinkling steamed cauliflower with bright green frozen peas.

With Red

Red, too, enhances cauliflower's white color. Sprinkle chopped sweet red pepper over a head of cauliflower. Make a salad of cold cooked cauliflower, rings of Spanish onion and red pepper. For protein, add kidney beans (red) and feta cheese (white).

With Yellow

For a yellow and white composition, sprinkle sieved hard-boiled eggs or lemon zest over cooked cauliflower.

Cover the vegetable with a golden cheese sauce. Hold back a cluster of flowerets, and place it in the center of the melted cheese, flanked with parsley and tomato wedges.

You can make yellow cauliflower for an Indian meal by cooking it with yellow turmeric. Make a circle of the golden cauliflower around a mass of coriander leaves or cooked spinach, on which you arrange chutney, chopped nuts and kumquats.

With Brown

Add contrast to pale cauliflower with brown garnishes. Cook bread crumbs in butter. Flavor them with chopped nuts or cooked bacon bits. Use a beurre noir over a whole head of cauliflower.

Use the flowerets to make a white border around a roast or serving of meat. Make a plain linear border, or make groupings of cauliflower, cherry tomatoes and snow peas to place here and there around a roast. *(Fig. 91)*

The English, great lovers of all cabbage-flavored vegetables, cook cauliflower whole and serve it still enveloped in its leaves—which are, by the way, not only edible, but delicious. Unseparated cauliflower is, however, hard to portion out. Instead, mimic a whole cauliflower by separating the flowerets, then reforming and cooking them in a bowl over a steamer.

Caviar

If it was merely expensive, that would be one thing. But good caviar is more than costly. It's an international symbol of elegance. Like champagne, the presence of caviar makes any meal a celebration.

Before the Revolution, there was a legendary golden caviar in Russia, which was reserved only for the family of the czar. Today, the best we have is the large-egg gray-black caviar from the Beluga sturgeon, and the slightly smaller but still beautiful eggs of the Sevruga and Osetrova sturgeons.

Then come the hearty and salty red caviar from salmon, and dyed and pressed black lumpfish caviar.

Very good caviar should be served very simply. As the quality declines—the eggs become smaller and more salt is added—the presentation becomes more complicated. At one end of the scale we have gray Beluga caviar served in its can. At the other end, a baked potato with a spoonful of red caviar, or a platter of canapés done with black lumpfish caviar and cream cheese.

If you're making deviled eggs or cream cheese balls or yogurt dip with caviar, you will use, thriftily, red or black lumpfish caviar. But remember that the dye in the black caviar smudges, and will turn everything sooty green.

Traditionally, caviar is served in the can in order to avoid damaging the fragile eggs. But the can is more than protection for its contents. It is as much a part of the caviar as the grill on the Rolls-Royce or the green bottle containing Dom Perignon. These symbols exist at a level beyond mannerly reticence over displaying trademarks.

Serve it chilled. Set the can into a mound of crushed ice or a bowl filled with ice cubes. Surround the ice with green leaves and lemon slices.

92

93

Make an ice shape with a ring mold. Line the indentation in the center with a lettuce leaf and empty the can of caviar into it. The lettuce leaf will act as waterproofing. Do the same with an individual ring mold for single servings.

Don't be modest with the crockery. Use the most elegant you have, whether it's a piece of red lacquer, a crystal bowl or a gold-banded service plate. In Russia, the tradition was that any metal baser than silver would damage the caviar, so it was always served with a gold or silver spoon.

Don't be skimpy. If you can't afford caviar, then serve something else. An individual serving of caviar should measure around one ounce. A large old-fashioned soup spoon is a good measure and makes an egg-shaped mold.

For a single serving, cut a square of dark pumpernickel diagonally into four triangles. Shingle three of them on a dessert plate, and turn the fourth around. Place a spoonful of caviar where this triangle meets the other three. Garnish with the traditional chopped egg, onion and lemon wedge. *(Fig. 92)*

Cut the crusts from a slice of thin white toast, or make this arrangement directly on the plate and serve toast on the side. On the toast, make lines of parsley, onion, caviar and chopped egg with the tip of a teaspoon. The row of caviar can be as narrow as it needs to be, but it's more sporting to keep it close to the traditional one-ounce measure. *(Fig. 93)*

Canapés

If you plan to serve caviar to a crowd, you'll find that preassembled canapés are neater than serving from the can. They also let you stay in control of the portioning, foiling the greedy guest. It's legitimate to use less-expensive black lumpfish caviar for canapés.

You can scarcely make a bad design. On a triangle of dark pumpernickel, place a section of hard-boiled egg and, on that, a mound of caviar.

Make strict geometrical designs on small toast squares. Cover half the square diagonally with an index card and spread soft cream cheese or brie on the exposed area. Then fill in the blank space with caviar, setting a tiny cluster of parsley leaves where they meet.

Red Caviar

Red caviar is made from the roe of salmon or lumpfish. It's cheap and salty. But it has a nice cheerful color, and the saltiness is dissipated when you serve it with lots of bland or creamy foods.

You may have had red caviar with baked potatoes. Just now, it's very chic to serve it with pasta.

Mix red caviar with cottage cheese, and use it to fill a tomato or green pepper casing.

Float a raft of sour cream on soup, and place on it a few grains of red caviar.

Beautiful, but austere, is the presentation we saw in a Japanese restaurant: a meager spoonful of red caviar nestled in the natural hollow of a gray rock.

Yellow Caviar

With the price of Russian and Iranian caviar spinning out of sight, a very good American caviar has come on the market. It's pale yellow and delicately flavored. It presents a problem, because it isn't black Beluga, and shouldn't pretend to be the real stuff. But on the other hand, the flavor and color are both more subtle than that of red caviar. It's too delicate to be spooned onto baked potatoes or mixed with whipped cream cheese. It's still new, but our guess is that it should be served without apologies, with all the trappings of Beluga.

Celery

Celery, like carrots, is available all year round. Choose green Pascal celery with firm clean stalks. Reserve the outer stalks, which may be damaged, to cut up in soups and salads, and use the leafy tops for flavoring sauces, chopped up in mixed-herb dishes such as omelettes fines herbes and as an emergency garnish, a pleasant if unemphatic change from parsley and watercress.

Celery has to be washed clean of the soil between the stalks. Old celery should be scraped if it's going to be eaten raw. Otherwise, the strings turn into inedible wires in the teeth.

94

95

96

Although braised celery is delicious, in America we usually eat it raw. There used to be a standard piece of tableware called a celery glass, a vase of cut glass or milk glass in which celery stalks stood on end, their leaves pretending to be blossoms. You can still serve it that way, standing the whole stalks on end in brightly colored mugs or vases. Or serve whole celery stalks lying flat in a long basket, like a bread basket, with the leaves hanging over one end. For color, add a pile of cherry tomatoes and washed mushrooms.

To cut celery into neat matchsticks, remove the leaves and base and scrape the stalks. Cut each stalk into two or three equal lengths. Holding the lengths together, slice them into long thin sticks. Serve them raw with carrot and zucchini sticks and sautéed in butter with other julienne vegetables.

Celery Curls

Celery curls up when it is slashed and soaked in ice water.

Let the leaves remain in place on a whole stalk of celery. Cut the other end of the stalk in ¼-inch-wide slashes 2 inches long, and put the stalk in ice water. The slashed end will curl up, giving you celery that's frilly at both ends. *(Fig. 94)*

Make short diagonal incisions down each side of a stalk of celery. Put it in ice water, and all the little slits will curl back. *(Fig. 95)*

Stuffed Celery

To make sections of celery for stuffing, cut 2½- to 3-inch lengths of stalk straight across or on the slant. Stuff them with something bright, such as cream cheese and red caviar, Cheddar spread or guacamole.

Make a celery rosette to use as a garnish or a canapé. Trim off the top and base of a bunch of celery. Wash the stalks and reassemble them, using flavored cream cheese as the cement. Starting with the central stalks, press each one firmly into place. Wrap in foil and refrigerate for a few hours. Just before serving, cut across the bunch in thin slices. *(Fig. 96)*

Cheese

A cheese tray doesn't have to be a supermarket. You aren't obliged to offer your guests a taste of every cheese in the store. You want to show that you have chosen a few very special cheeses for them.

Be generous with amount, not variety. Serve fewer cheeses, usually not more than three. Serve large wedges. As the crowd gets bigger, increase the size, not the number, of the wedges.

A plate can hold a whole wheel of Stilton and nothing else. Or a wedge of Cheddar and a half-circle of Brie. Or a triangle of Swiss, a small round Camembert and a tube of chèvre. The choice, of course, is primarily for taste and texture. But after that, choose for contrast in shape as well.

97

Cover a wooden board or a flat wicker basket with dark leaves or ferns. Spinach leaves do very well. Set the cheese on the greenery, and provide a knife or slicer for each one.

The plate should be unadorned except for the leaves and the cheese. If, however, you're doing a very large platter for a buffet, you could put an arrangement of edible fruit or vegetables at the back of it: grapes, pears and apples or celery (very English, with cheese), radishes and Brussels sprouts. But it's better to have only the cheese on the board, with a bowl of fruit or vegetables nearby.

When serving a whole wheel of Brie or Camembert, some people score the rind lightly as a guide for guests who'll be cutting their own portions.

Present crackers separately in a low basket. If you're serving bread, be very French and place it right on the tablecloth.

It's nice, too, to serve a small piece of cheese as part of the salad course. After the main dish, every diner gets a plate holding a small tossed salad, a circle of chèvre or a narrow triangle of Brie, and two pale water biscuits. Flank the cheese with the crackers, and place the salad on the other half of the plate. It's just enough to refresh the palate.

Cheese before the meal or after it? It depends on the kind of meal. If it's Italian, then by all means have a wedge of cheese and some sliced salami in the living room. If it's Greek, you'll serve feta cheese and black olives with drinks. But when the meal is formal, you never serve cheese at the beginning. And it's probably not a good idea, quite apart from any question of style, just because cheese is such a filling food.

Cherries

Cherries arrive in early summer, plump and sweet, so red that they're nearly black. In some parts of the country, you can find fresh golden cherries with a rosy blush.

Fresh cherries should be served in abundance. Heap them in a basket lined with leaves or ferns. Put them in a white bowl with green grapes, or in a black or celadon bowl. Add fresh pitted cherries to any fruit bowl.

(An old-fashioned cherry pitter was a cranked machine that dropped the pits out of one spigot and the cherries out another. A rather specialized tool, they're almost impossible to find these days. Cookbooks used to recommend that you pit cherries with an immaculately clean pen point. But now that they're disappearing from sight, you'll have to do the job with a sharp paring knife, and accept the fact that you may have to cut the cherry in half.)

Fresh cherries make a lovely garnish during the few weeks when they are in season. Use them anyplace where you might put a strawberry or a maraschino cherry: on a Charlotte Russe, a hot fudge sundae or in a Manhattan.

Frost the cherries for a more formal garnish. Using the stem as a handle, dip each cherry in egg white and then in powdered sugar. Let the cherries dry on a cookie rack before you use them. Then set two on a plate holding a pot of chocolate mousse, or a whole cluster on a plate of cookies.

Canned and Frozen Cherries

For cooking, we buy tart canned cherries. For eating, we can get sweet canned and frozen cherries, either dark burgundy or pale peachy gold. The dark frozen cherries are good layered with vanilla ice cream in parfait glasses, each red layer covered with a thin layer of pale green pistachio nuts. But remember that the juice of the canned dark cherries stains everything in sight.

Maraschino Cherries

Cherries come fresh, canned and poisonous. But if maraschino cherries are so bad for us, why do we love them so?

They're full of dye. They taste like chemicals. And, frankly, their color isn't all that great. But the intent is right: a touch of bright color, a miniature fruit to put a cap on a scoop of ice cream or to float in a glass of lemonade. And all the memories from the days when we drank Shirley Temple cocktails and the nicest thing we could have for dessert was red gelatin with whipped cream and a cherry.

If you worry about the dye—and you should—substitute a fresh strawberry, now available all year round. And for the few weeks of the year when we get fresh cherries, use the real thing.

Chestnuts

Chestnuts are actually nuts, but are often treated as vegetables when they are cooked. They have hard shells that look like finely finished wood, with a shape that's blunt at one end and pointed at the other. It takes some work to get at them, but that seems to be part of the pleasure of the food, part of cold weather, street vendors on windy corners and the warmth of the chestnuts held between mittened hands.

To peel and cook chestnuts, you first cut an X-shaped slash in the flat end of the nut. Then either bake or boil them until you can easily peel off both the hard outer shell and the thin inner skin. More fun, but less efficient, is the roasting pan, made like a skillet, in which you cook chestnuts over an open fireplace.

Cut shelled, freshly cooked chestnuts into quarters and mix them with red cabbage or Brussels sprouts and bacon. They are traditionally served with game.

You can make your own marrons glacés, dipping the nuts in a sugar syrup. Or buy them in cans and serve them with ice cream or in a compote of fresh fruit.

Canned chestnut puree is a useful addition to the larder. It can be added to vegetable dishes or used in making a Mont Blanc. Force the puree through a sieve into a ring mold or on a plate. Then cover the mountain of chestnut puree with whipped cream and decorate it with candied violets. It's a very poetic, very substantial dessert.

Chicken Parts

In the modern world, we buy our chicken in parts. Small families and single people buy few plump roasters. The whole bird shows up only

86

on Sundays, for company, and at Thanksgiving. But night after night, we cook our two chicken breasts or our broiler-fryer cut up in eighths.

There are thousands of ways to cook them. We sauté and fry them, grill and broil them, poach or stew them. We bake them in the oven. But what in the world do we do with them once they're cooked and ready to go on the serving plate?

The aim is to make a neat presentation. The best way to do that is to lay down the chicken parts in a symmetrical pattern that echoes the way they were joined on the chicken.

We'll describe methods of arranging a chicken cut in half, in quarters, in sixths (breast and wing joined) and in eighths (breast and wing disjointed). Then we'll give a suggestion for plates of one part only, just breasts or just drumsticks.

We've garnished these model plates with carrots and watercress, but that's only as a model. You could just as well use shoestring potatoes and tomatoes, or mushrooms and string beans. And you can place the chicken on a bed of rice or noodles just as well as on a bare platter.

Halves

Sometimes very small broilers, weighing 1½ pounds each, are simply split in half. Place the chicken halves back to back on a platter. This is a very proper, very old method of presentation, called *en accolade*. Between the halves, put a fence of cress. *(Fig. 98)*

98

Quarters

We often buy small chickens cut into four parts. Put the four pieces in the four corners of a platter. Lay cress between the pieces, with heaps of carrots in the center and at the outer ends of the cress.

Or tilt the breast quarters over the thigh quarters. Place a big puff of cress in the center of the space between them, with shredded carrots forming a line out from it on either side. *(Fig. 99)*

99

100

101

Sixths: Two Breast-Wing Sections, Two Thighs, Two Drumsticks

Place a row of carrots down the center, bisecting the platter. To either side, the legs should form a base, with the thighs tipped over them, and the breast-wing sections tipped over them. Cress goes at the top and bottom. *(Fig. 100)*

Eighths: Two Breasts, Two Wings, Two Drumsticks, Two Thighs

Place the thighs in the center of a platter, head to foot. Cress goes between them. The legs to either side, one up and one down. Finally, the breasts, with the wings alongside them, again one up and one down. Carrots go at the top and bottom of the platter. *(Fig. 101)*

One Part Only: A Plate of Wings, or Breasts or Drumsticks

On a round platter, make a tuft of cress in the center, and have the breasts radiating out from it. Carrots between the chicken.

On an oval platter, a row of breasts down the center. On either side, a bed of cress with carrots over it.

Again on an oval platter, a wide display of cress and carrots across the center. On either side, a heap of chicken breasts, narrowing toward the narrow part of the oval.

For a whole cold chicken, remove the breast meat from both sides, leaving the breast bone intact. Fill the cavity with a cold stuffing, slice the breast meat on the diagonal and reassemble on the frame. The joining point of the slices can be garnished with fruit, vegetables and greenery. *(Fig. 102)*

A whole chicken, served on a platter, is improved with greenery tucked fore and aft, at the neck and between the ends of the drumsticks. For a Sunday special, clusters of green grapes, kumquats or baby carrots can be added.

102

Children's Food

When we cook for children, we attempt to appeal to a taste that is at once more conservative and more baroque than our own. On the one hand, we have the finicky taste of a four-year-old, who likes everything clean and crunchy and *separate,* with the chop never touching the potatoes. On the other hand, we have to cope with a comic-book aesthetic, which favors animal crackers in the soup and loves everything decorated to look like a smiling face.

Children like food that is small: two Ritz crackers and a half-slice of American cheese on a plate. They like things crunchy: raw (never cooked) vegetables. And they like it clean: nothing covered with sauce. They like foods whose boundaries they understand. For that reason, they prefer cookies to cake, hot dogs to stew. They like real colors, and they loathe anything green.

Because he lacks the dexterity to spoon it up, a bowl of soup looks like an ocean to a child. Better to serve it in a teacup, so he can drink it.

For the same reason, children prefer pasta in small shapes, such as elbows and twists, to long, slippery spaghetti. In fact, the more you can transform everything to a finger food, the better chance you have of seeing it "all gone."

On the other hand, the fastidious little classicist sees nothing wrong in eating a hunk of chocolate shaped like the family dog, or in having his name written in mustard all over the salami. He revels in the worst excesses of the commercial food world, automatically adoring everything made with cherry gelatin, canned pear halves and chocolate sprinkles.

It helps to think of a child's plate as Japanese: an arrangement in restraint. That way, you won't think that you're starving him.

Vegetables

Cut raw vegetables into fingers and make a sunburst with them on a salad plate. Try two sticks of carrot, two of celery and two string beans.

Serve a bowl of raw peas in the pod, and show the child how to get at them.

Buy a tiny birthday-party basket, and put in single bits of raw vegetable: a bean, a carrot flower, a piece of cauliflower, some raw peas.

None of these salads is to be polluted with dressing (yik, gross). But you may put a small cup of dressing at the side of the plate for use as a dip.

Fruit

Restraint is the world for fruit as well as vegetables.

Arrange three apple wedges in a fan. Between them, place two fingers of cheese. Nothing else. And no fancy cheese—American.

Serve three strawberries around a mound of sugar for dipping. Instead of sugar, try a small saucer of honey.

Cut a banana in half crosswise, leaving the peel intact. Pull the peel back from the cut surface, flowerlike, and serve half a banana to each child. Make him ask for the second half.

Sandwiches

Children like sandwiches that are made on crackers or on bread cut to cracker-size. And they like open-faced sandwiches, so that they don't have to worry that there's something nasty hiding inside.

Cut sandwiches into small pieces. Cut the bread into four long fingers, and then cut them in half. A serving is four of the eight sections.

Try the trick of making a sandwich from one slice of white bread and another of whole wheat. Cut it into four pieces, and turn over alternating sections for a checkerboard pattern.

Give in to kids' passion for cookies by cutting the sandwich bread with a cookie cutter shaped like a star or a heart. Fill it after, not before, you cut it, or you'll waste too much filling (unless, of course, you're the kind of parent who happily eats the cutaway scraps).

Cut bologna slices with a star-shaped cookie cutter, and lay two stars on a plate with two crackers alongside.

Family Meals

Serve soup in a teacup or dessert bowl. Float something crunchy on top. Fish-shaped crackers are nice. Breakfast cereal and popcorn are good, too.

One of us loved pink foods as a child, was gently persuaded to drink pale pink milk with, usually, a cherry hidden in the bottom of the mug. She thinks that cottage cheese colored with strawberry jam might please a little girl.

Don't forget the seductiveness of a mug or bowl with a favorite picture or saying on the bottom.

We won't tell you how to get children to eat their desserts. They will.

Party Food

At parties, children can indulge in their utter lack of good taste. They *adore* commercial gelatin in every form. They *faint* when they see it layered in different colors in parfait glasses. It's so haute cuisine, yet so safe.

Mix your gelatin, then let it set in a ½-inch-thick sheet in a jelly-roll pan. When it gels, cut shapes with cookie cutters. Put a gelatin star on a cake plate for each child.

If you're not dealing with a bunch of wild boys, you will have the party of the season if you pass around a spray can of whipped cream and let the children decorate their own gelatin.

Serve plain cookies or cupcakes, and pass around a can of ready-made icing. Let each child ice his or her own cake. Have bowls of sprinkles, M&M's and chopped nuts nearby for garnishing.

Cut an apple in half, and put it cut-side down on a dessert plate. It won't be eaten. Then pierce apple cubes, grapes and strawberries with toothpicks and stick them into the apple.

Fill flat-bottomed ice-cream cones with chocolate pudding or gelatin. Or set them in muffin tins and fill them two-thirds full with cake mix. (The kids can do this at the start of the party.) Bake, then serve topped with whipped cream or a scoop of ice cream.

103

Stick a sparkler into a cupcake. Better still, stick it into a hamburger bun. If they don't die of fright, maybe they'll eat the hamburger. And remember to make little patties: ⅛ pound of meat is about right.

Decorate cupcakes with "balloons" made with round mints and strings of licorice.

Place a personal message underneath the sandwich on a child's plate.

Tie a small sandwich in ribbons, with a sprig of grapes on the bow. But first be sure that the children are old enough to be able to untie the bow.

Stuff a peach half with cottage cheese, and stick a paper parasol into it.

At a party, you can forget about the main course. You aren't responsible for the guests getting their RDAs. It's enough that they don't go home sick.

But pizza isn't bad for them. Nor is a fried drumstick or a dab of tuna salad. You might do a platter of tuna or egg salad, give the children plates holding three Ritz crackers and a plastic knife, and let them help themselves.

We made a sensational clown's head with egg salad. We spread it out into a round pancake shape. The eyes were half-slices of cucumber, with its green skin left on. Narrow strips of cucumber skin were placed vertically through the eyes. We used a radish with an upward point for the nose and half an apple slice for the mouth. The hair was made with lots of grated carrot and the ruff at the neck with leaves of Boston lettuce. *(Fig. 103)*

Inspired, we made a cat's face from tuna, beginning with the same flat pancake shape. We used a triangle of black olive for the nose, with carrot-stick whiskers on either side. The eyes were radish rounds with pupils of black olive ovals. We made rounded ears out of more tuna. Another time, the ears were round slices cut from a green apple. Caution: pointed ears will make your cat look like a wolf, and nobody will eat anything at all. *(Fig. 104)*

The children adored both of these platters. They didn't eat much more than usual, but they thought we were awfully clever to have made them.

104

Chocolate

Chocolate is made from a liquid extracted from cacao beans. This liquor is made into blocks, and some of the blocks have some of their cocoa butter removed. The chocolate we buy is composed of different proportions of solid chocolate, cocoa butter, sugar and milk.

There are several reliable American brands, as well as excellent imported cooking chocolate. You have to look out for artificial chocolate, which has sneaked onto the market now that the price of real chocolate has gone up.

The most common chocolates used in baking are unsweetened or bitter chocolate in squares or melted in envelopes, semisweet squares and chips, so-called sweet chocolate, which has extra sugar and cocoa butter added to it, and cocoa, both sweet and unsweetened. Milk chocolate is similar to semisweet, but it has sugar and milk added to it and is seldom used in baking.

We love it, try not to eat too much of it, since it's all fat, cholesterol and calories, with no redeeming qualities save bliss.

But if you use chocolate for decoration, you get some of the taste without too much of the sin. The dark color and bittersweet bite contrast well with many creamy rich foods and add a depth of flavor to citrus fruits.

Start with chocolate that is already processed in forms useful for decorating.

Sift cocoa through a stencil onto iced cakes and cupcakes.

Sprinkle chocolate shot and chocolate chips on cookies or ice cream.

Spin plain chocolate wafers in the food processor or roll them between sheets of wax paper to make fine crumbs. Then press these crumbs into cake icings or make layers with ice cream in parfaits.

Thin chocolate mints, lying flat, slanted against one another or standing on end, make an elegant border on a layer cake.

You can create your own decorations with melted chocolate. Melt it in the top of a double boiler or in a slow oven. Semisweet chocolate chips are probably the most reliable consistency for melting. Most of these decorations can be made ahead of time and frozen. They are also, unfortunately, somewhat unreliable, with the malleability of the chocolate dependent on its age, the temperature and the position of the planets.

To make chocolate leaves, melt semisweet chocolate bits. Wash rose, gardenia or ivy leaves, and trail them, one at a time, over the top of the melted chocolate. Cool, chocolate side up, and, when it has hardened, peel the leaf off of its chocolate backing.

Dip fruit into melted chocolate chips, working quickly in a cool kitchen. Put the fruit, half-dipped in chocolate, into the freezer for a few minutes. Once it has set, move it into the refrigerator. Serve with cookies, alongside custards or on top of layer cakes.

It's a little harder to make chocolate cones, but they are very attractive adorning the top of a cake. Make wax-paper cones, securing the cone by tucking in the pointed end. The smaller the cone, the more elegant the finished product will be. Spread melted chocolate chips *inside* the cone. Cool in the freezer. When the chocolate has set, peel off the paper.

To make chocolate slabs, spread melted chocolate on wax paper. When it has hardened in the freezer, cut and break the chocolate into large spiky slabs. Stick them upright in puddings or whipped cream or lay on top of an iced cake. You're supposed to be able to cut these slabs with truffle cutters, but we've never been able to manage it.

Buy small cupcake papers for chocolate cups. Spread the melted chocolate inside them. Put the chocolate-lined papers in muffin tins and then in the freezer. When the chocolate hardens, peel off the papers, and you'll have semisweet chocolate cups to fill with pudding or softened ice cream. Top with a strawberry, a mandarin orange section or a nut.

Chocolate curls are hard to do. You're supposed to be able to make them by scraping a block of chocolate with your vegetable peeler, but once again, we've had difficulty making this work. Commercial bakers use special chocolate that has a great deal of cocoa butter in it, which makes it more malleable than any we can get.

Grated chocolate, on the other hand, is easy to do in the food processor, with a hand grater or a Mouli.

When you're serving chocolate sauce, don't forget to put it under, not over, other things. Put it under the poached pears (a whole pear, standing up in a pool of chocolate, with some more drizzled just on its top), under strawberries, scoops of ice cream or sherbet.

Clams and Oysters

Although there are hundreds of recipes using clams and oysters, these mollusks are at their most distinctive when served in their shells, either raw or baked. Remove them from the shell and they might, visually speaking, be anything. In the shell, they are triumphant.

It's not easy to open raw oysters, but the prize is worth the game. Using a special blunt oyster knife, pry the shells apart, letting the liquid drip through a strainer into a bowl. When the shell is open, release the oyster with a knife, rinse it under cold water and put it back in the deeper half of the shell. Spoon on some of the strained oyster liquor.

Raw clams open more easily. The problem with them is that they are often very gritty and need serious scrubbing and soaking in brine before they should be opened. Some people eat raw mussels on the half shell, but this practice is uncommon because mussels have been implicated in gastric infections.

The aim when you serve clams and oysters in their shells is to hold them steady. You don't want them skittering all over the plate. Oyster plates help, metal platters with indentations for half shells. The metal even helps to keep the hot food hot, the cold oysters chilled. But they are unquestionably restaurantlike in looks.

If you don't have oyster plates, you can serve raw clams or oysters on beds of chopped ice set into shallow plates. Decorate the ice with parsley or seaweed. (Seaweed is sold dried in oriental food shops.)

Cooked clams and oysters are wedged in beds of rock salt in the same shallow plates. The French sometimes serve hot oysters in the shell nestled in crumpled white napkins, but in America, we use aluminum foil instead. It certainly doesn't have the same style.

You could set raw clams or oysters on a bed of parsley or watercress in a small gratin pan. It works quite well if the pan is of the right size to hold six shells snugly, with the greens peeping out between them.

In general, clams and oysters are among the foods that look best with the least adornment. For one thing, they must be opened just before they are eaten. Too much decoration, and we begin to wonder how long ago the presentation began. To go with raw clams and oysters, therefore, use nothing but lemon wedges, tiny pots of vinegary mignonette sauce and baskets of crackers. Epicures would add caviar to the list. The most extravagant presentation we know for oysters is the oyster canapé on black bread. Just butter, a raw oyster and a dab of black caviar.

Steamed clams are served in deep bowls and wire baskets. They could be placed in the French style, in a crumpled napkin. Don't forget the pot of broth, the pot of melted butter and a bowl to hold the shells.

Clams and oysters that are removed from the shells and cooked are served like any other sauced food: in scallop shells, in croustades, on toast or rice. They are also cooked on skewers, alternating with squares of bacon and mushrooms, then grilled and pushed off the skewers onto toast.

Cocoa and Chocolate Milk

Cocoa used to be a respectable adult drink on the order of tea and coffee. There were china cocoa sets designed just for this brew, which was considered, on the whole, a little too stimulating for children.

Now cocoa has been relegated to the nursery and the ski slopes, where it is always served in thick mugs. But it can still use some of the additions and garnishes that it acquired during its more sophisticated days.

(To prevent the formation of skin on hot cocoa, beat it with a wire whisk as you cook it. In Mexico, they have a special tool for this, a knobby wooden stirrer.)

In Spain, they used to pour sherry into hot cocoa. In Vienna, it often came with coffee and always with *schlag*—whipped cream.

Serve cocoa topped with melting marshmallows, with vanilla or coffee ice cream, whipped cream or curls of orange rind. Put in a cinnamon or peppermint stick. Sprinkle with powdered cinnamon or shaved chocolate.

All the same adornments go into chocolate milk. And you might put candied or chocolate-dipped cherries on the saucer to nibble with the chocolate drink.

Coffee

Coffee is the national drink. In England they have afternoon tea, but in America, the meal is called a coffee break, even when it consists of orange juice or a soft drink.

We pride ourselves on making good coffee and argue the advantages of drip over percolator. We buy espresso makers, burn ourselves on the steam of cappuccino makers. We boil the grounds in water on camping trips and assure ourselves that we've never had such good coffee. And when we begin to get caffeine-induced fidgets, we switch to decaffeinated rather than give up the rich, brown brew.

There are traditional cups for different kinds of coffee. If you're lucky, you can find huge café-au-lait bowls from France for your breakfast coffee. Most of them have no handle at all. American coffee is served in medium-sized cups and mugs, while espresso and Turkish coffee, black as sin, go in tiny demitasse cups. There are also tall thin mugs for Irish coffee and, of course, tall highball glasses for iced coffee.

Always serve coffee on a tray, even if it's only two mugs of instant. And remember that all coffee tastes better when you have seen and heard it being poured from the pot. On the tray goes the pot, cups or mugs, a sugar bowl and a milk pitcher. And, if you are serving Viennese coffee, a bowl of whipped cream.

On a breakfast tray, provide a pitcher of steamed milk for making café au lait.

After dinner, you should have only small cups, a bowl of sugar and a plate of lemon peel. No milk is required.

Never serve instant coffee from the jar. The English put their tea bags into the pot; you can do the same with your instant coffee.

Pour leftover coffee into ice-cube trays. When they are frozen, empty the cubes into a plastic bag. Use them to chill glasses of iced coffee. Or whir them in the blender with milk for a foamy coffee milk shake. With iced coffee, serve stirrers made of cinnamon sticks, or

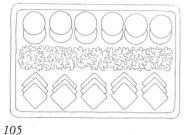

105

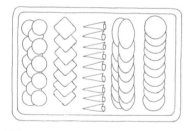

106

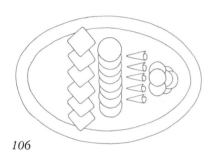

107

108

garnish the glass with whipped cream and chocolate shavings or bits of candied orange peel. Most wonderful of all, put a scoop of vanilla or coffee ice cream into a tall glass of iced coffee.

Cold Cuts

There you stand with the platter in front of you. The salami is in one hand, the ham or provolone is in the other. What do you do now? How do you put them all together?

This is one time when you can't skimp on the quality of your basic materials. There's no way to hide the watery pink of cheap ham, the slippery texture of overprocessed turkey roll, the hardening edges of cheese that was sliced too long ago.

The arrangement of a platter of cold cuts should fall somewhere between casual and contrived. You surely don't want to toss a pile of flesh on the plate. But neither do you want it to look as though it had just been delivered from the deli, and that you had, at that moment, ripped off the plastic wrap.

A good approach is to make areas of each meat, rather than neatly alternating slices of ham and cheese. Avoid—just because caterers do it—the common radiating and concentric patterns made with tidy strips of meat extending from a central accent. Shun overly symmetrical designs, tired parsley and radish roses on cellophane-frilled toothpicks.

What to do instead? If you have two kinds of meat, cover the left side of the platter with one and the right side with the other. At the point where they meet, make a row of cherry tomatoes.

Turn the design 90 degrees, and cover the top half of the platter with the ham and the bottom half with the cheese, with clusters of olives or a strip of shredded greens at the joining. *(Fig. 105)*

Do three diagonal areas: ham at the south-west, cheese across the diagonal axis and turkey at the north-east.

The areas don't have to be symmetrical. Set a focal point to one side of the platter. Then lay down an area of bologna and, next to it, a much wider area of turkey breast. *(Fig. 106)*

On a large platter, do simple stripes. Across the width, a whole stripe of ham, then a whole stripe of salami and so forth. Or turn the stripes lengthwise. Try a round plate too. *(Figs. 107, 108)*

Height

Once the basic arrangement has been established, you will want to add height to it. The obvious way is with a central focus. That's the stuffed tomato on the caterer's tray. You should be able to find one more interesting. Like an artichoke filled with mustard-flavored mayonnaise. A green pepper filled with black olives. A potato half, facedown, into which you stick a cluster of vegetable skewers. Even a pile of cold marinated cauliflower and broccoli. Look at the section on focal points for more ideas.

Once you have chosen a focal point and laid out the arrangement of the meat, you can add volume and height to the sections of meat. Make a neat hem in every—or every other—slice of ham on the plate, so that one edge looks fuller. Not only will this add height, but there will seem to be more ham than really is there. *(Fig. 109)*

Gather an occasional slice of meat into a butterfly, a fan or a fold to add volume. At the point where it is gathered, place a cherry tomato, a few leaves of watercress or a slice of pickle. Don't crumple every slice; use it as an accent, one or two to a row. *(Figs. 110, 111)*

Caterers deal with stiff deli meats that don't fold easily by rolling them into cornucopias. They fold salami slices in half, then in half again, and secure the corners with a radish or pickle on a toothpick. They make pinwheels by cutting into the meat in four places to within ½ inch of its center, then folding every other corner in to the center and fastening it with a toothpick. Try it on an occasional slice of meat on a platter. *(Figs. 112, 113)*

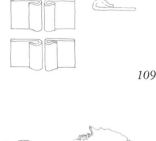

109

110

111

Garnishes

After the platter is arranged, interrupt the look of too much sameness with garnishes. Add softness by tucking sprigs of parsley under the edges of individual slices.

Avoid using rows of parsley to separate areas, unless the rows are really full, the parsley really fresh. If you have half a platter of bologna and half of roast beef, make a graduated chain of leaves and vegetables at the place where they meet. Begin with Italian parsley. Build

112

113

114

115

through green and black olives. The peak is a cluster of red-orange peppers and cauliflower flowerets, after which you descend again through the chain. *(Fig. 114)*

Separate areas with a herringbone pattern made of julienne-cut zucchini, carrot and fennel. Soften the platter with mounds of alfalfa sprouts holding green olives and cherry tomatoes. Use cucumber slices, cut nearly in half and standing upright like lemon slices. Or a row of pickled mixed vegetables. Round and curved foods help to break up the rigid look of machine-sliced meat. Use arcs of orange, tomato wedges, apple slices. Try laying a green olive slice on a half-slice of orange. *(Fig. 115)*

A Sample Arrangement

This is how it works. Make an arrangement on a tray 16 inches long and 10 inches wide. The ingredients will be ham ⬜ , salami ◯ , julienned carrots, zucchini and yellow squash ‖‖‖ , black olives ⦙ and green olives ⦙ .

You can do a composition like a Mondrian design, with the pink meat played off against the colors of the vegetables, and the olives serving as an accent. The round salami makes a contrast with the rectangular ham.

Lay out the top line first. When you do the second row, be careful not to have any edges matching vertically so as to create unintentional vertical patterns. Think of the vegetables as another flat area, the equal of the meat, rather than as a garnish. When all the rows are in place, use olives to frame an area or to interrupt a run of meat. *(Fig. 116)*

If you copy the pattern once, you'll feel more comfortable about creating your own designs in the future.

116

Containers Made from Food

Food makes good containers for other foods. Why else have there long been ceramic pots and bowls made in the shapes of cabbages, squashes and melons?

We're not talking about cooked edible casings. Not about sandwiches, crepes, stuffed cabbages or vine leaves. We mean a method of service in which a natural, often edible product takes the place of a man-made dish; in which the orange shell or the hollow loaf of bread isn't cooked with the food inside it, and is eaten only incidentally or not at all.

Imagine, for example, a still life of squash and melon on a buffet table, clustered on wicker trays and in deep baskets. Here and there among them is a ceramic mushroom or cucumber. Some of the real vegetables are filled, while others are left empty. It looks sensational.

Or imagine a round loaf of peasant bread with the top cut off and a glass bowl placed in the center. Spicy dip goes into the bowl, and the loaf is surrounded by slim breadsticks meant to be used as dippers.

There are rules to making a neat container. Most fruits and vegetables stand more steadily when you cut a thin slice off the bottom. Then cut off the tops straight across and scoop out the insides. If you cut the top in a zigzag, it won't hold as much filling: not bad when the filling is something expensive, such as lobster salad. Lean the top against the base or replace it and let the diner take it off himself.

Some foods, such as bread and leafy vegetables, work best as containers when a clear glass bowl is set into them to keep things tidy.

Keep the food appropriate to the container. Ice cream goes in fruit shells, rice salad in peppers, salads in bowls set into whole cabbages and heads of lettuce.

Fruit Containers

Fill half an apple or pear with chutney to go with cooked meat.

Fill a baking apple with hot potato salad and serve it with roast pork.

Coconuts, pineapples and melons hold fruit salad.

Lemon shells hold tartar sauce and cocktail sauce for fish and shellfish.

In France, they serve small melons with the caps cut off, seeds removed and red wine poured inside. The caps are replaced, and the melon served as a first course.

An orange shell makes a container for ambrosia or ice cream.

Traditionally, pumpkins are used as tureens for pumpkin soup. If you get one really cleaned and dried out, you can use it to serve a salad at a big party.

Tomatoes, of course, hold all kinds of salads. They hold chopped shrimp, crab meat, tuna and all the foods that were supposed to make you gasp when the lid was lifted, that went by the name of *Tomato Surprise.*

Fill tomato shells with currant-rice salad or with spinach puree.

We filled a tomato with orange sherbet, then set it in the freezer until it was well chilled but the casing not frozen. We served it in the southern tradition, as a pleasant refreshment in the middle of a long meal.

Vegetable Containers

Artichokes, because of their flowerlike shape, make spectacular and usually edible containers. Remove the middle leaves, cook the artichokes and drain them facedown to make a commodious space for salads.

To make cucumber containers, copy a Chinese technique. Cut 2-inch lengths of cucumber and scoop out a cone-shaped hollow in each.

The Chinese fill them with ground pork, then steam them, but we can use them raw to hold russian dressing or cocktail sauce.

Instead of baking stuffed peppers, leave them raw. Slice off the top third, fill the insides with ham salad or corn relish and stick sprigs of watercress around the filling.

Leafy vegetables are fillable if you use clear glass bowls in them. Remove the central leaves from a cabbage and set a bowl into the space. Fill it with pink shrimp salad or with guacamole.

Use a savoy cabbage with lots of leaves. Place it directly on the table so that the leaves fan out opulently. A glass bowl goes into the center. Fill the bowl with a mixed salad and place some of the salad elements between the leaves of the cabbage. A salad with lots of tomato looks radiant spilling out on the pale leaves.

Buy a large round loaf of firm bread. Scoop out the center and put a glass bowl in the hollow. Fill it with scrambled eggs, mounded high, and garnish with cress and tomatoes.

Remove the center of a raw eggplant. Set a bowl into it and fill it with ratatouille.

Egg Shells

For a very special presentation, fill eggshells with scrambled eggs and caviar. Using a sharp knife, cut off the top third of a hard-boiled egg at a slant. Scoop out the inside of the egg and trim the edges of the cut with a sharp scissor. Put the shell in an eggcup, fill it with scrambled eggs and top with a few grains of caviar.

The Russians cut hard-boiled eggs in half lengthwise through the shells. One push with a sharp knife will do it, and the edges can be trimmed after the inside is removed. They chop the whole egg with dill pickles and mayonnaise, then spoon the seasoned filling back into the shell, from which it is eaten with a spoon.

Cookies

Cookie decoration is determined by tradition. If there's a new way to decorate a cookie, we're not sure that we want to know it. Just now, there is a vogue for huge, plate-sized chocolate chip cookies. To us, they seem trendy, unmanageable. When you finish eating a cookie, you should want another one.

The way they are made determines the appearance. Cookies are either dropped, cut into squares and bars, rolled and cut or forced through a cookie press.

Drop cookies are placed in heaping teaspoonfuls on cool cookie sheets. They spread as they bake. These are chocolate chip and oatmeal-raisin cookies. If you do them in standard amounts, you can use drop cookies to make cookie sandwiches. In general, they are the simplest and also the least decorated variety.

Bar cookies are made in shallow square or rectangular pans. Spread the dough evenly with a spatula. When the dough is baked, let it cool for a while, then cut it into bars. You can press a nut half onto each butterscotch bar or a chocolate mint onto each brownie square.

Hand-molded cookies are usually made from rather firm dough that won't flatten by itself. These are the ginger cookies that you roll into a ball between your palms, then flatten with a sugar-dipped glass, or the peanut butter cookies that you press down with the tines of a fork. You can also make thin ropes of two shades of cookie dough, cut them into 3-inch lengths, twist them around one another and bend into candy canes to hang on the Christmas tree.

118

You can also hand-mold dough to use for refrigerator cookies. Make a long cylinder of dough shaped in a round, an oval or a square. Wrap it in a thin sheet of dough in a contrasting color. When you slice it up, you'll have two-layered cookies. *(Fig. 118)*

119

Make a stack of layers of differently colored cookie dough. When you slice it, the cookies will be striped. *(Fig. 119)*

Use two colors of dough rolled into flat ribbons. Fold them into each other to make a pinwheel design. *(Fig. 120)*

120

Rolled cookies are the ones we cut with cookie cutters. Although there are hundreds of different cookie-cutter shapes, you may want one that hasn't been invented yet. If you do, cut it out of stiff cardboard. Then use it stencil-style with a very sharp knife to cut the dough. It helps to work with chilled dough and to roll small amounts at a time.

104

Pressed cookies are forced through cookie presses in sculptured shapes. Best to use the instructions that come with your machine. The only trick is in keeping an even pressure, so that the cookies turn out to be the same size and bake evenly.

To decorate the cookies, make thin icings. Dip half a cookie in the icing, holding the other half in your fingers. Spread icing on the top of the cookie with a knife.

Paint a glaze on a cookie by thinning a beaten egg yolk with water and a little food coloring. Spread thin jam on another cookie. Or put a square of chocolate on a still-hot cookie and spread it as it softens.

For the top, sprinkle on colored sugar, chocolate shot or sprinkles. Press in chopped or halved nuts, coconut, bits of preserved fruit and real candies: M&M's, gumdrops, jelly beans.

Serving

The best serving dish for cookies is a shallow basket. Arrange them as you would crackers. Stand one variety of cookie on end in the basket, and then put a different colored or shaped cookie here and there among the first.

On a flat plate, serve several different kinds of cookies. Do a row of overlapping round molasses cookies down the middle of the plate, with nut crescents on either side.

When you serve more than one variety of cookie together, make sure that they can be told apart. Don't use chocolate chips and oatmeal cookies together, both of which are round, beige and lumpy.

To add formality, serve the cookies on a footed plate, as the English do on the tea table.

Or serve them from a tin. Use a French box with an Art Nouveau design, an English tin with the queen's picture on it or an Italian box covered with medallions and insignias from the proud manufacturer.

Christmas Cookies

Christmas cookies are crisp, often spicy and always decorative. They're often made in holiday shapes, then covered with tinted icing, powdered sugar and sprinkles. Their one common factor is that they are made of firm, long-keeping doughs which are intended to be baked ahead of time and to ripen and harden until the Christmas season.

You can find cutters shaped like gingerbread men, stars, bells, trees and wreaths. If you want a shape you can't find, a snowman or an angel, draw it on heavy cardboard. Cut out the cardboard, leaving the frame intact. After you roll out the dough, use a sharp knife to cut around the empty space in the cardboard.

(This kind of frame works, too, when you stencil a Christmas shape on an iced cake. Make a tree-shaped stencil. Lay it over a white-frosted cake and pour chocolate or green sprinkles through the opening. Then decorate the tree with jelly beans and gumdrops.)

To hang Christmas cookies on a tree, cut holes in them before you bake them. Or make the candy-cane cookies we described above.

When the cookies are cool, they are ready to be iced. Use thin sugar icings tinted with vegetable dyes. Spread icing on a logical section of the cookie: Santa's cap or the top two thirds of a bell. When the icing is dry, fill a pastry tube with white icing or use one of the little icing tubes you buy in the supermarket and outline the remaining space with straight and scallopped lines.

Corn

Of all the foods that originated in this hemisphere, corn is the most distinctively American. New England Indians brought succotash to the first Thanksgiving. Mexicans eat tortillas. In the South we eat corn fritters, corn oysters and corn pudding. Now the food most identified with the United States—more than hamburgers or clam chowder or blueberry pie—is corn on the cob, boiled in salt water or roasted on a grill, and eaten with lots of butter, salt and freshly ground pepper.

Buy the freshest corn you can get, from the farmer who picked it, if that is possible. The sugar in corn turns quickly to starch, which is why so many people are fanatical about eating corn the day it is picked. It comes in varieties with tiny white kernels or large yellow kernels. Always check fresh corn by pulling back some of the green husks to make sure that the kernels are well developed and free from rot.

If you must keep it longer than a few hours, leave it in the husks and store in the refrigerator. When it's time to cook it, remove the husks and the silk—a messy job at best—and drop it into boiling water to cook for just a few minutes. Parboiled corn can be painted with melted butter and placed over the coals for a few minutes. If you want to cook it on the coals from scratch, soak the husks with water and lay the corn, still in its husks, on the rack.

Use your biggest oval platter to serve corn on the cob. Pile the ears lengthwise. In a V at one end of the platter, place two ears, still in their husks, but with the husks pulled halfway back. Make a heap of cherry tomatoes and greens where they touch at the base of the V.

Serve individual ears of corns on leaves from the husks. Remove the husks and soak them in water to keep them flat until you're ready to use them.

Some people spread butter on corncobs with pieces of bread. It's less slippery that way than with a knife. Each plate gets dark rye or pumpernickel bread for the job. It can be yesterday's bread, since it won't be eaten.

Holders—those cute little ceramic skewers that are stuck into the ends of ears of corn—are not to our taste. There's something overly genteel about refusing to touch the corn with your fingers while you're down there gobbling it up. Just accept the fact that it isn't a neat food to eat.

Frozen corn on the cob is well below second best. But frozen corn off the cob is quite good, as is some canned corn. To cut fresh corn off the cob, you can use a paring knife or a special corn-scraping tool.

Serve corn kernels in tomato cups, in green pepper halves or in split, hollowed zucchini. Mix it with brightly colored vegetables, such as black olives, pimiento, diced green or sweet red pepper. American Indians cooked it with lima beans, but it's much better looking with red kidney beans.

Creamed corn isn't really creamed at all. The sauce comes from the inside of the corn kernels. It's runny and colorless, and needs to be served in a vegetable container to give it shape. Try a green pepper or a tomato casing or even an orange shell. Or put it into a small bowl and top it with chopped green peppers, a tomato slice or with croutons of toasted corn bread and green olives.

Corn Bread

Corn bread is a variety of muffin because it is raised with baking powder. It's homely and familiar when it is baked in muffins and sticks or in a black iron spider. But it can also be done in fancy molds. The quality of the metal doesn't seem to matter. We had no trouble making star-shaped corn bread in strongly fluted gelatin molds or round corn bread in ring molds. The breads slipped right out of the buttered molds when they were done. The sharply creased shapes added to the appeal of the bread's golden-brown surface. And we did bake the molds on cookie sheets to keep the bread from burning.

Bake corn bread in a ring mold, and fill its center with red beans and corn kernels or with creamed chicken.

For color and texture, add bits of ham or bacon, whole kernels of corn, chopped red onions or pecans to the corn bread batter before you bake it.

Serve the muffins, sticks or squares in a basket lined with a brightly colored napkin.

Cottage Cheese

Cottage cheese is pure white, a soft fresh cheese with a creamy or tangy flavor. Like the very best cream and butter, it tastes of nothing but milk, and the purity of its flavor is reflected in the purity of its appearance.

Serve cottage cheese in a blue-and-white-striped bowl and it looks fresh from the dairy. Serve it in a dark bowl and garnish with a single radish or some sprigs of arugula, and you have emphasized the white color.

Add chopped parsley and scallions, and it looks and tastes garden-green. Add sweet red pepper and chopped carrots and you have a multicolored health salad.

On a mound of cottage cheese, stand a slice of cucumber flanked with carrot slivers or black olives—anything that sets off the snowy whiteness of the cheese. *(Fig. 121)*

121

If you want to serve it on a bed of greens, make them dark green, such as spinach or escarole. Sprinkle with chopped dill, and put a cluster of watercress leaves on top.

Layer cottage cheese in a wine goblet with strawberries or sliced peaches. When you puree it in the blender, it turns into mock sour cream. This can be swirled with cooked fruit in a parfait glass to look like a rich dessert.

Crackers

No one makes his own crackers. These crisp unleavened breads and biscuits were developed as a long-keeping form of bread, but now appeal simply to our desire for something crunchy, snappy, salty. What a variety there is available to us, from the sturdiest whole-grain cracker in the health-food stores to the cheesiest, saltiest, most additive-stuffed product of the American food industry.

We eat them with cheese, with peanut butter, with jam. We serve them with salads and seafood cocktails and soup. We eat them out of the box for snacks. We buy large round crisp breads and dark rye thins from Scandinavia, matzos that were invented in biblical times, water biscuits, soda crackers, melba toast, zwieback, Montpelier biscuits and English wholemeal biscuits. Plus all the crackers that we call by their first names: Ritz and Triscuits and Wheat Thins and Uneeda Biscuits.

Beware of a too-orderly arrangement when you serve crackers. The first guest to take one will destroy the symmetry. Try, instead, for a look of haphazard abundance.

If it is possible, stand the crackers on end. Choose a container that's small enough to crowd the crackers. Baskets and earthenware bowls are good. A colorful napkin crinkled in the basket helps to stabilize the crackers and adds color to the table. For a party, hollow out a loaf of dark bread and fill it with crackers, or serve them in a terra-cotta flowerpot or child's tin bucket.

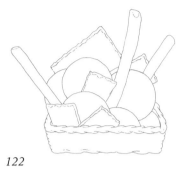

122

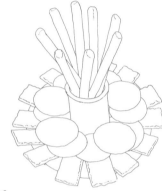

123

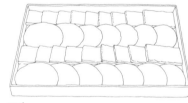

124

The best arrangements use at least four varieties of cracker, chosen for contrast in shape and color. Don't try to segregate them by type. In a long, narrow basket, first put in the largest, a big disk of Swedish flatbread or two matzo boards. Fill in around them with the smaller varieties, standing them on edge. Finally, punctuate with long thin breadsticks or zwieback. *(Fig. 122)*

Fill a low tumbler with breadsticks, and put it in the center of a round plate. Surround it with rows of rye crisps, with round water biscuits laid on top of them. *(Fig. 123)*

A generous assortment is best. But if you have only two kinds of crackers, it's more than twice as good as one.

Fill a small basket with round crackers standing on edge. Place long crackers on their sides among them, in spokes or in roughly parallel lines.

Build a heap of wheatmeal biscuits at one end of an oval basket, sesame sticks at the other end. Then place two sesame sticks among the biscuits, and vice versa.

If you want an orderly arrangement, you can shingle the biscuits on a flat plate. Do it in concentric circles, alternating types of crackers in the ring or alternating circle by circle. Or do parallel straight lines, shingled in opposite directions. *(Fig. 124)*

Even a tidy arrangement can look a little haphazard. On a flat plate, put long dark rye toasts at the four compass points, and pile round water biscuits between them. *(Fig. 125)*

If you have only one kind of cracker, it's hard to keep the arrangement from looking commercial, as though you had emptied the Ritz right out of the box onto the plate. Do your best. Stand them up, tightly wedged, in a long narrow basket or bowl. The bowls meant for celery and olives are perfect for this.

Cranberry Sauce

Dark red cranberry sauce is itself an accompaniment to other foods, setting off the brown roast or turkey of holiday dinners, adding tang to both eye and taste.

Most people use it from the can, either jellied or in chunks, although there are still those who make raw cranberry conserves with their children at Thanksgiving, cook cranberry relish full of raisins, orange peel and nuts.

If you do make your own sauce, let it set in a ring mold. Turn it out, and fill the center with mandarin orange sections and watercress leaves.

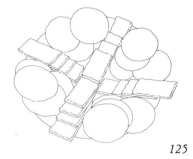

125

Spoon chunky sauce into scooped-out lemon or orange halves, and garnish the sauce with thin strips of peel tied into knots.

Line a clear glass bowl with thin orange slices. Spoon chunky sauce into the bowl and lay half-slices of orange on the top around the edge of the bowl. Place greenery where the slices meet.

If your family prefers plain jellied cranberry sauce, remove it from the can. Cut the cylinder into ½-inch slices. Lay the circles, overlapping, in a cut glass bowl or opaque white dish. Garnish with kumquats and holly leaves, or with walnuts and watercress. Or make an orange loop, by cutting a slice of orange in half, then making a cut between the skin and the orange almost to the end, and curling the skin under to form a loop. Place one orange loop at the end of the overlapping slices of cranberry sauce.

Leave the log whole. Stick short parsley stems into the jelly, tracing a gentle curve that outlines both ends and crosses the cylinder diagonally. *(Fig. 126)*

126

Make thin slices of cranberry jelly. Cut out diamonds and flowers, using small cookie cutters. Place the shapes flat on orange or lemon slices, and use them as a border around the sliced turkey.

Crepes

Pale, supple crepes are thinner than pancakes, and more elegant. We stuff them with jam and fruit, roll them around ice cream and soufflé mixtures, fill them with savory seafood and chicken.

A few years ago there was a vogue for crepe parties, at which one person made crepes all evening long, while the guests chose their own fillings from bowls set out on the table.

We serve them flat with powdered sugar, folded in half over berries, in quarters as in crepes Suzette or folded in wedges with some of the filling showing through. *(Figs. 127–29.)* We also roll them in tubes around fillings, then arrange them overlapped in a row on a plate. *(Fig. 130)*

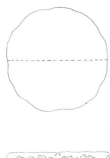

127

128

Garnish filled crepes according to their filling. Add mussels in their shells and lemon wedges to seafood crepes, nuts and dried fruit to a plate of Hungarian apricot palacsinta, or dessert pancakes. Stuff crepes with seasoned ricotta and serve them on a plate covered with tomato sauce. Garnish with basil leaves.

A nice trick, and easier than it looks, is to drizzle a lacy network pattern in batter on a well-oiled crepe pan. Slide it off onto wax paper and repeat. Make as many of the filigree patterns as you have crepes. Then spread a whole crepe with filling—strawberry jam or sour cream and caviar—and put a lacework crepe on top of it.

129

Croquettes

Croquettes are patties of finely chopped cooked food bound together with a sauce, usually a white sauce, then breaded and fried. As the name implies, the outside is crunchy, but in a proper croquette, the inside remains creamy and delicately flavored with chicken, ham, salmon, oysters or whatever other morsels it contains.

American croquettes are usually cone shaped, while the French make them into tubes. You can also make them into round balls or flat patties, then cover with bread crumbs and fry to a golden brown.

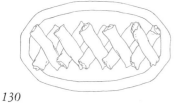

130

Serve croquettes on a light plate that is covered with tomato sauce or on a dark plate that is covered with cream sauce. Drizzle some sauce over the patties, and garnish with pea pods or parsley.

Croustade

A croustade is a bread casing for hot sauced food, easier to make but just as serviceable as a patty shell. It can be large, and take the place of a serving bowl, or it can be a small container, meant to be put on a dinner plate and filled with creamed chicken or shrimp Newburg.

112

To make a large croustade, slice off the top of a whole loaf of unsliced white bread. Remove the center of the loaf with your fingers and then with a knife, leaving walls that are ½ inch thick. Brush all the surfaces with melted butter, and bake the casing on a cookie sheet in a very slow oven for about an hour, or until it is golden brown. A more decorative casing can be made by scoring the outer walls of the loaf or by cutting off the top edge of the shell in zigzags or scallops.

To make individual croustades, use unsliced firm-textured white bread. Cut it into slices 2½ inches thick. Trim the crusts and leave the slices square or cut them into circles or ovals. Carve the outer edges of these slices in shallow scallops or zigzags. Hollow out the center of the slice to make a shell, leaving a ½-inch base and 1-inch walls. Then deep fry the shell or dry it in a slow oven.

Fill croustades lavishly with hot cooked food, and garnish the food with thin croutons cut in fancy shapes that you dip in melted butter and then in parsley.

An easier method is to buy round rolls with good firm crusts. Cut a slice off the top of each roll, then pull out the centers with your fingers, leaving a casing. Instead of garnishing with croutons, tilt the lid of the roll against the base and garnish the food with parsley.

Croutons

Croutons are more than the little cubes of dried-out bread that are tossed in a Caesar salad. They are a decorative staple of the haute cuisine, crisply toasted triangles, diamonds and hearts that surround a platter of fish or float on a clear soup. They're easy to make, fit well into everyday cooking and are a good way to use up slightly stale bread.

Make crouton cubes by cutting slices of bread into strips, and then into cubes. Dry them in a 300°F oven, or fry them in seasoned butter. Dry, cool and store in airtight containers.

For fancy croutons, cut the slices of bread into shapes with a cookie cutter or a sharp knife. A slice of packaged white bread makes two right-angled triangles, four equilateral triangles or three rectangular strips.

131

Make a heart by slicing the bread in half on the diagonal, cutting off one of the acute angles, and then trimming the pointed shape into a long heart. *(Fig. 131)*

Make a doughnut by cutting the bread with a cookie cutter or with a large, then a smaller glass. If you collect enough doughnuts, make a chain by cutting a slit in every other one, and then linking them into a chain.

Toast, fry or brush with melted butter and bake the shaped bread in a 300°F oven for about 30 minutes. The leftover bread gets whirred in the blender to make bread crumbs.

Use diamond-shaped croutons around a platter of roast chicken. The points can overlap or stand ½ inch apart, with olive slices or parsley tufts between them.

Stand a toasted diamond or oval crouton aslant on a bowl of chicken salad or creamed salmon.

Use croutons laid flat as a topping for an oven-baked casserole. Play a little. Cut out fish shapes, toast them, and serve one minnow on each portion of codfish.

Decorate the croutons by dipping one end into the soup or stew, and then in finely minced parsley or dill.

Crudités

When raw vegetables became party food they took the French name of *crudités*. Crudités can look haphazard or just right, depending on the way they are carved, the combination of vegetables used and the care taken in the arrangement.

The vegetables should be cut uniformly and neatly, convenient to being used as finger foods. Save the scraps and curvy bits for vegetable soup. Don't try to be thrifty by using them on the platter.

The rule is to make the shapes as uncomplicated as possible. Then carve one or two piece. in a more ornate manner and use them as accents. An overworked, oversculptured platter looks silly and catered.

Trim and scrape the vegetables early in the day, and store them in ice water until you are ready to arrange the platter. Use lemon juice when it is required to keep the food from discoloring. Just before you serve it, spray the arrangement with a flower mister. Grocers do this every Monday morning to restore Saturday's lettuce to garden freshness.

There are three steps to a beautiful arrangement: (1) select the vegetable in accordance with a color scheme. (2) Choose an appropriate container. (3) Design a composition that fits the container and has, possibly, a focal point and accents.

Choosing the Vegetables

The best arrangements are based on only two or three colors. More than that, and you have a mixed vegetable salad. Most vegetables are green and white. Some are red, and a few, like carrots and sweet potatoes, are yellow-orange. Look at the color appendix for ideas on combining colors.

Try an arrangement using only green and white vegetables: zucchini, mushrooms, broccoli, cauliflower, green beans and fennel. Accent with tomatoes and black olives. Do an arrangement in red and white: radishes, cauliflower, cherry tomatoes, white turnips and thin strips of raw beets, accented with dark-green scallion brushes.

Make an all-green arrangement on a round platter, moving from dark green at the rim to the palest shade in the center. Go from broccoli to scallions to romaine leaves to endive to celery.

Try an arrangement in orange: carrots, thin strips of sweet potato, turnips and cauliflower, with a garnish of black olives.

Containers

Choose a big enough container. You'll need more vegetables than you think. Crudités are always eaten right away by people who are trying to quiet appetites aroused by the smell of the main meal, and whose determination to diet has not yet been dulled by the drinks.

Ceramic and straw baskets make good containers. So do low bowls in terra-cotta, clear glass and wood. Think of platters, clay flowerpots, huge wineglasses—even a French wire salad basket.

115

132

Three wine goblets, filled to overflowing with radishes, mushrooms and celery stalks. A bouquet of tall vegetables instead of flowers in a ceramic flowerpot. A three-tiered cake dish heaped with vegetables, the bottom level spilling off onto the table.

Use a vegetable as the container. Take a leafy savoy cabbage and place it on a basket, its leaves opened out generously. Remove the central core of the cabbage and fill it with dip in a glass bowl. Arrange vegetable sticks, chunks and circles between the leaves. *(Fig. 132)*

Arrangement

The simplest arrangement is best. Choose a concentric design, a striped design or one made of pie-shaped wedges.

To make stripes, cross the short axis of an oval platter with stripes of cucumber, radishes, green beans, tiny onions and tomato slices. Don't make this symmetrical, beginning and ending with the cucumbers. Just read it from left to right, getting a contrast in color or tone with each change. *(Fig. 133)*

Make four pie-shaped wedges on a round platter, alternating green and white vegetables, covering each quarter of the plate with broccoli, cauliflower, green beans and turnip disks. *(Fig. 134)*

116

To make neat edges to the sections, lay a piece of cardboard or the side of a spatula where you want each section to end. Slide it out when the vegetables are in place. Over the border, lay sprigs of parsley, cherry tomatoes or black olives.

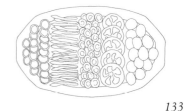

When you finish an arrangement, if you feel that it looks wrong, you have probably used too many different kinds of vegetables for the size of the container. Weed some out. You can always refill when your guests' first hunger has been quelled.

If the arrangement has been made in a basket or shallow bowl, it might have a base made from a bed of different leaves.

If it extends from some central point, you might emphasize that fact with a focal point. Use something that contrasts with the carved vegetables. Something larger and taller that catches the eye, like a pepper stuffed with olives, a big carved turnip or a collection of skewered greens.

134

If the plate looks boring, try adding accents. Choose accents from foods that contrast in color and texture with the principal vegetables. Parsley, olives and tomatoes are possibilities. A carved vegetable can be an accent to its uncarved mates: a radish rose among heaps of smooth radishes, a carrot spiral on top of a bundle of carrot sticks. Try flowers: an orange day lily looks surprisingly right on a tray of green and white vegetables.

A Plan

Here's an easy arrangement for a basket of crudités. Use it as you would a recipe. Follow the directions the first time and then, as you become more confident of your taste and ability, make up your own variations.

Use a basic assortment of winter vegetables: carrots, celery, radishes, scallions, cucumber and watercress. Nothing that you can't get in your supermarket in February.

For a group of four friends meeting for drinks, choose a basket that's about 8 inches in diameter.

Early in the day, do the fancy carving on a few vegetables so that they can open out in ice water. Take three scallions with full tops. Cut them off on the diagonal and sliver the ends. Cut three radish flowers. Then trim the rest of the vegetables into even slices and spears. Place everything in ice water.

Cut a potato in half and place it, cut-side down, in the bottom of the basket. This is the base for the skewers. Skewer a few leaves of Boston or leaf lettuce, and stick the skewers into the potato. Lay other leaves around them, falling over the sides of the basket. The greenery forms a good base to hold up the rest of the vegetables. Push in spears of carrot and celery. Stand scallions on end. Finally, lay cucumber slices and radishes low in the arrangement. Use clusters of vegetables rather than an even mix. Place the basket in the refrigerator, where it should keep well for half a day. When the guests arrive, take it out and spray it with a flower mister. *(Fig. 135)*

135

Cucumbers

Cucumbers used to be sliced crosswise, showing both the green rind and the pale center. For a party, the skin would first be scored with the tines of a fork to make a pattern around the edges when the slices were cut.

Those days are gone, thanks to modern agriculture. Farmers have developed cucumbers with tough, bitter skins and the middlemen, aiming for longer shelf life, have finished the job of making the skins inedible by dipping them in wax. Nobody who doesn't grow his own wants to eat an unpeeled cucumber anymore.

Peel off most, but not quite all, of the skin. Thin strips of green left in place won't hurt the taste and will add a visual contrast.

Slice them straight across in circles, or on the diagonal, with your knife held nearly parallel to the cutting board, to make ovals. If you leave some skin on the round slice, you can cut it nearly all the way through and make a standing cucumber twist on the model of a lemon twist. *(Fig. 136)*

Unfortunately, there's often a problem with too many seeds. When a cucumber is more than mature—"of a certain age"—the center becomes a mass of seeds and pulp. You ought to remove this before you serve the cucumber. The most palatable way of preparing raw cucumber is usually to peel it, cut it lengthwise, scoop out the seeds and then, finally, slice the cucumber into half-rounds.

136

118

There are several ways to cut cucumbers for stuffing. In China, they cut 2-inch lengths, push out the seed section and stuff the cases with chopped pork and ginger. You can do the same, leaving a base on the bottom of the section, and fill the cups with russian dressing, cranberry sauce or red caviar. A more decorative way to make cucumber cups is by cutting off the end of the vegetable so that it will stand steadily, and then making three slanted cuts in toward the center, like flower petals. Twist out the rest of the vegetable and scoop out some of the insides.

Cut a cucumber in half lengthwise. Scoop out the seeds, and fill the centers with seasoned cheese or cold chopped vegetable salads.

For stuffed hors d'oeuvres, cut off both ends of a cucumber. Remove the seeds with a special tool, such as a zucchini or cucumber corer, or with an iced-tea spoon. Then stuff the center with Roquefort cheese or seasoned cream cheese. Chill and, just before serving, slice it into rounds.

There are several garnishes to be made of cucumbers that use the dark skin decoratively.

Make cucumber triangles. Slice down one side of a cucumber, removing a shallow strip of skin. Cut the skin into rectangles 1 inch wide and 2 inches long. Make cuts in the short edges, one high and in from the left side and one low and in from the right; do not cut all the way through. You should now have a Z-shape. Twist the upper and lower arms of the Z so that they cross one another, forming a triangle. Float these on cold soups.

Make cucumber chain. Cut off the ends of the cucumber, push out the seeds and cut the vegetable in thin rings. Slit every other ring and make a chain of the links. This can be a border for a salad, or can be used in a short chain of only three rings alongside a portion of fish.

To make a cucumber feather, cut off a side of cucumber about 4 inches long to get a flattish piece of dark skin. Trim this slice so that it is 1 inch wide. Make six lengthwise cuts, each 1/8th inch, not cutting through at one end, so that the resulting strips remain attached. Soak in salted water to soften the skin. Then fold strips two, four and six into loops, leaving every other strip unbent. This feather can be varied by bending just the inner or outer strips. Place on an open-faced sandwich or garnish a whole baked fish. *(Fig. 137)*

137

119

To make a jet trail, once again cut off the side of a cucumber so that you have a flattish piece of green skin. Make cuts ⅛ inch wide down the whole length of the piece, leaving a narrow spine attaching them on one side. Soak in salt water until it is malleable. Then splay out and use it around half of a scoop of salad or vegetables. To be even fancier, place a flat carrot flower at one end of the trail.

More difficult still, but lots of fun, is a cucumber spring. Cut off the ends of a whole cucumber. Stick a skewer or a chopstick through the center of the vegetable. Using a sharp knife, cut into the stick at a slight angle. Turn the cucumber so that the knife continues to cut a spiral down its whole length. Pull out the skewer, and you will have a cucumber spring, to use in its whole length or in short sections.

Dips

Dips are good, messy and very easy to eat. They encourage gluttony, save work for the hostess and are, therefore, suited to large informal parties where the guests fix their own drinks. Although they seem totally twentieth-century American, they have a respectable culinary ancestry in fondues, rarebits, hotpots and bagna cauda.

The Dips

We think of them as party food. But there's no reason not to serve a dip at a family supper in place of a salad: a basket of raw vegetables with an earthenware bowl of flavored yogurt, for example, or, after the main course, a plate of apple and pear slices with a bowl of Roquefort cheese dip.

For parties, you will want to make more of a fuss over the presentation.

Peel back the outer leaves of a savoy cabbage and cut a bowl-shaped chunk out of the core. Set a clear glass bowl into it and fill it with dip. On a smaller scale, hollow out a head of Boston lettuce and set your bowl into that space. Save the tender leaves you removed, and use them for dipping. And anytime you serve greens as a container, remember to freshen them with a flower mister just before you serve them.

Cut off the top of a round loaf of crusty bread. Remove the inside of the loaf, cutting it into croutons for dipping. Place the bowl of dip into the hollow.

Use any bowl-shaped vegetable as a container, such as tomatoes, bell peppers, artichokes, acorn squash or eggplant. Or use an assortment of different vegetable containers, linking them visually by sticking a tortilla chip or a red-tipped lettuce leaf into each one. Set them on a flat basket with the largest container—the eggplant or the cabbage—in the center, and the smaller ones around it.

Serve dips in oversized red-wine glasses, with dill-green dip in one, red tomato in another, creamy yogurt in a third.

If you serve dip in a clear glass bowl, line it first with greens. Cluster escarole or endive, curled scallions or young asparagus spears at intervals around the inside of the bowl. If you're serving guacamole, line the container with corn husks.

The Dippers

There's logic in the pairing of dip to dipped. Why break up the comfortable marriage of guacamole and tortilla chips? Could you really devise something better to dunk in horseradish cocktail sauce than cold shrimp, scallops and clams? Or to go with mustard sauce than tiny meatballs and sausages? Can you imagine sour cream-onion soup dip without potato chips?

Avoid the trendy commercial nibbles for dipping, the ones shaped in curls and squiggles with ingredient lists suggesting that they were made of industrial by-products. Use honest potato chips, tortilla chips, strips and cubes of homemade toast and good-quality breadsticks and crackers. And vegetables, of course: an assortment of crisp cold vegetables, not only carrot and celery sticks but, perhaps, a mound of broccoli and cauliflower flowerets or a trayful of cooked cold artichoke leaves.

Easter Eggs

There is a very old tradition of making colored and decorated eggs at Easter time. The custom is older than Christianity, as old as the association of eggs with new life and rebirth.

In Greece, Easter eggs are dyed red, then wiped with an oiled cloth to make them shine. In the Ukraine and in Poland, they draw on the shells with a waxed crayon, then dip the eggs in dye. When the wax is pulled off, the area underneath the drawing appears in white. In Russia, they blow the raw egg out of the shell before they decorate it. The empty shells are often filled with confetti, poured in through small funnels made of stiff paper.

Chinese tea eggs aren't made for Easter, of course. But they are made by a technique we can copy at Easter time. Hard-boiled eggs are cooled in their shells. Then they are rolled gently under the palm so that the shells are covered with a tracery of fine cracks, and simmered and soaked in a solution of strong tea. The tea soaks through the cracks, making spidery lines on the egg whites underneath.

You can adapt any of these techniques to use on plain American Easter eggs. Most of the time, you'll be using commercial egg dyes or beet juice. Felt-tipped marking pens are invaluable additions to your egg-decorating equipment, as is a wire egg tree to hold the eggs steady while you work on them.

Dye an egg red in the Greek manner. If you draw on the shells with pinpricks, tattoo fashion, before you soak the hard-boiled egg in dye, you will have a pointillist design underneath when you peel off the shell.

If you're very good with your hands, you can dye a shelled hard-boiled egg with beet juice, then make a pattern by drawing with the point of a paring knife on the surface, and removing a thin layer of egg to reveal the white underneath.

An easier trick is to do reverse coloring, Ukrainian-style, by pasting gummed stars and labels and bits of paper doilies on the eggshell. Dye the egg, and pull off the appliqués to reveal the white shell underneath. *(Fig. 138)*

138

122

Easiest of all, dip an egg in colored egg dye. Then draw on it with your felt-tipped marker. The best designs are the most abstract. Think of Imperial Russian eggs when you make up a pattern. It can be quite ornate, but it should not be realistic. Rather, try to do lines and circles that fit the curve of the eggshell.

Gilding the lily, take your marker-decorated egg and apply fripperies from the notions counter, like sequins and bits of lace and tinsel.

Come Easter morning, present the eggs on a nest made of sprouts or shredded vegetables. Put them in a wire egg stand, in a shallow white earthenware bowl, in a basket lined with a snowy linen napkin, or in an egg carton that the children have painted white.

Eggs

No food is more changeable than an egg. You can present it pristine-white in its shell or let it explode with baroque decorations in an Easter basket. At breakfast, it's a mass of yellow curds; at lunch, an austere ring of yellow and white on an open-faced sandwich; at dinner, it becomes a white web floating in golden chicken broth.

Boiled Eggs

Eggcups remain the best way to serve soft-boiled eggs. Set one on a small plate. Surround it with fingers or triangles of toast, strips of bacon or spears of asparagus for dunking.

On a Sunday morning or a birthday, tie a ribbon bow around the narrow part of an eggcup. Stick a sprig of parsley between shell and cup. A simple special-breakfast idea is to stick a gold star on top of the egg's unbroken shell.

Boiled eggs that are broken into a bowl or the wide side of an eggcup can be sprinkled with crumbled bacon, chives or croutons. Cut a toast star with a cookie cutter, and lay it over two soft-boiled eggs in a bowl.

Fried and Poached Eggs

Fried and poached eggs are nearly identical in appearance. We serve fried eggs on the naked plate, but never offer poached eggs without some buffer between the plate and its slippery self. Actually, both look best when they are framed on a bed of another food. Serve them on toast, English muffins, hollowed-out rolls. Put them on beds of flavored rice, chopped cooked vegetables, with asparagus, on artichoke bottoms, chili and, of course, on hash. *(See Figs. 12, 14)*

Poached eggs cook tidily if you add a bit of vinegar to the cooking water and stir the water into a whirlpool before you drop in the raw egg. Trim the whites with scissors after you scoop them out of the water; they aren't as fragile as you might think.

Scrambled Eggs

Scrambled eggs have no shape of their own, but they can be gathered into whatever form the cook prefers. Beat them furiously and you get a chopped texture. Stir them languorously and you get large yellow curds.

Spoon scrambled eggs over any of the beds we suggested for poached eggs, and garnish the top with a bit of the base: a spoonful of hash or two toast triangles with some parsley.

Fill an empty eggshell with scrambled eggs. This is easier than it sounds. Take a hard-boiled egg and cut off the top, using a heavy knife in one downward push. Trim the ragged edges, if there are any, with scissors. Spoon in the eggs, garnish with parsley, and serve in an eggcup.

Fill edible containers, such as baked tomatoes or baked potato skins, with scrambled eggs.

Arrange the scrambled eggs in a long oval shape, making a kind of mock omelet, and lay a line of garnish down the center. Chopped parsley does very well for the garnish. Accompany the eggs with fried tomato slices, chicken livers or kidneys. *(Fig. 139)*

On a serving platter, flank a wide band of smoked salmon with widths of scrambled eggs. On a round platter, gather the eggs into a circular mound with an indentation in the top, like a ring mold. Fill the hollow with chunks of ham, and edge the cavity with sprigs of watercress. Surround with ham and tomato slices. *(Fig. 140)*

Omelets

Visually, the problem is to relate the oval envelope to the round plate. Omelets are never served on beds of other foods. If, however, you have a sauce to go with the omelet, you should pour a thin layer of it on the plate before you put the omelet down. The sauce will frame the eggs.

Tuck parsley under the edges of the omelet.

Spoon some of the stuffing alongside the omelet so that the diner will know what to expect inside. With a mushroom omelet, add a few whole sautéed mushroom caps.

140

Cut a slit in the top of a rolled omelet, and spoon a little extra stuffing into the slit. A complicated presentation involves stuffing the omelet with one mixture—say, cheese—and spooning another, complementary mixture—say, spinach—alongside it.

To glaze an omelet, rub it with a pat of butter or brush with melted butter. Sweet omelets get a sprinkling of sugar.

Frittatas

The flat omelets called frittatas or tortillas are made with vegetables and sausages. They are peasant dishes and should look that way—studded with bright green peppers and zucchini, red tomato chunks and cubes of potato. Scramble them all together with the eggs, or arrange them deliberately in the pan for the last minute of cooking. But do it roughly, casually.

For example, have sticks of zucchini radiating out from three overlapping red pepper rings in the center of the omelet. Dot pepperoni slices between the zucchini.

A sprinkle of grated cheese will produce a golden glaze as it melts. Hold the skillet under the broiler before you take it to the table to serve the frittata. Serve it in wedges, like pizza, onto bright heavy pottery.

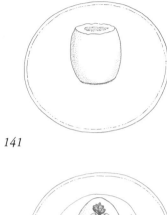

141

142

Hard-boiled Eggs

Small tricks add up to a good-looking hard-boiled egg. To keep the egg from bursting in the hot water, prick one end of it, either with a needle or with the totally unnecessary little tool that is sold for this purpose. To keep the yolk in the center of the egg, turn it over in the water several times during the first few minutes of cooking, until the egg white is lightly set. And to prevent the nasty dark line from forming around the yolk, try not to overcook the egg, and stop the cooking as soon as it comes from the water by plunging it into cold water.

It's almost too simple to mention, but you can make a surprising change in the look of hard-boiled eggs by cutting them crosswise, through the short axis, instead of lengthwise. Take a slice off the bottom, so that the egg half will stand upright, and you'll have chubby little barrels instead of the too-familiar ovals. *(Fig. 141)*

Serve them cut-side up or down.

Use disks of sliced hard-boiled egg in a border. Surround a heap of chicken salad with a border of hard-boiled egg slices alternating with clusters of 2½-inch carrot sticks and scallions.

Making disks means having lots of ends left over. They're all protein and very good for you. If you have just a little bit, chop the whites with parsley and sprinkle them on sliced tomatoes or asparagus.

In the haute cuisine, it's traditional to cut tiny diamonds from egg white with truffle cutters. With them, chefs decorate aspics, canapés and cold poached fish. Identical shapes cut from black olives or truffles make a dramatic contrast. If you don't have a truffle cutter, use a sharp knife dipped in water to make neat shapes. *(Fig. 142)*

And for a really unusual look, copy the Japanese, who make cone-shaped hard-boiled eggs in a paper pocket. Take a regular sheet of paper (8½ by 11 inches) and fold it in quarters. Pin three adjacent corners together and leave the fourth detached. Break a raw egg into the resulting pocket and gently slip the paper, corners up, into a pot of water for cooking. *(Fig. 143)*

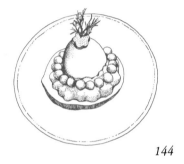

Deviled Eggs

Deviled eggs have to sit on something or they slide all over the plate. Put them on platforms of toast, vegetable slices, pâté or cheese. First, of course, cut a thin slice from the bottom for stability.

143

Set stuffed eggs, cut-side down, on sliced tomatoes. Pipe extra stuffing around the egg, add peas, and place a carrot flower and a dill sprig on top. *(Fig. 144)*

Or place the egg on a tomato slice and garnish with parsley, piped mayonnaise and a black olive slice. *(Fig. 145)*

Once you've filled the egg cavity, create a texture on the stuffing. Use the tines of a fork or the zigzag edge of a bread knife. Or feed the stuffing through the flower tip of a pastry tube. The thicker the filling, the sharper the contours of the design will be.

Slip a sprig of dill or parsley between stuffing and white. Place half a cherry tomato or a row of capers on top of it. Cut a sunburst from a carrot slice, and stick it in the soft stuffing. *(Fig. 146)*

144

Slice the egg lengthwise and stuff the halves. Place them alongside one another, tipped to form a peak and facing out. Fill the space between them with cress.

Cut off both ends of hard-boiled eggs to make squat barrels. Stuff, and stand a ring of them around salads or cold fish. Place them on toast, artichoke bottoms, disks of pâté. Decorate, and serve as a first course, cloaked with sauce.

Eggs in Aspic

145

There are molds made for eggs in aspic, but you can make do with 6½-ounce cans of tuna, the tops and bottoms removed, and the insides well scrubbed.

Prepare aspic and let it partially set. Put the cans into a flat cake pan and spoon in some of the aspic. Decorate with chopped herbs, with red caviar, with bits of tomato or green or black olive. Then place a cold poached egg or half a hard-boiled egg on the aspic, and spoon in more aspic to cover the eggs completely. Refrigerate. When it is set, unmold it, and decorate with more chopped aspic.

146

Baked Eggs

Collect clear glass dishes for baked eggs. Make two layers beneath the eggs. For example, rice covered with red beans, or toast underneath asparagus. Then, of course, the eggs, with a garnish made with a bit of the base. For a browned top, sprinkle with grated cheese.

Egg Drop

A stream of beaten egg dropped into boiling soup cooks into a web of filmy threads. In Greece, it's *avgolemono,* in Italy, *stracciatelle,* and in China, egg drop soup. Pour the lightly beaten egg from a cup into the soup in a fine stream, and stir the soup gently as you pour.

Eggplants

Eggplants are beautiful vegetables, with gently curved pear shapes, shiny purple or white skins and green caps. They are in season throughout the summer, come in sizes from tiny 2-inch eggplants to gigantic overgrown foot-long vegetables. Buy them firm, smooth and unblemished, and there should be no problem keeping them in the refrigerator from a few days to a week. Out-of-season eggplants are another story, since you can't know how long they traveled before they came to you.

The taste is rich but bland, and most presentations require the addition of green or red peppers, tomatoes, onions and spices. Luckily, the same foods improve the eggplant's appearance, because once its purple skin has been removed it's ugly and shapeless, a pale green that begins to turn gray the moment you cut into it.

It's not difficult to peel an eggplant. Do it with a vegetable scraper when the eggplant is uncooked. Broil eggplant halves cut-side down or sear the whole vegetable over a gas jet. If you don't want to keep the inside of the vegetable neatly sliced, the skin will just peel away, and you can chop the rest. For moussaka, the Greek dish that is most impressive when the filling is encased in shiny purple eggplant skins, you should bake split eggplants, then scoop out the flesh, leaving the delicate skin intact.

(Sheets of cooked eggplant skin can be used to line molds in other dishes besides moussaka. Line a bowl with skin, and fill it with ratatouille. Bake, and turn it out so that the purple skin shows. Garnish with parsley, tomato, lemon slices and pale green grapes.)

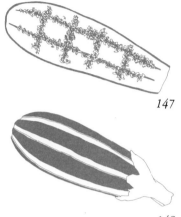

147

Cut small eggplants in half lengthwise and slice into them as though you were making garlic bread. Brush with melted oil or butter seasoned with garlic, and stuff fresh basil or parsley into the slits. Broil or bake until the eggplant is tender. *(Fig. 147)*

148

For fried and broiled eggplant slices, cut straight across into circles. Although some people find the skins bitter, they do undoubtedly help to hold the eggplant together when it's heated. Chop the eggplant, with or without its skin, to use in casseroles.

Eggplants are among the vegetables that are most frequently stuffed with other foods, with lamb mixtures, rice and vegetable combinations. They are often combined on a stuffed-vegetable platter with red and green stuffed peppers. Although it is usual to cut them along the long axis, you can make an effective presentation by removing a thin slice from the round end of the eggplant, standing it up, and cutting off the top just under the stem. Remove the insides carefully, and stuff the vegetable through the narrow opening. This then creates height on a platter of low stuffed peppers and zucchini.

Tiny eggplants can have their skin peeled away in stripes with a vegetable peeler. Brush them with seasoned oil and bake or broil. *(Fig. 148)*

In a Japanese restaurant, we saw medium-sized eggplants decorated with sgraffiti, the technique of removing areas of the surface to make designs with the contrasting color below. The whitish flesh formed a decoration on the purple skin, and it was quite beautiful. If you want to try this as part of a vegetable centerpiece, carve away parts of the skin in abstract patterns, and then rub the cut surfaces with lemon to keep the flesh from discoloring and turning an unhealthy gray. Surround the purple eggplant with basil or Italian parsley. If you can find them, add tiny white eggplants. If not, use lemons.

149

Endive

This small whitish lettuce with its tight head of elongated leaves has a crisp, slightly bitter flavor and an invariably steep price. It should look as special as its taste and price deserve.

For individual salad plates, fan six whole endive leaves on each plate. Garnish the center with olives, walnuts, with sweet red pepper or with shredded beets, and add dressing.

If you have too little endive to serve everyone generously, cut the leaves into lengthwise strips or crosswise arcs, and toss them with darker greens, such as arugula.

Use the leaves as scoops for a dip. Arrange them, spokelike, around a small colored bowl or a vegetable container. Instead of making a whole circle of endive, place it at the four compass points, and fill in the empty angles with julienned carrots and cold cooked beets.

Use the leaves in place of celery on a canapé tray. Fill them with deviled ham, Roquefort butter or shredded raw vegetables. *(Fig. 149)*

The best plates for serving endive are not pale and fine, in keeping with its special quality. Instead choose highly glazed dark brown or black pottery to set off the nearly white color and precise shape.

Fennel

Fennel looks like celery with an overdeveloped bulb. The stalks are like slender celery stalks, pale green in color and ending in feathery, dill-like leaves. When it is raw, it has an insistent licoricelike flavor that fades when the vegetable is cooked.

When the bulb is sliced horizontally, it reveals a pattern of tightly closed arcs, not unlike the tight heart of celery but more sharply angled. Cut into vertical slices, it looks like a cross section through an artichoke. In Italy, these vertical slices are frequently breaded and fried like fried zucchini.

To serve raw in salads and in plates of crudités, slice the bulbs horizontally or vertically, and slice the stalks in 2-inch pieces.

Cooked fennel loses most of its sweet flavor, and the bulbs are often cut into quarters and braised, or in vertical slices and sautéed, and then finished with a topping of butter and cheese. The stalks, when dried, are served in a bed underneath bland-tasting fish. The lacy tops resemble dill and can be used for garnishing in place of parsley or watercress.

Figs

An ancient fruit from the Middle East, the fig is now grown in California, picked tree-ripened, then packed with respect for its fragility and shipped to us. We most often get purple or pale green figs, with golden or pink centers. Buy them soft but smooth-skinned. There are also very good canned figs in sweet syrups and, of course, a worldwide commerce in dried figs.

Serve ripe figs split, in a bowl, with crème fraîche, sour cream or sweet cream. Serve them with white chèvre or a fresh cream cheese for dessert. Lay a half-circle of provolone on one side of a flat plate and a fig cut in half on the other. *(Fig. 150)*

Ripe figs are an alternative to cantaloupe or honeydew to serve with prosciutto. Each plate gets a whole fig standing in the center. A second fig is cut into four vertical sections that radiate out from the center, with four slices of prosciutto crumpled between them.

Or lay slices of prosciutto flat, covering half the dessert plate. Cut a fig in half vertically, then one of the halves in half again. On the bare half of the plate, place the half fig in the middle, with a quarter fig on either side of it. A black plate would be attractive against the pale pink ham and the pink or green of the figs.

Dried figs are often stuffed with almonds, walnuts or orange peel. We eat them out of hand or use them in baking, making jams and pickled figs.

Canned Kadota figs are a pale pretty green. Serve them in a white or clear glass bowl, cover them with cream and place a spoonful of raspberry jam or lingonberries on the top.

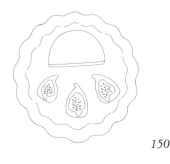

150

131

Fish

It's true of everything, but truer of fish: to make it look good, you must cook it properly. Overcook it, and it just falls apart. Use the guidelines of the Canadian Department of Fisheries, who recommend that you cook fish (by any method) for precisely ten minutes for each inch of thickness. According to this rule, a ½-inch fillet should be cooked for 5 minutes, while a 3-inch-thick stuffed snapper takes a full 30 minutes.

You can avoid the traditional coating of paprika by learning how to produce a truly browned crust on broiled fish. Pat the surface dry, then rub it with oil or butter. Sprinkle with a tiny bit of flour: ½ teaspoon will do for a good-sized steak or fillet. Slide it under a broiler that has been preheated for at least 10 minutes.

Whole Fish

Whole fish is served both hot and cold. Only the faint of heart remove the head and the tail. If you have to quiet the sensibilities of someone who can't bear to be stared at by his dinner, just cover the real eye with a false one cut from a cross section of stuffed olive or a circle of black olive on a larger circle of egg white.

In France they twist whole fish into shapes that look grotesque to the American eye, forcing the tail out through the fish's open mouth. In Japan, they skewer whole fish lengthwise, broil them on the skewers, then prop three skewered fish upright, tripod style, on a platter. But the shape of a whole fish lying on an oval plate is so pleasant that there is no reason to distort it. If you must reshape it, skewer the fish through the tail, body and head to hold it in a flowing S curve reminiscent of a fish swimming. *(Fig. 151)*

Or make a slit along the back of the fish, clean and debone. Run a string around the head and tail, curving the fish into an arc and fill the cavity with savory stuffing. *(Fig. 152)*

Apply garnishes in relation to the line of the fish's body. Make a line of lemon slices or half-slices down the side of the fish. *(Fig. 153)*

151

152

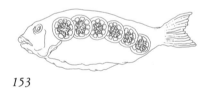

153

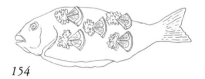

154

Or cut each slice into thirds and make staggered rows of these. Place a bit of parsley or caper at the point of each slice. *(Fig. 154)*

Repeat the shape of the back of the fish with a hedge of parsley or watercress set an inch away from it on the plate. Place cherry tomatoes or green grapes and blanched almonds on the parsley.

Decorate the side of the fish. Before you bake it, cover it with strips of scallion laid in a jagged pattern, like one in a penmanship book: a slanted line, a vertical line and so forth. The scallion will bake onto the fish so that, once it's cooked, you can move it to a platter without disrupting the design. Then add two carrot disks that you've sautéed just long enough to get rid of the raw look, and you'll have a lot of looks for a little effort. *(Fig. 155)*

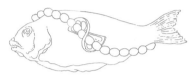

155

Decorate a really big fish with a string of green grapes. Drape the necklace over the fish's head, down across its body and under its tail in an S curve. Echo the curve with a lemon twist slipped between the grapes halfway down the chain. *(Fig. 156)*

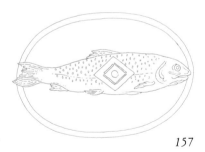

156

Cold Fish

Any of these designs can be used on a whole cold fish just as well. The difference is the surface, which, on cold fish, is likely to be cloaked with an opaque sauce.

You can cover the fish with an aspic made with the fish poaching broth, so that the silvery skin shows through. First remove a diamond of skin from the side of the fish. On the bare flesh, make a diamond with strips of pimiento, and place a circle of black olive in its center. Then spoon on chilled, syrupy aspic. Repeat until it is well coated. *(Fig. 157)*

157

Or remove the skin in a wide rectangular band from behind the head to above the tail. Decorate the bare area with sprays of dill and vegetable flowers before covering it with aspic. *(Fig. 158)*

Whole cold fish is party food and can absorb a complicated presentation. It's a good idea to fillet the fish and then reassemble it, with the fillets trimmed into a fish shape, tail and all. (The part you cut away can go between the fillets and into a constructed "tail.") The fillet is then covered with an opaque masking sauce such as a

158

mayonnaise collée and is decorated like a fish. It's a good buffet presentation, since it leaves no bones for guests to contend with.

Glaze a cold fish with mayonnaise collée or a chaudfroid sauce. If you make the glaze thick enough, you can spread it as you would a frosting, with a spatula or knife, working quickly because it sets rapidly. Chill for a while, and then decorate. Make an eye from a radish or an olive slice or from egg white and black olive. Simulate scales by laying on paper-thin slices of cucumber that overlap down the whole body of the fish, and make gills with a strip of green cucumber skin. *(Fig. 159)*

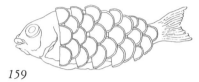

159

Make a design on the glaze that has nothing to do with the fact that there's a fish underneath. This is commonly done on ham in very formal presentations. Build the design of parsley leaves and blanched vegetables: petals cut from turnips, radish and carrots, leeks, scallions, tomatoes. You can make a bouquet or an abstract design. We built one from strips of scallion, hearts cut from egg white, red pepper fans, orange peel and black olive. *(Fig. 160)*

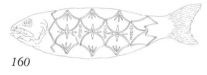

160

Fillets and Steaks

A family fish dinner usually means fillets or steaks. They are endlessly smooth, flat and white. Too often, they come served with equally smooth and white boiled potatoes, when what they really need is a bushy pile of shoestring potatoes or a mound of red cabbage slaw. Add textural interest to the plate with grated carrot salad, add color with stir-fried spinach and crunch with fried potato slices.

You can add height to the plate by rolling and skewering the fillet before you bake it. The roll will stay closed if you start at the wider end, keeping the side of the fillet that was nearest the bone at the outside of the roll. Add something for color—smoked salmon, dark spinach or tomato sauce—before you roll up the fillets. To be safe, skewer the roll and decorate the skewer with a cherry tomato or a mushroom cap over a spray of parsley.

Use two fillets or steaks, sandwichlike, as a substitute for whole stuffed fish in recipes for baked fish. Good for small families, dinner for one. Fill the sandwich with something colorful, such as spinach and carrot puree or peas and saffron rice.

Salmon steaks are an exception to the rule only because they are pink rather than white. Serve them with something green: with lime, avocado or dill. Or serve with a spoonful of green mayonnaise to one side and a surprising bunch of purple grapes. *(Fig. 161)*

161

Flaked Fish

Shredded leftover fish is delicious and thrifty, albeit somewhat shapeless. Most canned fish go into this category, too, such as tuna, salmon, mackerel and sardines. Curried haddock, cod Newburg, tuna a la king. Serve them in individual scallop shells, in large flat gratin dishes, over toast, rice or in bread cases.

Decorate them with chopped parsley and lemon slices. If the mixture is too white, add some buttered bread crumbs and broil briefly to brown the crust.

If you're giving a party, see if your fish dealer will give you the head and tail of a good-sized fish. Rinse and steam them until they are cooked. Then set them at both ends of an oval platter and fill the space between with a mound of cooked fish in the shape of the fish's body. Then garnish as you would a whole cooked fish.

Shape cold tuna or salmon salad into a make-believe fish. Do it with a knife or spatula, and with humor. Make a flat flounderlike shape, and cover it with chaudfroid sauce or mayonnaise. Then do a silly face with a green pepper smile and a leering radish eye. Or make a pursed kissing mouth with strips of pimiento and an eye with long lashes of black olive.

Garnishes

As hamburgers go with catsup, as strawberries go with cream, so fish goes with butter, lemon and parsley. The butter adds voluptuousness, the lemon piques with acid and the parsley's color and bushiness improve the visual texture. (You can, of course, use other fats, acids and greens, such as olive oil, capers or cream and dill.)

The old-fashioned way of serving lemon with fish is to wrap each lemon half in cheesecloth, which is knotted to hold it in place. This keeps the pits from falling onto the fish. You can get rid of pits in a lemon wedge by flicking them out with a knife or cutting away the membrane at the point of the wedge.

Combine lemon juice, chopped parsley and softened butter into a prepared butter. Mash them together, roll them into a tube and freeze them. Just before you serve the fish, slice off a disk and set it to melt over the hot fish.

Cook butter, parsley and lemon juice briefly and pour it, sizzling, over plain fish.

Decorate lemon slices with chopped parsley and lay them alongside a fish.

Use lemon wedges to weight down parsley sprays. Alternate the lemons with blue-black mussel shells for color contrast. We laid a fillet across the middle of a round plate, set three mussels in the shell on one side of it and a lemon-weighted parsley spray on the other. (*Fig. 162*)

162

Use citrus fruits other than lemon. Cut a thin slice through the center of a grapefruit, and place a mound of watercress in its center as a focus on a platter of fried fish.

Whenever you buy fish, buy a few shrimp or mussels as well. You will find ways to use them as garnishes on the fish plate.

Look for ways to add dark tones to fish. Use dark plates with pale fillets. Present the fish on beds of dark greens or alongside brightly colored food: julienned zucchini, carrots and red cabbage, cooked spinach or romaine, pureed turnips or broccoli.

The Japanese make a wild and difficult garnish for fish, one that's too hard to describe, much less to copy. It begins with a large carrot or icicle radish. By intricate shaving and slicing, using nothing but his cleaver, a skewer and iron nerves, the master chef produces a frail lacy net from the vegetable. This is then laid over a whole fish.

Smoked Fish

In some circles, Sunday morning breakfast is always smoked fish: salty pink lox or delicate Nova Scotia, fat whitefish with crackly golden skin, silvery sturgeon and sable, thick pink baked salmon. It's an Eastern European Jewish meal whose popularity has spread with the popularity of the bagels that go with it.

A good smoked fish platter is the result of good shopping and arrangement. Avoid presliced fish, which is often overprocessed, somewhat dried out. Look for fish that is shiny, supple and moist. Find a fish man you trust and who takes pride in his skill with the slicing knife.

Once you bring it home, there's nothing to do but put it on platters. Salmon shines against black platters; if you don't have one, supply a color contrast by surrounding the fish with watercress.

Look at the section on ARRANGEMENT (see pages 1–7) and choose a simple plan. Cover half a round plate with sliced sable, half with lox, and make a line of black olives down the middle. Put a chunk of baked salmon or half a whitefish on a plate, and surround it with cucumber slices.

Don't get too fancy with the accompaniments. You'll want sliced tomatoes, Spanish onions and cucumbers to go on the sandwiches. Tiny black olives to nibble on. A basket of bagels and bialys. A pot or bar of cream cheese. Some pickled or chopped herring to eat while you wait to regain your appetite between sandwiches. Some families add sliced Swiss cheese to the meal. There should be a pot of coffee on the stove and a yeasty coffee cake waiting on the sideboard.

Flowers as Garnishes

There is a whole cuisine based on flowers, and not only confections. It is described in a book called *The Forgotten Art of Flower Cookery* by Leona Woodring Smith (Harper & Row, 1973).

There is also a tradition of using flowers as part of the decoration of the table, of flower centerpieces and individual nosegays at each place setting.

But you have to be careful when you garnish with flowers, when you actually mix flowers with food.

It has to look intentional. You don't want anyone saying, "Oh, look, there's a flower in my soup."

Then there's the matter of style. Flowers look marvelous with Indian, Indonesian, Mexican and Polynesian food, and fine on wedding cakes. They look silly with sandwiches and cupcakes.

Making them work with roast pork or chicken is a matter of exercising taste and daring.

But most of all, you have to be careful about toxicity. Some flowers are definitely not to be eaten: azalea, crocus, daffodil, foxglove, jack-in-the-pulpit, lily of the valley, oleander, poinsettia, rhododendron, star of Bethlehem, wisteria. They'll make you sick.

Even edible flowers may have been sprayed with poisonous chemicals. You must make it very clear that the flower is a decoration, not food. Even then, it must be chosen with care and washed thoroughly.

On the other hand, flowers can add flash and glamour to a platter. We once had a huge dish of Mexican chicken and rice spectacularly surrounded with orange and red African daisies.

Imagine the effect of wedding cakes covered with real gardenias, not blossoms made of sugar. Or candied real violets on petits fours. We've seen flowers on layer cakes that were dipped in lightly beaten egg white, then in fine granulated sugar. Even more elegant was the flower that was egg-painted here and there with a fine brush, so that only the tips of its petals glittered with sugar.

The best rule is to decorate food with flowers only when you're serving a cuisine from a hot climate or when the flowers are obviously not meant to be eaten. When, for example, they are used for candleholders. Or when a flower is laid on the serving plate underneath a wine goblet or glass bowl of ice cream. Or when they become a focal point on a cheeseboard or part of a fresh-fruit centerpiece. Or when they decorate real flowers that are in fact to be eaten, such as a platter of fried zucchini blossoms.

French Toast

There is a very old recipe for something called pain perdu, which involved soaking stale bread in egg yolks and then frying the bread in butter. Several centuries later, we recognize french toast, a breakfast favorite, a dish related to English fried bread and Passover matzo brei.

Although it was clearly invented as a way to use up stale bread, french toast is now made from whatever bread you choose. One restaurant in New York makes a specialty of french toast made from hazelnut brioche bread. The best french toast is made when you start with thick slices of airy bread that puffs up as it cooks. If you're lucky enough to have an unsliced loaf of challah or brioche dough, cut it into slices 1½ to 2 inches thick, and soak the slices in beaten eggs.

Starting with square pieces of bread, cut each into four squares, soak and fry them and heap them overlapping in the center of a dish. (Sausages on one side, fried apples on the other?)

Or cut each slice into three rectangular strips, and fan them out from a simple garnish or else from a heap of sausages set on one side of the plate. *(Fig. 163)*

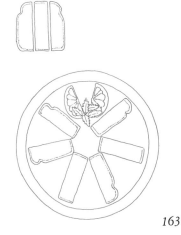

163

Fool the eye by cutting the bread into three triangles—two from the sides and one from the center. Arrange them overlapping on a plate, and the dieter will think he is being served an immense amount of bread. *(Fig. 164)*

Another variation is to leave the bread slices uncut and press them in a buttered waffle iron instead of sautéeing them in butter.

Make a self-garnish by cutting one slice of bread into a decorative shape with a cookie cutter. Soak it, fry it, and serve alongside the ordinary rectangular french toast. These garnishes are good on fried and scrambled eggs, too.

Other garnishes can be made with breakfast fruits, such as strawberries, sugar-frosted green grapes or thin slices of orange cut through to the opposite rind, then twisted so that they stand upright.

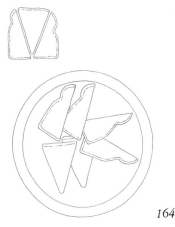

164

Sift powdered sugar over the whole serving. If you have left the bread in whole slices, you can hold a paper doily over each one and sift the sugar through it, making a sugar snowflake.

Serve with a dollop of red raspberry jam, lingonberries or a pitcher of warm maple syrup.

Fruit, Mixed

Just as all flowers look fine with all other flowers, so all fruits look fine with all other fruits. But in both cases, you can do even better if, when you mix them in a basket, a fruit cup or on a plate or platter, you consider scale, shape and color.

139

Fruit Bowls and Baskets

Two factors make all the difference: careful selection of your fruit and using the right container to hold it. Choose a container that's pleasing to look at even when it's empty.

When buying the fruit, be sure that you choose a good mixture of colors and a contrast in size and shape. Don't have only peaches, nectarines and apricots. Mix cantaloupes, plums and green grapes. Mix tall pineapples with round nectarines and curved bananas.

Cluster similar fruits together to give your composition impact. Put all the apples in the center of the basket, all the Seckel pears to one side of them and all the tangerines to the other.

Bunches of grapes are indispensable, because grapes are the only fruit whose shape can be changed to adapt to the composition. If your arrangement is on an oval platter, place bunches of grapes at either

165

140

end of it, the points tapering away from the mass of the design. If you have fruit piled in a bowl, use the bunches to fill in and soften the awkward transitions. Lady apples, figs, walnuts and cherries are also good at filling small spaces. *(Fig. 165)*

Make a line of whole fruit at the back of a long platter. Use a pear, standing on end with its stem on, as the tall center of the line. Put small round plums on either side and berries and grapes at the ends. Tuck berries and small bunches of grapes among the larger fruit, and add green leaves to the center and both ends of the garland.

Dark leaves look good with fresh fruit, adding a nice contrast in tone. When you accent the arrangement with leaves—or with flowers—place one here, three there.

Think in terms of color. Although any colored fruit does look good with any other, you can make a sophisticated *ordered* grouping by choosing only warm-colored fruits like peaches, nectarines, strawberries and oranges. Or only cool-colored fruits such as green apples, grapes, honeydew melons, limes and purple plums.

Fruit Cup

Fruit salad, like tossed green salad, gets its look from the mixture of perfectly cut elements, not from a controlled composition. Just see to it that the fruit is neatly cut. Bananas and berries go in at the last minute, so that they don't turn mushy, and it doesn't hurt to pour in some lemon, orange or pineapple juice to keep the apples and pears from turning brown.

Vary the shapes. Make cubes of pear and apple, arcs of peach, round cherries, circles of banana. Vary the size by using melon ballers of different sizes.

Serve mixed fruit in glass bowls and stemmed wineglasses. Garnish with sprigs of mint, nut halves and with creamy mixtures, such as colored fruit yogurts, crème fraîche and sour cream.

Present cut fruit in orderly layers in a glass bowl. Line the bottom with peaches. Make layers of blueberries, banana ovals, pears, cantaloupe and so forth. Whole strawberries go on top as though on a cheesecake, with mint leaves sticking out among them. Mix the fruit when you serve it.

Serve fruit cup to a party in several glass bowls, each one holding just one or two varieties, with the guests invited to make their own mixtures, and with bowls of yogurt and chopped nuts to sprinkle on top.

Arranged Fruit Plates and Platters

These are serving dishes and side dishes made of cut fruit. The serving dishes explain themselves; the side dishes are eaten as salads along with cold suppers or as dessert.

It's a style of presentation very much in vogue right now, the design depending on a juxtaposition of lively colors. Put the fruit on plates that don't fight back. Use clear glass, plain white or black china.

The examples here are for both individual servings and large platters. Pinwheels, for example, are easy. Make radiating circular patterns of wedges or slices of fruit, with strawberries piled in the center. You can do one pinwheel on a salad plate or six on a platter. *(Fig. 166)*

Do a fan, or a segment of a fan, using five honeydew sections, anchored by berries and grapes. *(Fig. 167)*

Arrange three arcs of sliced cantaloupe across a plate, all going in the same direction, with blueberries outlining the curve of the melon. *(Fig. 168)*

Use a wedge of melon or pineapple as a platform for other fruits. A wedge of honeydew can carry thin arcs of purple plum on its top surface.

Make an asymmetrical design by placing a melon slice on its side to one side of the plate. On the other half, in the arc of the curved melon, put a slice of orange flanked by strawberries. Sprinkle with blueberries. *(Fig. 169)*

Cut a pear in half and place it facedown on the plate. (Cut it in slices crosswise, so you can eat it with a fork.) Flank with half-circles of orange, and put mint leaves and strawberries at the stem. *(Fig. 170)*

Slice an orange. Use the biggest slice for the center of a line, then put the smaller slices, in diminishing order, to either side of it. Garnish with berries.

166

167

168

142

Make sequential bands of cut fruit. This is a layout especially suited to serving platters, but can also be copied on individual plates. It's very new, very fresh-looking. The stripes can go either lengthwise or crosswise on the platter. And you don't want symmetrical arrangements, simply beginning and ending with green grapes. Instead, place different-colored fruits next to one another on the platter, and don't repeat any fruit.

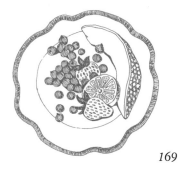

169

Reading from left to right, make stripes of strawberries/honeydew/plums/pears/mangoes; or green grapes/plums/banana rings/mandarin orange sections. Or avocado/nectarines/bananas/strawberries/peaches.

This way of arranging cut fruit looks especially good on white serving platters.

If you want to do something special for a party, lay fruit on a large rectangular platter or basket, using a coconut half filled with creamy dressing as a focal point. Then tuck one or two large fern or palm fronds under the fruit as an accent.

170

Or arrange a sampler of fruit, making clusters of five or six types. Look for contrast of shape and color. In the center use a single, larger fruit garnished with mint. *(Fig. 171)*

Gefilte Fish

Gefilte fish is a classic of Jewish cooking, a cold poached fish dumpling that is a year-round appetizer and always appears in the Passover Seder. Some people make their own; more buy the fish in jars. The dumplings are round or oval, beige to white. A guest at a Seder in Japan reports that there the gefilte fish was black, being made of local dark-fleshed fish and seasoned with soy sauce.

171

Just because gefilte fish has always been served with carrot slices and horseradish doesn't mean that you have to take the carrots from the jar. Shred fresh carrots in the food processor and use them on either side of the fish. Make stripes of magenta horseradish diagonally across the fish, or place it in an oval on top. Tuck parsley underneath the fish. Then watch your mother faint.

Gelatin

For decorating gelatin molds, see the section on MOLDS—ASPICS, GELATINS, MOUSSES (see pages 23–26). But there are other uses for gelatin, too.

In the haute cuisine, chefs use tiny chopped cubes of tomato or veal aspic to surround a platter of cold sliced meat or a ring mold of egg salad. You can do the same with fruit gelatin. Pour a thin layer into a pan, and let it harden. Then chop it fine. Use it as a base for ice cream or cottage cheese. Stir it into whipped cream, and pile into a champagne glass.

Cut fancy shapes out of the same thin layer of gelatin. Cut a large star, for example, and serve it on a dessert plate, surrounded by smaller stars.

Cut doughnuts out of green and red gelatin. Then push the hole from both of them, and put the red hole into the green doughnut and vice versa.

Cut a spade or diamond of gelatin and place it on a small bowl of yogurt.

For a very fancy dessert, draw simple figures on wax paper. Line the jelly-roll pan with the wax paper and pour a thin sheet of colored gelatin over it. When it has set, use a paring knife to cut through the gelatin, following the lines you have drawn on the wax paper. Remove them, and make a scene on the top of a sheet cake in gelatin: a house, a tree, the sun in the sky, with some birds flying by, all in gelatin.

Gifts of Food

People have always given gifts of food. In less prosperous eras, Christmas stockings held oranges and gingerbread men. Boys went courting with boxes of candy tucked under their arms. We bring casseroles to the parents of new babies, hoping to save them the trouble of one night's dinner. And when we go to dinner at the home of close friends, we ask, "What can I bring? Shall I make the salad?"

Recently, there has been a surge of making proud gifts of homemade foods. A friend with a country house brings us a basket of truly ripe tomatoes, knowing that we can't get them at our supermarket. A weekend guest brings pickles she has put up herself, and a jar of her special beach plum jelly. A sophisticated young man, who has been experimenting with making different-flavored vodkas, brings a carafe of what he claims is dynamite: commercial vodka in which he has soaked hot red peppers.

The simplest way to give food as a gift is to give it just the way it comes, with only a ribbon tied round it to show that it's a present.

The next time you bring a bottle of wine to dinner, just tie a bow around the neck of the bottle, and leave the ends in long streamers. It's a lot better than a brown paper bag. If it's New Year's Eve, or a special anniversary, or if the wine is champagne, then tie a flower to the end of each streamer.

Homemade bread and cakes should be covered in heavy transparent wrap, clear or colored, then tied round with a bright ribbon. That way, the baked goods are properly wrapped for storage.

Many food containers are so well designed that you can do no better than to give food in them. If you have baked muffins, give them in a brand-new unused muffin tin. (Not the one you baked them in.) If you've made jam, give it in a china jam jar. Present a special tea in a colorful tea caddy. Put mushroom-shaped meringues or special produce from your garden in real mushroom and berry boxes. We think anyone would be thrilled to get a long mushroom box full of fresh basil in August.

None of these serviceable containers need be hidden under wrapping paper. But if you decide to wrap a box of special cookies or a collection of different mustards or an imported vinegar and olive oil, then free yourself from the dominant taste of the gift-wrap designers. Think about using other papers. Buy paper in art-supply stores. Look at foreign-language newspapers and magazines: Italian for homemade pasta, Spanish for olive oil, Chinese for an assortment of Chinese spices.

Use fabric as gift wrap. You can wrap gift food in new dish towels or napkins. Dish towels are probably better, since one napkin serves little purpose, while one dish towel is useful. Best of all are the

145

French blue-and-white dish towels, tied into place with a big red bow.

Line a straw basket or a wire salad basket with a printed dishcloth or Provençal napkin. Put an assortment of food in it, and thread ribbon or yarn through the spaces in the basketry. For a wedding shower, fill the basket with kitchen gadgets.

The whole gift doesn't have to be covered. If you are giving a Mason jar of homemade jam or pickles, just fasten a circle of bright fabric over the lid with a rubber band, then hide the band under colored yarn.

Use a bow to attach a small utensil to a food gift, choosing a gadget appropriate to the gift. To the ribbon on a wine bottle, tie a corkscrew. To a canned ham, tie a meat thermometer or a small crock of really good mustard.

Think of it: the most common gift wrap for food is the boring white box that bakery cake comes in. Make it special by tying ribbon around it, or putting it in a small shopping bag and tying the handles together with a bow of bright yarn. (The shopping bag should have no advertising on it, or should be from some impossibly elegant establishment.)

Tie food to the wrappings of kitchen gifts. For beer mugs, thread pretzels through the bow. Attach a bouquet of leeks and radishes to the ribbon around a set of salad servers.

And any present for a child becomes a double treat when you fasten candies to the ends of the bow. It's even better when you make a bow with many ends and tie on lots of candy.

Grapefruit

Grapefruit is available all year round, but is less good in midsummer than it is the rest of the year. Choose a firm, heavy grapefruit without soft spots or puffy skin. If it's light in weight, there will be little juice inside. Whether the flesh is pale yellow, pale pink or bright pink is more a matter of looks than of taste.

Store the grapefruit in the refrigerator. Once you have cut it in half, cover the other half with plastic wrap or simply place it, cut-side down, on a dessert plate.

Halves

We are most familiar with grapefruits cut in half with their segments loosened from the membranes. Cut the fruit straight across, or in shallow zigzags. For a dramatic look that's a little hard to eat, cut the fruit in half in slanted zigzags. *(Fig. 173)*

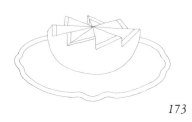

173

A grapefruit knife is a big help in loosening the flesh from the membranes. This slightly curved knife with its serrated edge slips inside the membrane and around the outside of each section. You can use a paring knife, but it doesn't do the job as easily.

Garnish grapefruit halves with mint leaves, with a fresh

147

strawberry, blueberries or a dab of apricot or raspberry jam. Sprinkle it with brown sugar or honey and place the grapefruit under the broiler until the sugar melts.

For a buffet breakfast, arrange a platter of grapefruit halves, each with one section removed and filled with a different fruit garnish.

Sections

Cookbooks tell you that citrus sections are easy to make once you know how. They're lying. Not only is it hard to do, but you inevitably lose most of the juice, which gets into the cuts in your fingers and stings like crazy. Still, if you must, you must.

First, peel the grapefruit, removing not only the peel and white, but also the thin outer membrane that covers the sections. Holding the fruit over a bowl to catch the juice, slice in toward the center with a sharp knife, removing one segment at a time.

Use these sections in fresh fruit cups with orange sections and melon wedges. Use them with avocado on platters of fish. Garnish them with dark blueberries or mint leaves.

Make a grapefruit basket by cutting in toward the center from each side and down on either side of the stem to make a handle, then removing all the fruit. Fill the basket with grapefruit sections and avocado slices. Or make a cup from the shell of half a grapefruit and fill it with sherbet and grapefruit sections. It tastes and looks great with slightly bitter dark chocolate.

For a really spectacular dessert, serve a whole grapefruit. With a knife, cut through only the rind around the equator of the fruit. Then gently pry off the half-shells, using your thumbs with steady pressure.

When the whole fruit has been removed, take off the bitter white membrane. Cut apart the sections, or slice the fruit horizontally. Replace it in the bottom shell, adding sweet liqueur between the slices. Put the top back on, and serve a whole grapefruit surprise to every diner. *(Fig. 174)*

174

Grapes

Table grapes come in pale green, purple and black, seeded and seedless. Choose them when they are plump, have good color and are firmly attached to their green stems. Although they used to be a seasonal fruit, the season has been extended, and we get good grapes not only in the summer and early fall, but throughout the year. Take advantage of the fact that they're one of the few fresh fruits that can legitimately be tasted before you buy them.

You don't have to arrange grapes. They do it all by themselves, falling into graceful attitudes over the edge of a bowl or platter, forming instant compositions on plates of baked chicken or fish.

There are two rules to follow when you do arrange grapes, either by themselves or as a garnish. First, it really is better to cut them than to break them off. That way, you won't be left looking at the ends of twigs.

And second, always place the wider part of the cluster toward the center of the composition, whether that composition is a bowl of grapes or a plate of cakes that you are decorating with grapes.

Serve bunches of grapes on leaves or ferns. Mix green and purple. And remember that grapes seem to look and taste best when they are served in abundance. Because of their cool refreshing taste, you might want to serve them as Europeans do, with a bowl of cool water for last-minute rinsing.

Serve them off the stem in wine goblets, topped with sour cream and brown sugar, with whipped cream flavored with kirsch or with crème fraîche and pistachio nuts.

Fill a lime gelatin mold with green seedless grapes, and garnish the platter with purple grapes and lots of leaves.

When arranging a fruit bowl or platter, always add the grapes last, using them to fill in the empty and awkward spots. Stick bunches of green grapes between the fronds of a pineapple in a centerpiece. Put bunches of purple grapes here and there around a roasted turkey.

Place a tiny cluster of green grapes in the middle of a chocolate-frosted cake or on a dish of pale custard.

To frost grapes, dip them in beaten egg white and then roll them in granulated sugar. Place them on a cake rack until they are dry. You can do a whole bunch that way, or one grape from a cluster of four. Frosted purple grapes are prettiest. Put frosted grapes on the plate alongside a dish of sherbet or next to a slice of cake.

You can stick grapes right into the freezer. They make instant sweet treats when they are frozen, and are attractive chillers in glasses of lemonade.

And small green grapes, without seeds, are part of the preparation of sole Véronique.

Green Beans

There once were vegetables called string beans because they had strings that had to be removed to make them palatable. But modern agriculture bred out the strings, and now we call them green beans or, more descriptively, snap beans.

Firm, small green beans should snap and not bend when you press them into an arch between your fingers. Buy them crisp and small, all year round, and choose beans with a good green or yellow color and without surface blemishes.

An English friend used to start every recipe for green beans by telling us to "top them and tail them": remove the ends and the strings. Now we just snip off the ends with a paring knife or kitchen scissors. If the beans look as though they might be tough—if they have large seeds or are thickly made—we french them.

To do this, lay the beans, one at a time, on a chopping board, and slice them lengthwise. Some vegetable scrapers have short blades on their nonscraping ends that can be used for frenching beans, too, but the hand-done method works just as well.

The best way to preserve the brilliant green color of the beans is to cook them just to the point of doneness, when they are still crunchy. And the best way to get them there is by stir-frying or steaming, testing as you go. Otherwise, plunge the beans into boiling water, cook them for a minute, drain and sauté them in melted butter or oil and garlic.

Serve green beans with lightly sautéed cherry tomato halves, with black mushrooms, water chestnuts, flowers cut from carrots, bean sprouts, diced red peppers, walnuts, almonds, peanuts. Garnish them with sieved hard-boiled eggs.

Serve cold green beans in a salad with chopped red onion and tomato wedges.

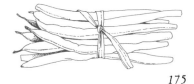

For a composed salad, tie ten long beans together with strips of scallion green. Steam them over boiling water until they are tender. Cool, and spoon on vinaigrette livened with chopped sweet red pepper. *(Fig. 175)*

Use green beans as a garnish for Bloody Marys served in wineglasses. Stick them into small glasses of plain tomato juice. Combine them with other vegetables to use as garnishes: make clusters of three green beans flanked with cauliflower flowerets or with bits of sweet red pepper.

Ham

Ham is pork that has been salt-cured, smoked and sometimes aged. Most of the ham we get is supposed to be ready-to-eat. It has been lightly cured and is safe but not delicious until it gets further attention.

Country hams are more heavily cured and smoked. They can be bought by mail, and when they come they need extensive soaking and slow baking, but reward the effort with wonderful taste. Smithfield ham is a top-notch country ham that is cured by a special process.

Canned hams are practical, good to have on hand for emergencies. Read the can carefully, because some canned hams need refrigeration, while others are real pantry-shelf foods. As with "ready-to-eat" ham, canned hams improve with loving care.

And fresh ham is not ham at all, but pork.

Cook ham according to the directions on the package or can or in a good cookbook. The inside must reach a temperature of 160°F in order to get rid of any chance of trichinosis. Score the surface, cutting through the fat but not into the meat. This helps to melt away the fat and lets you make a neat design in diamonds, squares or parallel lines on the surface of the meat.

Instead of the traditional pineapple rings and cloves on the surface of the ham, try scoring the fat, applying a glaze and baking it to a crusty brown. The simplest glaze is one made of brown sugar and mustard, but you can also cover the surface with a fruit sauce, with mustard and bread crumbs or with sliced almonds pressed into the brown sugar glaze.

You don't need any more decoration, nothing but a wonderfully flavored brown surface. When you have such a ham, you can surround it with wonderful things. Like bunches of green and purple grapes, sautéed sweet potato balls, tiny baked apples and Seckel pears, or puffy black prunes.

But if you do want to decorate the ham, be adventurous. Decorate in the last half hour of cooking, during the glazing stage. And have plenty of toothpicks on hand to attach the slippery decorations into the slippery glaze.

If you can't think beyond pineapple, make a necklace around the cut end of a half ham. Use pineapple rings cut in half. Reverse them, so that the rounded sides face one another, and place a canned apricot inside the arcs. *(Fig. 176)*

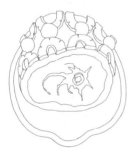

176

Arrange clusters of oranges and prunes. Cut thin orange slices in half. Pierce prunes with toothpicks to hold them in place between the oranges. Put a tuft of watercress on each toothpick. *(Fig. 177)*

Create a zigzag with narrow segments of canned pear. Where they meet, place a canned apricot half. *(Fig. 178)*

177

Sprinkle fine strips of lemon zest all over the surface of a ham, and make a chain of apricot halves and blanched almonds down the length of the meat.

If you're serving a half ham, pile garnishes against the "northern face" of the ham: apples, pears, sweet potatoes.

For a buffet table, you can cut off the top of a whole ham and decorate the plateau. Make radiating cornucopias of thin-sliced deli ham filled with parsley, using them to surround a mound of dried fruit.

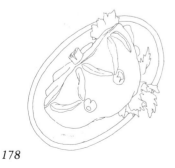

178

Ham can be baked ahead of time, cooled and then completely coated with a mayonnaiselike chaudfroid glaze. Spread it on thickly, then decorate the surface with scallion and carrot flowers. Then cover the decorations with spoonfuls of partially set aspic. It will take several coats of aspic to cover the decorations completely.

Ham Slices

Garnishes that are good with ham are good with ham slices, too. On a dinner plate, place a serving of ham to one side. Next to it, make a fan of orange slices alternating with fig wedges, and garnish with greenery.

On a platter, make a row of overlapping ham slices. Flank the row with stewed apricots and prunes, and put steamed broccoli on the outer edges.

Cover ham slices with clear aspic that is full of finely chopped parsley. Serve at room temperature.

Lay overlapping slices of ham on a platter. Sprinkle it heavily with parsley, and set new potatoes and olive-shaped carved carrots and yellow turnips to either side of the meat.

Hamburgers

A hamburger is an American classic. It evokes summer barbecues, drive-ins, simple family suppers. Along with pizza, it is the universal adolescent American meal, which we now share with the rest of the world. The visual appeal comes from familiarity and quality: a nicely toasted bun or English muffin, a dark-brown patty slightly larger than the bun and plenty of catsup or relish.

The permissible variations come with the relishes. These tend to be regional. In some places people eat mustard on their hamburgers. Other folks prefer lettuce and tomatoes, or dill pickles, or yellow cheese, or bacon or chili.

The top of the bun stays in place to keep the meat warm. If you've got a heaping garnish, such as bacon curls or spoons of chili, you can tilt the top of the bun alongside.

Add an extra serving of garnish to the plate: extra strips of bacon, fried onions, raw onion rings, a spoonful of chili, pickle slices. Carrot sticks, potato chips and french fries are side dishes that many people like with hamburgers.

For a party, make a platter of several hamburgers; serve the

179

relishes and accompaniments in individual bowls for the guests to take themselves.

For a dressed-up party hamburger, you might cover the bottom of the bun with a large lettuce leaf. Put the meat in place, and cover it with a tomato slice. Then stick it through with two bamboo skewers, one threaded with cooked bacon and a pickle chip, the other with cherry tomatoes or with a short length of fringed scallion or a carrot ribbon and a black olive. This is knife-and-fork food, and to the purist not properly a hamburger at all. *(Fig. 179)*

If you really want to expand, make a huge Pop Art hamburger for a party. Cut it into pie-shaped wedges for individual servings. Buy a 6-inch-round loaf of bread. Cut it in half and scoop out some of the insides (otherwise the hamburger will have the wrong balance of bread to meat). Then make the patty with a pound of ground beef. Cook it in a skillet or under the broiler and place it on the oversized bun. Garnish opulently with whole dill pickles, and serve accompanied by a basket of potato chips, scraped carrots and celery sticks standing in a flower vase.

154

Hash

Hash is the apotheosis of leftovers. You take some leftover beef, corned beef, tongue, chicken or turkey. You add some leftover gravy, sauce or cream. You mix in some leftover potatoes, mushrooms, peppers, onions—even beets. And when you've cooked it together, you've got something that's better than anything you started with.

Hash can be flat or lumpy, look like a brown pancake or a ladle full of creamed chicken. It all depends on whether you've cooked it in a skillet or a double boiler.

If you have the lumpy kind (chicken hash, roast beef hash with lots of gravy), serve it in a pastry shell, a bread case or inside a rice or noodle ring. After Thanksgiving, make a ring with the leftover stuffing, and serve turkey hash in the center. Spoon hash into baked potato shells or green pepper cases.

If you have the flat kind (corned beef hash, red flannel hash), brown it well in the skillet, turn it out onto a flat plate and garnish with parsley, hard-boiled egg, tomato slices and small sweet pickles. Serve individual portions of hash fried in patties or in small gratin dishes, topped with poached eggs and parsley.

For a serious presentation, make a ring of corned beef hash, and fill the center with creamed eggs or with succotash.

Three things go with nearly every form of hash: parsley, fried or poached eggs and catsup.

Honey

Honey comes in a variety of colors, from pale gold to rich brown. It varies in quality and consistency according to the region it comes from and the plants that the bees were visiting. You can buy honey in the comb or in a liquid, and the liquid either clear or in a crystallized creamed form.

Store all forms of honey in a covered crock at room temperature. When it is refrigerated, it will crystallize, becoming thick and opaque. If this happens, place the jar in a pan of warm water to melt it.

155

Serving honey is a sticky problem. You can buy special wooden twisters for serving it. You sort of unwind the honey in the air over your toast. But even the twisters don't solve the problem of getting honey from pot to plate without drips.

Put it on the table in a low crystal or glass bowl so that everyone can admire the golden color. If you prefer, everyone can get his own portion of honey. On each plate of biscuits, serve a small shot glass or votive-candle holder with honey in it. Or, for a change, place a chunk of honeycomb on each bread plate.

There are many attractive ceramic pots for storing and serving honey. There is also a very efficient, very ugly plastic squeeze bottle sold. It solves all drip problems, but it looks awful. Take your choice.

Hot Dogs

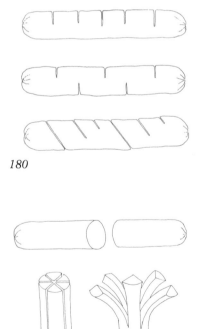

180

181

More than any other food, hot dogs are eaten out of doors, at backyard barbecues, picnics, beach parties, at ball parks and from street-corner vendors. Everything about them is portable, nothing is formal.

They are boiled, fried or grilled. Boiled hot dogs don't get a nice brown crust, sometimes split in the hot water unless you make some preventive slashes before you cook them. Fried hot dogs turn brown, but will curl up in the pan unless you cut them nearly in half vertically, leaving just a hinge of skin. Cooked out of doors over coals, a hot dog turns wonderfully charred, will stay reasonably flat if you pierce it through with a metal skewer or cut diagonal slashes down its length, rotating the frankfurter a quarter-turn before each new slash. (If you want a hot dog that opens up like a fan, make several parallel slashes crosswise on the outer surface of the arc.) *(Fig. 180)*

Serve on warmed or toasted buns with the expected: baked beans, coleslaw, sauerkraut or onion-tomato sauce, chili, dill pickles and a variety of mustards.

At a barbecue, cut the hot dogs into 1½-inch lengths. Stick each piece onto the end of a skewer or toasting fork, and make an X or a star of three crossed lines in the unpierced end. When it is cooked over the grill, it will open up like a flower. Have a bowl of mustard nearby for dipping. *(Fig. 181)*

156

Franks-and-beans are an American invention and are as formal as hot dogs get. Cook the beans yourself or use canned beans. Put them in the center of a platter, and surround them with cooked hot dogs. Serve with a bowl of coleslaw and some crisp rolls.

Ice Cream

We're a nation of would-be soda jerks. Give an American a scoop of vanilla ice cream, a pitcher of chocolate sauce and a handful of chopped nuts, and he feels the equal of any pastry chef. The results can be casual or elegant.

Make an elegant dessert for a crowd by making up a bowl of varicolored scoops of ice cream ahead of time and putting it in the freezer. Stick mint leaves or peppermint sticks throughout the bowl once it comes out of the freezer, and have someone who can serve it rapidly.

Make bombes and frozen molds with softened ice cream spooned into bowls and ring molds. Spoon chocolate ice cream against the walls and freeze it. Add a heavy sprinkle of chocolate cookie crumbs and fill with softened ice cream.

For an ice-cream dessert that looks like a watermelon, make an outer layer of pistachio ice cream, then a thin layer of vanilla, and fill the center with raspberry sherbet. Mix in chocolate chips pretending to be watermelon seeds.

You can create your own fancy ice-cream flavors by softening vanilla ice cream in the food processor, then stirring in a flavoring element. Gingersnaps, Oreo cookies, preserved ginger, nut brittle, coconut are all good. Then back into the freezer to harden again. And don't forget to reserve some of the added material to use as a garnish.

Because it melts quickly, ice cream is best served in individual portions. You'll need a good scoop, conical, spherical, spade-shaped or oval. Try one that has defrosting liquid in the handle, and dip it in water before each scoop.

Containers

Glass containers are best for serving this all-American treat. If you can't find the proper thick tulip-shaped glass dish, you can still create an effect in a low glass bowl or in a large red-wine goblet. And you absolutely can't go wrong when you serve ice cream with anything at all layered in tall champagne flutes.

It's also possible now to buy metal ice-cream dishes from restaurant supply houses. With their soda-fountain look, they're very appropriate and have the advantage, in a house with children, of being unbreakable.

Citrus shells make excellent ice-cream containers for formal dinners. Use large lemon shells, small orange shells, tangerine shells or a chrysanthemum of orange rind such as the one we describe in the ORANGE section (see page 182).

It's very fancy to frost the lemon shell by dipping it in egg white, and then in sugar. Fill it with dark chocolate ice cream and freeze. Garnish with a whole shelled almond and mint leaves or with candied violets.

Make fluted chocolate cups to hold ice cream. Melt chocolate chips and spread the chocolate inside small cupcake papers. Freeze them, held in muffin tins, then peel off the papers. You may be able to make cups of softened ice cream the same way, but it is harder to work with, harder to get it to fit in all the little pleats on the papers.

Sauce

It's a break with soda-fountain tradition, but you should try pouring the sauce into the dish before you add the scoop of ice cream. Make a pool of chocolate, butterscotch, pureed raspberries or crème de menthe. Place on it a mound of ice cream and garnish.

Garnish

With what? With whipped cream, of course.

With a cookie or slab of chocolate stuck into the ice cream. A fan-shaped French gaufrette cookie. A chocolate leaf or a plebeian oatmeal cookie. Then decorate both sides of the scoop with fruit or nuts.

Top with a cone, stuck upside down like a dunce's cap. Children love this.

With fruit, glacéed, canned or fresh. Or use frozen or sugar-frosted grapes.

Garnish with anything crunchy for texture, such as coconut, nuts, colored sprinkles, cookie crumbs, chocolate bits or granola.

For a special flourish, top with candied flowers, preserved ginger or with real candies: M&M's, mints or crushed toffee.

Be casual with the garnishes. Life is too short, and ice cream melts too quickly, to bother with a formal decoration.

Jam and Jelly

Unless the original jar is special—which means, frankly, unless the jam is either European or homemade—you should always remove the jam from the jar when you serve it. It's the old put-the-cheap-Scotch-in-the-crystal-carafe trick.

There are many attractive lidded pots around in which to put jam. They come in all forms from crystal lidded with silver to homely brown earthenware. Even a small Mason canning jar will make supermarket jam seem homemade.

Individual containers of jam at each place setting make for a neat breakfast or brunch table. Shot glasses and votive-candle holders hold portions of marmalade on bread plates. But then you don't get a choice.

Try serving three jams at breakfast—marmalade, apricot and raspberry. Put them in glass jars so that the colors show through. Place a teaspoon on the plate alongside the jelly jar, because spoons are for serving, knives for spreading.

Don't forget apple-green mint jelly to serve with lamb. And remember that melted jam makes the most convenient glaze imaginable for cooked fruits: not only for peaches or pears in a tart, but for baked apples or poached pears. You can paint skinned poached pears with red currant jelly to which you have added some red fruit coloring. Serve on a dark plate with a dab of crème fraîche.

Leeks

Leeks look like giant scallions, with their white ends and long green leaves. They're best in the early winter, but in the markets year round. Choose fresh green leaves without discoloration. They tend to be expensive, so don't throw away the trimmings. Use them instead in soups and stews, where the sweet onion flavor will add depth to the sauce.

Leeks trap sand between their layers. To clean them, slice off the roots and all but 2 inches of the greens. Cut the remaining vegetable in half and then in half again, and rinse well to remove all the grit.

Use the leek greens when you make flower designs in aspics and mayonnaise. Blanch them in boiling water, then rinse with cold water to stop the cooking. Pat dry with paper towels, and cut long thin strips of green for the stems and leaf-shaped pieces for the leaves of the flowers. The blossom itself might be a carved carrot slice, a series of petals made of egg white or a rose done in tomato peel.

Boiled leeks can be served cold with a vinaigrette sauce and can be garnished as asparagus are with chopped hard-boiled egg, with pimiento strips, with ham or mayonnaise. Braised leeks turn nicely brown in the oven. You can make a very good puree of leeks, cream and bread crumbs and use it to fill a tomato casing. And leeks are an integral part of the preparation of potato soup. Hold back some of the green leaves, chop them and sprinkle them over the smooth white surface of the soup.

For a properly oversized garnish on an enormous buffet platter, tie a bunch of leeks together with scallion greens and scatter over it a handful of cherry tomatoes and black olives.

Lemons and Limes

Lemons are an irreplaceable garnish for fish, shellfish, chicken, fruit and vegetables. The color is clear, and the flavor is nearly universally pleasing. Lemon juice helps to keep apples, mushrooms, avocados from discoloring when they are exposed to the air. But, on the other hand, the juice turns broccoli and green beans brownish yellow.

A lime is a visual surprise on the plate, just different enough from a lemon in color and flavor to make you notice it. Both fruits are available year-round. Buy them firm and heavy, but not hard, so that they will be full of juice. Look for brilliant yellow or green skins. Bottled lemon and lime juice are possible in emergencies––some cocktails require lime juice––but frozen lemon juice is somewhat better, and fresh, of course, is best of all.

182

Halves

The classic presentation is a lemon half wrapped in a twist of cheesecloth that catches the pits when you squeeze out the juice. It's a respectable method of service and proves that you know your manners.

183

But you can eliminate the cheesecloth and flick out the visible pits. Cut the lemon in half straight across, or cut deep zigzags. It's probably easiest to do this by cutting straight across, then cutting zigzags into the flat exposed surface. For a slightly different look, cut the zigzags on a slant. Put a bit of curly parsley in the center of each lemon half. *(Figs. 182, 183)*

Take a lemon half and cut a narrow strip of peel along its edge, leaving it attached at one end. Tie the sliver into a knot like a pig's tail. *(Fig. 184)*

184

Wedges

Whenever you make a lemon or lime wedge, slice down the central angle to remove the tough skin and annoying pits at the center of the fruit.

Remove vertical strips of peel from the outside of a lemon with a lemon stripper. Then cut the fruit into wedges, making the cuts between the strips so that each wedge has a stripe on its skin.

Cut a lemon or lime into six wedges. Gently pull away half the peel and curl it back over your forefinger so that it looks like a flower petal. *(Fig. 185)*

185

161

186

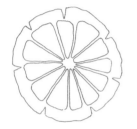

187

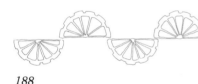

188

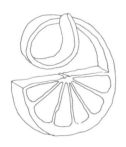

189

Slices

(Slices aren't the same as wedges. They are thin horizontal cross sections cut through the lemon or lime.)

To make a standing lemon slice, the kind that you see on Scandinavian open sandwiches, take a thin slice of lemon and cut through the rind and meat, three quarters of the way to the other rind. Then twist it so that it will stand up. *(Fig. 186)*

Color lemon slices with parsley. Roll the rind of a slice in chopped parsley. Fold a slice in half, and dip the fold into parsley. Or dip half a slice into a cup of chopped parsley.

Remove vertical strips of peel down the length of the lemon with a paring knife or a lemon stripper. Then cut slices across the lemon, so that there is a design on the edge of each slice. *(Fig. 187)*

These slices can be cut in half and used as a chain border. Put all the rinds on one side of the border, so that you have a scalloped design; or alternate rinds from slice to slice, so that you have a waving design. *(Fig. 188)*

Take a whole lemon slice and pare away half the rind from the meat, leaving one end attached. Curl the loose rind over the remaining half slice of lemon. *(Fig. 189)*

Take a whole lemon slice and pare away half the rind from the meat. This time, remove the meat from that half of the slice, and tie a knot in the loose rind.

Containers

Slice the end from a half lemon so that it will stand upright. Scoop out the meat, and use the cup to serve cocktail sauce or mayonnaise, or to fill with parsley as a garnish on a plate of fish.

Fill an empty lemon or lime shell with sherbet or ice cream.

Lemon and Lime Peel

The very outside of the fruit, the colored part, is called the zest. Just next to the zest is a thick white layer with a bitter taste. Whenever

162

possible, we try to remove strips and shreds of zest, leaving the bitter layer behind.

Grated lemon peel adds color and flavor. Mixed with finely chopped parsley and minced garlic, it becomes a garnish and seasoning called gremolata.

Remove 2-inch strips of peel. Tie them into knots. Cross them, with a slice of olive at the crossing. Drop long strips of peel into iced drinks for flavor and garnish.

Lettuce

By lettuce, we mean the many varieties of greens that we eat uncooked, in salads and sandwiches, under meat and fish. Because we don't cook them, they have to be perfect: fresh, clean, without browned edges or tired leaves.

Wash lettuce when you get it home. Then spin or towel it dry, wrap in paper towels and put in a plastic bag in the refrigerator. Some heads of lettuce, like Boston, can be washed most easily if you cut out the core, turn them upside down and run water through the opening. The others should be broken apart and rinsed in cold water.

Discard any browned leaves. If the outer leaves look wilted, set them aside to use as seasonings in soups and stuffings.

There's no agreement about whether to cut or tear greens into bite-sized pieces. Small central leaves, of course, can remain whole. Most of the food establishment says that the larger leaves should be torn apart rather than cut. But many like the regular look of neatly cut greens.

Choose from among the many varieties of lettuce not only for flavor and freshness, but for appearance. Bibb and Boston have pale, tender leaves and loosely joined heads. The small leaves can often be left whole. Chicory, also called curly endive, has dark, ruffly leaves and a bitter taste. Endive itself is expensive, with long pale leaves and a watery bitterness. Escarole is quite coarse, with ruffly bitter leaves.

Iceberg is scorned by many experts, but adored by the eating public for its consistent crunchiness, its clean watery flavor and the fact that its cup-shaped leaves are long-keeping. Shredded iceberg lettuce is a staple garnish in Mexican cooking.

Leaf lettuce and red-leaf lettuce have long loose heads and ruffly leaves. The red, especially, is beautiful, but both wilt easily. Romaine has dark color, stays crisp and will stand up under a vinegary dressing. It has a core of long pale leaves that look like endive.

Arugula is a dark, peppery and bitter green that is commonly used in Italian salads. Watercress and spinach, neither used primarily in salads, can appear in them. Watercress comes in bunches and wilts easily. Choose only fresh watercress. Spinach comes loose-leafed and in plastic bags. The already washed greens in plastic bags are too limp to be used in salads.

When you use lettuce as a garnish, it is usually underneath another food. The aim is to have a fringe of green peeping out from underneath the sandwich or the egg salad. The trouble is that most lettuce leaves are adamantly cup-shaped and won't lie flat. (This is always true of iceberg lettuce, which is, like it or not, the variety most people have in their kitchens most of the time.)

One solution is to turn the leaf over and squash it flat. Another is to cut away a triangle shape from the hard stem part of the leaf. Use that in a salad and tuck the outer, flatter (and usually greener) part under the hamburger or egg salad.

Americans learned about shredded lettuce from the Mexicans, who decorate hot foods with crunchy strips of green. Cut romaine and iceberg lettuce into thin ribbons and use them to make beds under deviled eggs or sliced ham and cheese.

Liver

Liver used to cost so little, be so little esteemed in America, that butchers would give it away free for pet food. Now it is both highly prized and high-priced, with calves' liver sometimes costing as much as beef fillet. Buy calf, beef or "baby beef" (actually mature veal) liver. Cook by sautéeing, braising or roasting. If you spread oil over it, you can cook liver over the coals, either in one piece that is sliced like a London broil, or in chunks, stuck onto skewers, with bacon weaving in and out between the chunks. It's best when it isn't overcooked.

But no matter what you do to it, liver turns out to be very very brown. And the things you serve it with—bacon and onions—are brown, too. That's why you have to enliven the plate with other foods.

Serve liver with green foods. Garnish with parsley and watercress. Serve green beans or green peas. Add avocado sections, lime wedges or pea pods to the plate.

Garnish with red foods, too. Put radishes and cherry tomatoes on the plate. Serve shredded beet salad or Harvard beets. Make a red cabbage slaw or cook sweet-and-sour red cabbage.

Add texture with fried shoestring potatoes. And take care with the way you cook the onions and bacon. Slice the onions very thin, and fry them crisply brown, nearly black. Drain, and make a bed of them on the plate, with Italian parsley beside it.

Lay fried bacon over the liver in a lattice pattern. If you want to do something special, put tufts of parsley here and there in the spaces made by the latticework. Thread bacon onto bamboo skewers, broil it and make caps for the skewers with cherry tomatoes.

Chicken livers are usually cooked in a sauce, which lends them some texture and color. Serve them on pasta, rice or on croutons. Be sure to dip the edges of the croutons in chopped parsley. Put chicken livers in a bright-yellow omelet and garnish with tomato slices. Add the same red and green foods to chicken livers that you did with other livers.

Chopped chicken liver takes a traditional presentation. It is pale brown, with visible chunks of white and yellow in it from chopped hard-boiled eggs. Garnish it with parsley, with tomato wedges, cucumber twists or with darkly fried onions or raw red onion slices. Serve it with dark pumpernickel or with pale round crackers. Add more chopped egg. Add pickles: spears and rounds if you want to be simple, pickle fans if you're dressing it up. To make a fan, split a gherkin lengthwise nearly all the way through. Make many thin slices parallel to the first one, and splay them out. You can put six of these on the plate around a mound of chopped liver.

Lobster

With lobster, as with artichokes, making them beautiful is less important than making them edible. There's all that impenetrable shell surrounding what is arguably the sweetest meat in the ocean. If we admire the courage of the first man to eat an oyster, we admire the persistence of the first man to eat a lobster.

By lobsters, we mean the large-clawed crustaceans that grow in the cold water off the coasts of Maine, Massachusetts and eastern Canada. Those that are best for eating weigh one to two pounds. They are blue-green ranging to near black but turn a cheerful scarlet when they are cooked.

You can't be a humanitarian when you shop for lobster. You buy them live, and buying a lobster is a little like buying a puppy: you're supposed to look for the most active one in the litter. That's awful, but it's true. Look for a lively lobster that is heavy for its size. Females are supposed to be the best because they have the luscious roe. Bring the lobster home and put it in the refrigerator in ice water.

If you're going to buy a split lobster for broiling, try to get it on the way home from work. It should be alive when you select it. Wait for the fish man to split it.

Lobsters are boiled, broiled, baked and sauced, and each technique has its advocates. Serve them hot with butter and lemon wedges, or cold with homemade mayonnaise. If you care about having the lobster stay flat when it's cooked, you can tie the head, the midsection and tail to a long wooden spoon before you throw it into the pot of boiling water.

When it comes out of the cooking water, boiled lobster needs some more attention from the cook. Cut off a small piece of the shell at the head, and drain out the liquid. If you are going to detach the claws from the body, do that now, too, and crack and drain them.

Serve the lobster so that the meat can be got to. Whole steamed or boiled lobster sits on the plate with its arched back up, the claws attached or detached and laid alongside. Nothing else goes on the plate, or it would be knocked off during the prolonged struggle involved in eating the lobster.

166

190

Broiled and stuffed lobsters are served with their shells down, and the claws alongside, and the underside split. Provide nutcrackers, small lobster forks, pots of butter and, to be really helpful, a plate for discarded shells.

A special presentation begins with cutting the tail section from the head and thorax. The head and thorax stand upright at one side of the plate, with lots of greens masking the bottom. The tail is laid behind it, with the meat exposed, and the disjointed claws are placed alongside it. Lemon wedges go here and there. (*Fig 190*)

If you are serving cooked lobster—au gratin, Newburg, thermidor, curried—you will put it over rice, in scallop shells, on toast rounds or in bread cases. You might like to serve it in the hollowed-out shells of lobster tails. To make a serving platter of such tails, reserve the head and thorax section from one of the lobsters after you cook it. Use it as a focal point, standing up in the center of the platter, with the tails radiating around it, and shiny marinated cauliflower, lemon, black olives and greens in between them.

167

But there are those who will never serve lobster with anything but corn on the cob, coleslaw and biscuits. Bibs, nutcrackers, picks, fish forks and more napkins than you think you're going to need. And we're not sure that they aren't right.

Mayonnaise

Mayonnaise is an emulsion of egg yolks and olive oil, seasoned with salt, mustard and lemon juice. It is made by hand, in an electric mixer, a blender or a food processor. (Or it is bought in jars; but that's something else again.)

There are many variations on basic mayonnaise, most of them changing the color as well as the flavor. Sauce verte is green; mustard mayonnaise is yellow; russian dressing and Thousand Island dressing are pink.

Serve extra mayonnaise alongside a salad or a sandwich, to let the guest decide how many calories he can stand. Instead of using a fluted paper cup, as in a sandwich shop, put the mayonnaise into a vegetable container—a hollowed-out tomato, a cucumber cup or a plate made from the bottom of a green pepper.

Mayonnaise works as a glaze and cover, like the icing on a cake. Mix it with gelatin to make a firm mayonnaise collée. Spread this on cold fish, chicken breasts or on open-faced tea sandwiches. Decorate the surfaces with blanched vegetables, citrus peel and olives, making flower shapes or abstract designs.

In Milan we saw mayonnaise borders piped onto plain metal platters. They mimicked traditional decorations on fine silver, demonstrating great skill on the part of the chef.

Meatballs

Meatballs are ethnic and plebeian. They're the homey, cozy food that everyone loves—hamburgers, Swedish meatballs, German klosse, spaghetti and meatballs. Nearly every cuisine has them, but they never show up in elegant cooking.

Meatballs are traditionally served with spaghetti, mashed potatoes or rice—anything that will keep them from rolling around on the plate. Spoon sauce over them, and sprinkle it with chopped scallions, parsley, bacon or chopped egg and parsley. For the best visual effect, serve them with something that isn't round, such as bright green broccoli, pea pods or green beans.

You can put cooked meatballs in a shallow gratin pan and slide it under the broiler to glaze the sauce just before serving. Stick triangular croutons of bread around the edges of the pan, which is then placed on a serving dish.

Melons

Serving melons properly begins with choosing them properly. We're never quite sure if they're going to be sweet and fragrant until we cut them. The best guarantee of quality is a reliable grocer. Failing that, try all the old unreliable tricks, pressing the stem end for softness, smelling for ripeness and shaking to hear the sound of seeds.

191

There are several varieties of melon on the market, some more seasonal than others, and all at their best in the late summer. Cantaloupe is, by now, available all year round at varying quality. It has become the strawberries and tomatoes of the melon world, always available and seldom topnotch. But when it's good, it's very good. Crenshaw has orange flesh, a smooth rind and wonderful fragrance. Honeydew has green flesh. When it's ripe it has an unparalleled sweetness, but it is often sold unripe and crunchy. Casaba has white flesh, is very good with prosciutto or Virginia ham. Persian melons are large, with orange flesh. Watermelon is something else again, the only melon without a hole in the center. It's one of those all-American foods, along with hamburgers and fried chicken, a red-fleshed fruit that seems designed to quench our thirst on a hot summer day.

Cut a melon in half, straight across or with zigzagged edges. If you cut widespread Vs around the circumference of the melon, you will have two star-shaped halves to serve. You can also cut the star shape smaller to make the lid of it a hollowed-out melon. (*Figs. 191, 192*)

192

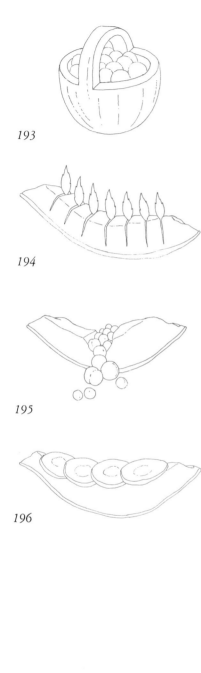

193

194

195

196

Serve a melon in a basket shape. The trick is to cut the handle first. Slice down on either side of the stem. Then slice in from both sides, leaving the handle intact. Scoop out the flesh, and fill the basket with a mixture of different fruits. *(Fig. 193)*

Cut a round melon into boat-shaped wedges. But don't serve them naked. Garnish them, if only with a lemon twist standing upright, or a lemon slice laid flat and weighted down with a strawberry. Mint leaves make an elegant garnish for melon slices. And, believe it or not, so does parsley. (Remember also that there is a whole school of people who eat melons with salt rather than lemon juice, and you might have to provide saltshakers for them.)

When serving melon wedges, cut the meat into neat pieces by running your knife between meat and rind, then slicing down in parallel lines through the meat. Put the cut sections back into place, with mint leaves sticking out from between them. *(Fig. 194)*

Cut a V-shaped piece out of a melon wedge, and spoon blueberries into the space, spilling out onto the plate. Or cover the flat surface of a melon wedge with shingled arcs or circles of fruit: deep red plums on honeydew, strawberries on cantaloupe. *(Figs. 195, 196)*

Individual servings can be made by cutting several 1-inch slices through the widest part of the melon, forming rings. (Scoop out the meat from the ends, mix the balls with berries and fill the centers with them.) Remove the rind from the rings in either a straight or scalloped circle. *(Figs. 197, 198)*

The Japanese cut melon pieces to resemble open fans—a fairly simple procedure. Start by cutting a whole melon into 1-inch-thick rounds. Cut each slice into thirds, remove the rind and cut away the seeds in the center. You now have a melon arc, the basic shape from which the fan is cut. Next, make four or five radiating cuts, about ¼-inch deep, on the face of the melon. At each radiating cut make a second, slanting cut (nearly parallel to the surface of the arc) that ends at the next radiating cut. Remove the resulting thin wedges of melon and you will find that you are left with an attractive fan.

Watermelon cuts are different from all the others, because watermelon is so large (individual portions are a smaller piece of the whole) and egg-shaped, and because it doesn't have a hollow center.

Basically, we cut watermelon into rings and the rings into semicircles. Or we cut the whole melon into lengthwise wedges and cut those wedges into slices. In the center of the watermelon is a fillet of fruit that lends itself to being cut into neat pieces. (It owes us that to make up for the messy part with the seeds!) If you remove that cylindrical piece of watermelon, you can slice it and cut the slices into triangles. Stand them on a plate, tilted against a cantaloupe wedge which has been laid on its side and sprinkle with blueberries. *(Fig. 199)*

For making melon pieces, a melon baller is essential. They come in different sizes, both round and oval. Buy several. Then you can make an arrangement with fruit balls and ovals of various sizes, all the way from watermelon balls (from that central solid piece) cut with a small ice-cream scoop down to much smaller blueberries.

Serve pieces and balls of melon on skewers. For color contrast, alternately spear honeydew, watermelon and cantaloupe balls. Then mint. Then another series of melon, with a triangular watermelon finial to finish off.

Whole melons make handsome centerpieces. You've seen it a hundred times—the watermelon boat or basket. Instead, try a centerpiece using a cantaloupe. Cut one wedge out of it, and cut this wedge into three slices. Fan these outward and arrange fountains of fruit so that they seem to pour from the opening. *(Fig. 200)*

Meringues

Making meringues is one of the great magic tricks of baking. The cook whips up mounds of snowy froth from egg whites and sugar, then dries out this froth in a slow oven, where it becomes rigid enough to last for days or to be frozen for weeks.

Some recipes call for a pinch of cream of tartar to help the egg whites rise and keep them up once they get there. Cooks have other aids. They are punctilious about eliminating every bit of yolk from the whites and any trace of grease from the bowl and beaters. They have the whites at room temperature, then beat them with a good electric beater or with a wire whisk in a copper bowl. They never make meringues on a rainy day, because the humidity inhibits the rising action.

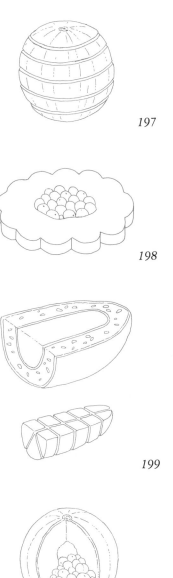

197

198

199

200

Meringues are used by teaspoonfuls, in cookie kisses, as well as in large elaborate desserts such as the Viennese Spanische Windtorte, a shell made of meringue layers decorated with baroque designs piped from more meringue. But in America we are most familiar with meringue as a topping for pies and baked Alaska.

The most common complaint about meringue toppings is that they shrink from the edges of the pie. This can be prevented by spooning the uncooked meringue onto the filling from the edges toward the center, and by cooking it in an oven set no higher than 350°F. Cool it away from drafts.

When the meringue is spooned in place on the pie filling, smooth it out with the back of a spoon or the end of a spatula. Then begin to create a pattern. Form a coil. Draw curved lines radiating from the center. Make a series of loops that look like flower petals. Lift the spatula from the meringue with a flourish, creating lots of peaks. If you're good with the pastry bag, make blobs and curls and ribbons all over the top of the pie. The idea is to have lots of edges, which will turn brown when the pie is in the oven.

You get a browner crust still if you sprinkle sugar on the meringue crust before you bake it.

Mushrooms

Mushrooms are always available in one form or another. Cultivated mushrooms, with their firm white caps, are sold year-round. If for some reason those fail you, there are dried and canned mushrooms. With the first, you sacrifice texture, with the second, taste; but sometimes you can make up for it with a judicious combination of the two. And for real mushroom-lovers, there is the adventure of hunting wild mushrooms: not a sport for the unknowledgeable, but worth learning about.

Never peel mushrooms, or you will get rid of most of the flavor. Instead, wipe the caps with a damp cloth. If there is a lot of soil remaining, rinse them in a colander, rubbing them with your thumbs to remove the grit.

Cook the mushrooms soon after you buy them. Fresh raw

mushrooms have a clean off-white color that disappears within days. Discolored mushrooms can be chopped and sautéed, so their wrinkled surfaces and dull color won't matter.

The shape is splendid. It's displayed best when the mushroom is sliced vertically, through cap and stem. Use this type of slice to float on soup, sprinkle on salads or make a finial for a skewer.

202

Use the whole cap as it comes, or flute the top with a sharp paring knife. Starting in the center of the cap, cut three or five curving lines out to the edges with the side of the blade, turning the mushroom and holding the knife steady, and removing a narrow channel of mushroom each time. Or cut an X into the top of the cap, and cross it with a second, smaller X. *(Figs. 201, 202)*

203

Make stamps from large mushroom caps. Slice off the top, making a flat surface. Then draw a simple shape—a star or a heart—with the point of your paring knife. Cut away a shallow layer of the background, leaving the design in relief. Then either slice off a ¼-inch disk, or leave the decorated cap on the stem. Use several to garnish a plate of sandwiches. *(Fig. 203)*

Stuffed Mushrooms

Stuffed mushrooms should be heaped high for a look of opulence. The stuffing will turn brown, no matter what it starts out to be: sausage, bread crumbs, chopped mushroom stems, even crab meat and vegetables. It benefits from a finishing roll along its edges in chopped parsley or from having a tiny sprig of fresh dill or parsley stuck in the edge between border and stuffing after it is cooked.

To make a low centerpiece of mushrooms, use gamy brown wild mushrooms and tiny pearl-white onions. Stand them in a flat basket with low greenery—parsley or watercress—packed between them.

Mussels

Mussels provide a rare opportunity to use black on a plate. Unless you're excessively fond of olives or able to afford great quantities of caviar and truffles, mussels are your best choice in this color.

204

They have elongated blue-black shells and golden meat inside. Uncooked mussels should be tightly closed when you take them home. Then take a scouring pad and a knife and scrub, scrape, snip and wash them until you have got rid of the hairy "beard" that hangs from the mussel shell.

Mussels are plebeian food. It's traditional to serve them abundantly, all in a heap. Increase the apparent amount in each serving by using bowls slightly smaller than you might (a pasta bowl rather than a soup bowl) and by standing the mussels on end in them. They should be piled up, with the sauce in a heap at their feet. Always provide a soup spoon for scooping up the copious broth.

Serve mussels in their shells on white or yellow plates. Serve them with yellow rice, with dark-red tomato sauce or brilliant green parsley sauce. Serve cold mussels with yellow curry mayonnaise or green sauce verte. Garnish them with parsley, lemons and cherry tomatoes. *(Fig. 204)*

It is less common, but quite possible, to eat mussels raw, like oysters, or simply cooked and on the half shell. Treat them as if they were as expensive as oysters by doing a flower-petal design on a bed of rock salt, filling the shells with chopped mussels and parsley.

It's not a bad idea to buy a few mussels whenever you buy fish. They make a good garnish for plate or platter, a welcome accent to white fillets, pale silvery trout or pink salmon. But use them along with something else, something green, like parsley, or bright red, like tomato wedges. Or put two black mussels on each plate with one pink shrimp.

Nuts

Nuts are served in and out of the shell. Once shelled, we get them whole, in halves, sliced or chopped into bits. They're around all the time, but best in the autumn, when the harvest is new. Nuts are a traditional part of every harvest or Thanksgiving feast.

If you do a lot of baking with nuts, try to buy them in bulk. Store them in the freezer, where they will keep forever. Warm air will make the oil on nuts turn rancid eventually.

We get them in great variety. There are oval almonds, big Brazil nuts tasting like coconut, filbert or hazelnuts with their heavy skin, pecans and walnuts, peanuts, which aren't nuts at all but legumes, as well as green pistachios and tiny pignolias. To blanch nuts—that is, to remove the skin—put them in boiling water for 15 seconds, then drain. The skin will pop right off of hazelnuts, almonds and Brazil nuts, but it won't work at all with wrinkled pecans and walnuts.

We eat them raw, as snacks. We mix them into foods, making nut tortes and oatmeal-walnut cookies. And we use them as garnishes.

Nuts in the shell go in flat baskets and wooden bowls. Mix different varieties, and add a handsome nutcracker. Or serve only one kind, and decorate the bowl with kumquats and autumn leaves. Use nuts in their shells to fill in the spaces in a basket of apples or pears. (And if you're serving nuts in the shell, there had better be an ashtray around to get the shells.)

For a gift, take a tall clear glass jar and put in distinct layers of different nuts out of the shell. You could do almonds, then pistachios, then walnuts, then pignolias, then pecans. Or you could make a stack of different forms of almond: whole in the shell, out of the shell, blanched, slivered and sliced. Emphasize the different layers with thin layers of dark raisins.

As garnish, nuts can be casual or orderly. The orderly garnishes go onto layer cakes and cupcakes. They are the perfect walnut halves pressed into a scoop of ice cream. The three nuts and sprig of mint that go on the crème fraîche topping a fruit dessert. The row of chopped pistachio around the circumference of the layer cake. Or the single almond pressed into the center of a macaroon.

The casual garnishes are usually sprinkled on. Sprinkle chopped nuts on ham, in salads and over soups. Salted peanuts are a surprisingly good and easy garnish for a thick soup. Add cashews to carrots and yams, pignolia on cooked chopped eggplant, pistachios sprinkled on cauliflower or walnuts on a green salad.

Amandine

A classic garnish, one that improves both the appearance and the taste of food. It is done by sautéing blanched, sliced or chopped almonds in butter until they are lightly browned, then spooning the nuts and butter over cooked fish fillets, chicken breasts or vegetables such as cauliflower and green beans.

Praline

A garnish made by crushing almond or hazelnut brittle and sprinkling it on desserts or icings. Make your own, or cheat by buying the nut brittle and breaking it up between sheets of wax paper. Then fold it into whipped cream and serve on coffee ice cream or sprinkle it over a caramel layer cake.

Okra

Okra is a small green podded vegetable that is typical of New Orleans cooking. In Louisiana they get it fresh, but the rest of us usually make do with frozen okra. It came originally from Africa, where it was called gombo; from that came the name for gumbo, the New Orleans soup-stew that is always thickened either with okra or with filé powder.

Because of its scalloped shape, okra has a lovely star shape when it is cut across its length. The pods are sometimes cooked whole, dusted with cornmeal and deep fried, or are boiled, then chilled and served in a salad. But more often you will eat okra cut into stars and added to a soup or gumbo.

Olives

Olives exist on the border between food and garnish. They are at the same time one of the oldest cultivated foods in the world and also the inevitable (and probably overused) accompaniment to a club sandwich.

Olives grow all around the Mediterranean and are cultivated in our own Southwest, especially in California. Look for new varieties. Try soft salty Greek olives, tiny dull-green Queen olives, big green

Spanish olives, purple kalamatas. The right olive can set the style of a dish. What would Salade Niçoise be without the small shriveled black olives of Nice?

Serve a variety of olives in an oversized wineglass. Serve only black olives, mixed with cherry tomatoes, in a silver bowl (but line the bowl, or the brine will discolor the silver). Serve olives with radishes and cauliflower flowerets.

There is a canapé made by wrapping stuffed olives in thin pastry dough and baking them only until the dough is browned. There is also an Italian olive salad, mixing green and black olives, pimiento and marinated vegetables in a strong oil and vinegar dressing.

Remove the pimiento stuffing from green olives and replace it with a piece of blanched almond, an anchovy roll, a bit of yellow cheese or a cube of ham.

Use large green olives as elements on skewers of meat, as part of a short *aba* chain of olive/tomato/olive.

Olives are wonderful garnishes because they are at the same time so colorful and so edible. They go on a plate of sandwiches. Remember not to serve a single olive—not one stuffed olive but three different olives or two olives with a tomato wedge.

Cut stuffed green olives across so that the red centers show. Place these on sliced hard-boiled eggs, on cooked carrot rings, on Danish open-faced sandwiches. Use three olive rings, overlapping, to float on a thick puree of cold soup. Make the olive ring the eye on a cold whole fish. Use them as round elements in very linear garnishes: cross two strips of scallion green and place a bit of pimiento-stuffed olive at the crossing. Or make a zigzag of thin slivers of lemon zest, creating a row of wide V's, and put an olive ring at the points where they meet. Make a design with olive rings on a baked ham.

Onions

Onions, thank heavens, are available year round to add flavor to nearly everything we cook. We know someone, however, from an old New York family who says that onions weren't allowed in her house when she was growing up. They were considered a common, low-class food.

On the rare occasions when an onion was required, the cook made a special trip to the market to buy a single onion.

The rest of us enjoy all the varieties of this large healthy family. The most common member is the Spanish or yellow onion, a medium-sized globe for general use. The Bermuda onion is large and white with a milder flavor, and the red Italian onion is sweetest of all, and very good eaten raw. There are also small white onions to use whole in stews and casseroles and tiny pearl onions that we pickle and use in Martinis or as garnishes.

There are also long green scallions or green onions, shallots, leeks and chives. Even garlic is a member of the onion family.

Buy globe-shaped onions when they are firm and unsprouted. They keep well if they are stored in a cool dry place. The other varieties keep best in the refrigerator, except for garlic, which should be stored at room temperature with air circulating around it.

There are any number of tricks guaranteed to let you peel onions without crying, from storing the onions in the refrigerator to holding a piece of bread between your teeth. Some of them work for some people some of the time. A good trick that helps you peel an onion easily, however, is to blanch it briefly, then rinse under cold water, at which time the skin will slide right off.

Raw Onions

If you love a thick slice of onion on your hamburger or bagel, why not make it red instead of white? The taste of a Spanish onion is mild, the color interesting.

Thin slices of raw onion are a surprisingly good sandwich filling when the bread is spread with lots of sweet butter or mayonnaise. This sandwich is an old-time remedy for a cold, guaranteed to get through the stuffed nose.

Chopped raw onion makes a piquant garnish for bean dishes: black bean soup, refried beans and several Tex-Mex dishes. The taste contrast is right, biting and crisp to go with bland and mushy. So's the look. Imagine how they'd be, then, on New England baked beans.

Chopped raw scallion looks wonderful on pale foods, on potato salad, scrambled eggs, vichyssoise.

Cooked Onions

We slice them, chunk them, chop them; we boil, fry, sauté and roast them.

The onion is one of nature's truly natural vegetable colorings. Cooked long and slow, its sugar caramelizes and turns the onion and everything around it to a beautiful mahogany brown—something good to know when a soup or stew turns pale and watery.

In India, they slice onions thin, then fry them until they're a deep brown, nearly black. Try this cooking method, making sure to blot the dark onions on paper towels before serving them as an accompaniment to broiled liver or chicken or on a chicken and rice casserole.

Cut thick onion slices and broil them under a hot flame or over charcoal. They will turn dark brown, look good with barbecued meat.

Roast onions under a chicken with the potatoes, and serve them with pan-roasted potatoes and sautéed carrots.

To make stuffed onions, first skin and parboil them. Then cut a slice off the top and scoop out most of the insides. Chop the insides and cook them with your filling. Stuff the shell, and sprinkle the filling with parsley. Cut a thin slice off the bottom of the onion so that it stands steadily, and place it on a tomato slice or a ring of pumpernickel bread for contrast.

Garnish flat, bland, creamed onions with chopped parsley, dill, cress or, of course, scallion greens.

Garnishes

There's one spectacular trick to do with an onion. It works as well on tiny pearl onions as on big ones. But it's at its most flamboyant with a huge red Italian onion.

Peel the onion. Then slice down through the stem, nearly all the way to the bottom. Cut each half in half, and then in half again. (If you can make still another cut, do so.) Then cook the onion. Parboil small ones for around 10 minutes, or wrap the large ones in foil and bake for 1½ hours. When you take the onion out of the oven, you should be able to pull each petal gently away from the center,

179

205

206

finishing with a huge red-and-white chrysanthemum. *(Fig. 205)*

Use white onion chrysanthemums around a roast, alternating them in an *abcba* pattern with clumps of watercress and tiny carrots.

Carve tiny pearl onions into chrysanthemums and serve three or four on a plate, surrounded by sprays of Chinese pea pods. Or use a few of the tiny white flowers in a bowl of fresh peas or green beans. *(Fig. 206)*

To make fried onion rings, a great garnish for hamburgers and hot dogs, cut thick slices of mild onion and soak them in milk for 10 minutes. This removes some of the biting taste and helps to hold the breading. Coat them with flour or batter, deep fry and serve in a heap. Instead of rings, you can do half-circles of onion.

Oranges

One of the advantages of modern transportation is that we now have fresh oranges all year round. Smooth-skinned Valencias, good for juice, rougher-skinned temples, navels, tangerines and tangelos for eating. Buy them when they have no scars or soft spots, and when they are heavy in the hand to show that they are full of juice. The

180

color is no guide to quality, since most oranges are picked green and are colored with dye to appeal to the consumer—an indication of the food industry's awareness of the importance of how food looks.

Whole Oranges

An orange makes a refreshing dessert, but you have to make it accessible. In a Japanese restaurant, we were served an orange from which the peel had been cut in one long spiral. The peel was arranged in an oval shape on the plate. The orange was sliced, and the overlapping slices were placed inside the oval peel.

You can also cut an orange rind to form lacy petals around a whole fruit. Choose an orange with a thin, flexible skin. With the point of a knife, score three large petals alternating with three small petals. (For a larger orange, score four and four.) Remove the rind between the petals. Then, within the large petals, score two more petals, one near the edge of the original and another the size of the small petals. Remove the center section of the large petal and bend back the petal strips to make a flower. *(Fig. 207)*

For a simpler presentation, start by scoring the orange with six or eight vertical cuts, going from top to bottom, but not all the way, so as to keep the base intact. Pull each segment of rind away from the meat of the orange and fold it in on itself, making a loop. Carefully remove the membrane from the outside of the segments and garnish the top with a sprig of mint. *(Fig. 208)*

In an elegant town house, we were served an orange that had been peeled and the peel discarded. The orange was sliced horizontally and reassembled in a shallow glass bowl, and port was poured over it.

You can peel and slice an orange, then arrange the slices on a plate in a circle or an overlapping line. Garnish with coconut, and you'll have made ambrosia. Garnish for color with a line of blueberries and one of strawberries.

Containers

Use orange and tangerine shells as containers for other foods. Fill with ice cream, with strawberry mousse, with a fruit soufflé.

207

208

181

Fill a half shell with cold shredded vegetables and serve it with a sandwich. Or fill it with cranberry sauce or applesauce to go with roast meat.

Cut a large cap off the top of an orange and remove all the fruit. (You won't be able to do it neatly.) Spoon it halfway full of softened raspberry sherbet. Then make a thin layer of orange sherbet, and continue filling with raspberry. Replace the top, and put the orange in the freezer so that the contents can harden again. Before you serve it, remove from the freezer and slice it vertically, cutting through the plug you made, so that each half shows raspberry sherbet bisected by a line of orange sherbet. Place on a bed of mint leaves garnished with fresh raspberries.

Hang four shrimp over the edge of a tangerine shell and pour cocktail sauce in the center.

Serve an orange shell heaped with tuna salad on a lunch plate. Fill shells with different salads, and make a platter with them on a buffet table. They're easy to take, are a neat way of serving mayonnaise salads.

It's surprisingly easy to make a chrysanthemum from an orange shell. Quarter the orange nearly to its base and remove the fruit. Using scissors, cut the rind into slender "petals," first cutting each quarter in half, and then cutting those halves in half again. All the petals remain attached to the base. On the flower, serve a scoop of crab meat salad, fruit salad or sherbet. *(Fig. 209)*

Garnishes

Use orange slices and wedges where you expect to see lemon: in drinks, with other fruit, alongside salads and vegetables. Combine orange strips and slices with darker foods in *aba* arrangements or in chains. Try them with green olive sections, black olives, parsley or hard-boiled egg slices.

Make slender orange strips with a citrus peeler. Tie them into knots. Cross two strips and place a dot of parsley at the crossing.

Take half-slices of orange and use them to form border chains with tiny black olives in between each loop. Put the rounded arcs all on one side of the chain or alternate, making a wavy effect.

209

Cut a thin orange slice nearly all the way through and stand it on end, like a lemon slice, on an open sandwich of sliced pork or on a chopped-beet salad. Make a border chain of orange slices alternating with hard-boiled egg slices.

Use orange wedges over the edges of drinks. To change the look, release the skin from one end, peel it back and curl it over your finger so that it looks like a flower petal.

In short, do everything with oranges that you do with lemons. They make a similar garnish in a different color and slightly larger scale.

Pancakes

Whether you call them pancakes or griddle cakes, they're a very American food, a delicately browned quick bread that could be made anyplace where there was a campfire and an iron frying pan. Although we now make them from mixes and frozen batter, save them for leisurely Sunday breakfasts; they still bear the atmosphere of simpler, more wholesome times.

Pancakes come in three sizes: 12-inch, regular and silver-dollar. The 12-inchers are done in frying pans, served in wedges and are topped with powdered sugar and preserves. The regular-sized pancakes are served in stacks with melted butter and maple syrup. Two-inch silver-dollar pancakes are spread on the plate in a wreath or piled in a heap. You can also make a small flower with four silver-dollar pancakes, topping each one with a dollop of sour cream and a strawberry.

Serve pancakes with a pitcher of warm syrup, with butter already melting on the pancakes and with a tub of extra whipped butter alongside. If you want to do more, garnish the plate with twisted strips of bacon, with strawberries or with a bamboo skewer piercing sausages and capped with an orange wedge.

Blueberry pancakes get a side order of fresh blueberries mixed with yogurt or sour cream. Apple pancakes get sautéed apple rings, and nut pancakes a garnish of perfect nut halves.

For a buffet breakfast, put pancakes on an oval platter, overlapping down the length of the platter. On either side, make a row of pancakes folded in quarters, with their points toward the middle of the platter. Put clusters of sausages and orange wedges between the points of the folded pancakes.

Paprika

Bad cooks use paprika as though it were tasteless. For some reason, there is a convention that paprika, sprinkled over fish or chicken, looks like a nice brown crust. It doesn't. It just turns the top of the fish red. Furthermore, when it is left uncooked, it adds a particularly raw and nasty flavor. Cooked paprika turns brown. But then, so does cooked fish, so why not just cook the fish properly to begin with?

Paprika is a spice made of ground sweet and hot capsicum peppers. Although it is most identified with Hungarian cooking, it is grown both in Hungary and Spain and was probably brought to Hungary from Turkey. It has a distinctive flavor and, when it is cooked, lends a rich reddish-brown color to goulashes and chicken paprikash.

If you can, buy paprika freshly ground in small amounts, and store it in a covered glass jar in the refrigerator. If the spice man asks you whether you want sweet or hot paprika, tell him you want sweet, since that's the kind called for in most recipes. But buy a small packet of hot and see if you like it.

Parsley

Even cooks who don't garnish, garnish with parsley. It's so widely used as a decoration that we hardly see it anymore. Unseen and almost always uneaten, it's noted mainly when it is absent, in the vague awareness that something is missing from the plate.

But just because it's overused, don't eliminate parsley from your palette. It's the basic of basic garnishes, the most widely available and most widely used of all the fresh herbs. Both the curly variety and the flat-leafed Italian variety add bushy texture to flat plates of sole, fill in the empty spaces on a bare dinner plate and make a color contrast with all but other bright-green foods.

It's OK to use parsley. Just look at what you're doing. Select only parsley that is dark emerald-green and bursting with freshness. Rinse it under cold water and shake it dry when you get it home. Then wrap it in paper towels and put it into the refrigerator in a plastic bag. Add it to the plate at the last possible moment.

Don't serve paltry amounts. Don't let a single cluster or a single leaf appear as a gesture toward garnishing, looking skimpy and shabby-genteel. Use at least one whole stem on every plate. Separate the branches so that the shape of the leaves and the curve of the stem can be seen.

Whenever you put parsley on a plate, think of putting something else with it, even if it's only a second sprig or a cluster of Italian flat-leafed parsley. Use parsley with black olives, radishes or walnuts.

Accompany the parsley with a bit of fruit or vegetable. Use half a cherry tomato, laid cut-side down; a twist of lemon; a slice of orange, with the parsley stem threaded through its center; a small cluster of grapes. Weight down the parsley stem with a wedge of hard-boiled egg, a mussel shell or a half-circle of orange. *(Fig. 210)*

210

Placement

One reason to use parsley is to fill space. If you have a plate on which there is a small steak and a half cup of carrots, the empty quadrant might be a place for parsley. It will make a low-calorie plate look fuller as well as more colorful.

You can also use parsley to separate or to join different foods on a plate. An oval serving dish that holds a line of sliced tomatoes and another line of sliced onions will profit from a border of parsley sprigs lying between the two.

With parsley, you can echo the shape of the food on the plate. Suppose you have a small whole trout. Tuck parsley sprigs under the tail, top and bottom, and make a line of sprigs along the curve of the back.

You can use it as a bridge, a transition between food and plate. A square sandwich is uncompromising on a round plate. Put two

185

generous tufts of parsley near opposite corners of the sandwich and the picture will be improved.

Use parsley on, as well as near, the food. Place a bush of parsley off-center on a fish fillet. Or divide the fillet in two parts lengthwise with an orderly line of leaves. Lay a small bouquet of parsley and a tomato wedge on a pale chicken breast or a slice of vitello tonnato.

Chopped Parsley

Chopped parsley is an all-purpose food coloring that does a great job of enlivening pale foods, such as rice, and red foods, such as tomatoes.

Snip the parsley in a cup with kitchen shears, or chop it on a board with a chef's knife. The food processor, of course, does the most efficient job of all. If you chop more than you need, store the surplus in a plastic bag in the freezer. Spoon it out as you need it, without bothering to defrost. It's second best to fresh as garnish, but good to have on hand for cooking. And whenever you use commercially dried herbs, a pinch of frozen parsley added to the mixture wakes up their flavor.

Chopped parsley keeps its color best when you chop it dry, then gather it in a twist of cloth and hold it under very hot water. This cleans and blanches the parsley at the same time. Twist the cloth to dry the parsley.

Parsley is not only pigment, but also a food. You can use it as one of the greens in a mixed salad. This is quite common in the Middle East, where it is part of mixed green salads and also of tabbouleh, a cold salad of mint, grain and parsley. A delicious pasta sauce is made with parsley, grated cheese and butter; we think it's better and fresher in midwinter than pesto.

And why not tip your hat to the whole idea of decorating with parsley by placing bunches of the herb in tiny vases on your dinner table? Let the greens make their point alone, or have them accompany a few daisies.

Pasta

In America we call them noodles, and we serve the same varieties most of the time: long thin spaghetti, flat fettuccine, curved elbows and shells. In Italy, they call it pasta, and they have hundreds of varieties, many with wonderfully evocative names such as butterflies (farfalli) and quill pens (penne), cockscombs (creste di galli) and priests' hats (capelli di prete), moustaches (mostaccioli), wolves' eyes (occhi di lupo), little worms (vermicelli), angel's hair (capelli d'angelo) and the suggestively named bridegrooms (ziti). Here are some of the more exotic pastas available in this country. *(Fig. 211)*

In Italy there are rules about what sauce goes with what pasta. Some shapes are considered right for thin sauces, others for creamier mixtures. Some go with seafood and others with soups. Despite the great surge of interest in pasta here, we have not yet learned to make that kind of distinction.

We do like to use different colored pastas. Eggless noodles, made with only flour and water, are white; egg noodles are yellow, becoming progressively more so as the dough becomes richer. There are green spinach noodles, and if you're lucky, you may find someone who makes basil noodles. There is red pasta, colored with tomato paste. And brown pasta, made of whole wheat flour or buckwheat flour, with its strong wheaty taste. The colors generally promise more than the flavors deliver, and you can mix colors without worrying about discordant flavorings.

In Italy, pasta is always served as a separate course. It should be presented in a shallow bowl, somewhat smaller than a soup bowl. The heavy crockery helps to hold the heat, and the sloping sides make it easy to get hold of the last elusive noodles. Never serve a soup spoon for assistance in eating pasta; never, that is, unless it is a pasta in brodo.

When you think about garnishing pasta, think plain. Nothing complicated: spaghetti with tomato sauce might have a single basil leaf or a few sautéed mushrooms laid on top. Noodles in a creamy sauce could take sautéed broccoli or ham slivers.

You can mix different sizes of noodles in the same dish if they are

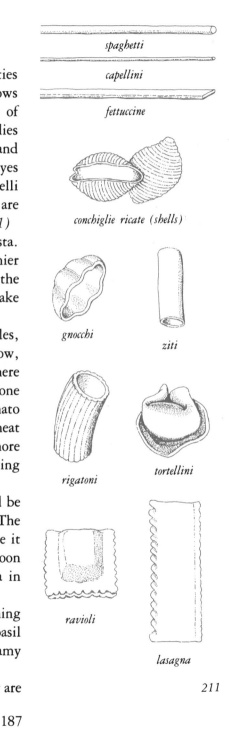

spaghetti

capellini

fettuccine

conchiglie ricate (shells)

gnocchi

ziti

rigatoni

tortellini

ravioli

lasagna

211

187

related in scale and shape. Not seashells with fragile vermicelli. But you can mix fettuccine with narrow fettuccelle, or small butterflies with large butterflies.

In some parts of Italy it is the custom to serve a plate of plain pasta cloaked with two different sauces. The noodles are mixed with the sauces before they are served. Each plate gets a coil of linguine with pesto and another coil of linguine marinara. The sauces, of course, must be compatible in taste.

But pasta, like salad, is more often an impulsive composition than a firm recipe. Think of spaghetti primavera, the springtime mixture of pasta and vegetables. The noodles are moistened with pesto, with a light cream or tomato sauce, or with butter and garlic. While the noodles cook, we steam or sauté vegetables. The plate comes alive when the vegetables are cut cleanly and cooked lightly in oil: slivers of red and green pepper, yellow squash, carrots and broccoli. Toss most of the vegetables into the pasta and sprinkle some on top for color.

Non-Italian Noodles

Pasta is Italian, but noodles are universal. Italians don't eat cold pasta dishes. They eat leftover pasta or hot noodles with uncooked sauces. But the practice of making cold pasta salads is very American.

You can make a cold pasta salad with nearly anything, chosen for color as well as taste. The noodles get a strong vinaigrette dressing (cold will kill some of the taste, so make it pungent). Then add something red, something green and something black or white. For example: chopped red pepper, broccoli and cubes of feta cheese. Ham cubes, green peas and pignolia nuts. Cherry tomatoes, lots of parsley and black olives.

In Eastern Europe, noodles are usually served as a side dish: wide egg noodles or spaetzle with chicken paprikash, bowknots and kasha with pot roast. Mix some of the pasta with sauce before you put it on the plate.

Serve buttered noodles in a vegetable container. Bake macaroni-and-cheese in a green pepper, or put cold macaroni salad in a tomato.

Press buttered noodles into a ring mold and turn them out onto a platter. Fill the center with a brightly colored food such as chicken a la king or vegetable curry. Hold back some of the ingredients and use them to garnish the base of the mold, along with lots of fresh green parsley.

Pâté

Pâté is a baked mixture of chopped or ground meat, chicken, fish or vegetables. It is usually cooked in an earthenware or porcelain terrine. It is then weighted down while it cools, so that some of the fat and liquid is pressed out to make a layer of aspic. It is always served cold.

There are perfectly plain pâtés. But one of the interesting things about pâtés visually is that they often have bits of whole food in them, which show when the loaf is sliced. Because these are traditionally rather opulent, the whole foods tend to be cubes and strips of tongue, ham or game, truffles, olives and pistachios. But a cold meat loaf holding whole hard-boiled eggs that appear when the loaf is sliced works on the same principle. We now have spinach and broccoli purees that hold steamed carrots and turnips; and we have even seen a recipe for a fruit pâté that, when sliced, revealed a pattern of cut strawberries and kiwi!

Pâtés are traditionally served with gherkins, pickled onions, olives, parsley and lemon. They are often accompanied by thin slices of dark bread or white toast.

Slices of Pâté

Plain sliced pâté has a nice neat shape, but an uninteresting brownish-gray color. Freshen the plate with Boston lettuce, with sprays of dill or watercress leaves. Serve it on good china in bright clear colors.

To enliven a dull slice of pâté, lay on a simple garnish of green, such as a spray of dill. Chop up carrot, egg yolk or egg white very fine and sprinkle it over the meat to add shimmer to the surface.

Put the rectangle of pâté on a plate, and surround it with tiny shimmering cubes of aspic made of beef or veal broth. On the plate's rim, put long narrow toast triangles.

212

213

Cut a slice from the center of a mushroom. Lay it flat on the pâté with some watercress leaves.

Place a scallion diagonally across the rectangle. Lay a flower-cut carrot over it, in the middle of the pâte slices, and tuck Italian parsley leaves under the carrot. *(Fig. 212)*

Other Ways with Pâté

Pâté can also be made in cylindrical crocks, then spooned out onto toast. For a large party, do this in a very big crock, and provide a big silver soup spoon to take it out in curls.

Slice off rounds of pâté with a cookie cutter, and place them on a cookie sheet with sides. Decorate each disk with a flower made of blanched scallion greens, egg white and bits of sweet red pepper. Pour beef aspic over the pâté rounds so that the slices are covered, and let the aspic set. Then cut the pâté out of the aspic, in circles that are slightly larger than the pâté, so that each one has an outer ring of jellied aspic. Put down beds of watercress on clear glass plates. On them, put the aspic-circled pâté. *(Fig. 213)*

Make your pâté in a soufflé dish, and cut individual serving wedges. Lay each one on its side, and make a half-circle of white water biscuits with parsley at either end.

For a picnic or a buffet, fill a hollowed-out loaf of Italian bread with pâté. First cut it in half lengthwise. Then scoop out the inside of the bread. Fill both halves with pâté, put them together, wrap in foil and chill. Put it on a breadboard on the buffet table, slicing off a few pieces so that the guests know what's inside. Or bring it to the picnic and slice it there.

Pâté en Croûte

Pâté is often covered with a tough, basically inedible dough. This helps to seal it for steaming. It is usually richly decorated with cutouts in the shape of leaves and flowers, and painted with an egg wash to make a golden color. When the pâté is cut into slices, there is dough on the outside, then a layer of aspic, and then the meat mixture.

190

Pâté en Gelée

A more edible covering for pâté is made with aspic, producing a pâté en gelée. Make the pâté in an attractive earthenware pan. Then cover it with aspic, and set a design in the aspic. Have a bowl of liquid aspic, made with veal or chicken stock. You can find a recipe in any general cookbook.

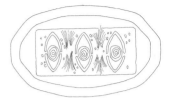

Choose the decorations and blanch them to make them pliable. The decorations can be quite formal, made with foodstuffs that suit the pâté such as orange slices for duck-liver pâté, or apples and sweet pickles for a pork pâté.

Spoon aspic over the surface of the meat. Then, using tweezers, dip the decorations in the liquid aspic and set them in place on the covering. Continue to spoon on aspic as it cools until it is completely covered. *(Fig. 214)*

Try a repetitive triangular design using string beans and carrot sticks, with egg slices in the centers.

Cut tiny needles of carrot and scallion and make a feathery V-shaped pattern on top of the pâté.

Make a flower from a spray of dill with egg white and radish blossoms.

Or make two rectangular outlines, one inside the other, using flat leaves of Italian parsley. Then lay strips of thinly sliced carrot and turnip diagonally between the rows of parsley leaves.

Create a sunburst with a round of hard-boiled egg in the center, slivers of carrot, radish, zucchini and parsley radiating from it. This design is dense in the center and becomes more diffuse as it nears the edge of the dish.

Tins of Pâté

Pâté comes in log-shaped cans of various sizes. The ones made with the most expensive ingredients, of course, come in the smallest can. With a can opener, cut off both ends of the log, just as you would a can of cranberry sauce. The pâté will slide out easily onto a plate. Once it is out of the can, it's easily decorated, since its surface is sticky and garnishes pressed into it stay in place.

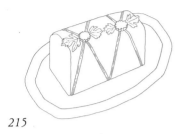

215

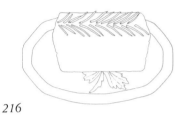

216

Use miniature garnishes on a small tin of expensive goose-liver loaf. Make a line of olive slices, and surround with Italian parsley.

To decorate a larger tin, first blanch scallion greens to make them malleable. Cross two over the loaf, one going the long way, the other crossing it. At the joining, place a steamed disk of carrot cut to look like a wax seal. Tuck a leaf of Italian parsley under each side of the carrot. *(Fig. 215)*

Press sprigs of dill into both ends of the loaf, standing them up so that they look like trees.

Cut tiny slivers of carrot and lay them in a feathery pattern along the top of the loaf. Have greens protruding from the middle of each long side of the pâté at its base. *(Fig. 216)*

Peaches

Summer's first peaches have clinging stones, delicate white flesh and the aroma of springtime. At the height of summer, when peaches are in full season, we get golden-fleshed freestone peaches that are fuzzy on the outside, juicy on the inside and red-stained around the pit.

At least, that's the way it's supposed to be. But it doesn't work that way, because what has happened is that for something like six months of the year we get beautiful, rock-hard peaches that are shipped miles and miles to come to us. They never ripen; they just wither. It's very hard to find a tree-ripened peach.

(And everything we say is equally true of nectarines, which, despite their fuzzless skins and slightly acid flavor, are nonetheless another variety of peach.)

Peaches should always be peeled unless they are to be eaten raw and by hand. It's a simple technique. Peel peaches as you do tomatoes, by dipping them in boiling water for 2 minutes. Remove them with a slotted spoon, and slip the skin right off.

But peaches, once the skin is removed, will discolor nearly as fast as apples do. A sprinkle of lemon juice helps a lot when you peel or cut peaches. Cut them in half through the stems. Freestone peaches will release the pit with no trouble. You may have to use your paring knife to take the pit from a clingstone.

192

Cooked Peaches

Peaches are poached, baked and broiled. Poach them, whole or in halves, in red wine or Bourbon. Bake them as you would apples, first removing the pits and filling the cavity after they have cooled with ricotta cheese and macaroon crumbs or cream cheese and nuts. Broil them sliced in half or in sections, sprinkled with brown sugar and Bourbon, and serve with duck and ham.

Fresh-poached peaches are part of a perfect peach Melba. Make a pool of raspberry sauce on a white or clear glass plate or in a shallow glass bowl. Set half a poached peach on it, cut-side up. Add a scoop of vanilla ice cream, a drizzle of sauce and a finial of whipped cream. Finish with a green mint leaf and three blanched almonds.

Cover a whole poached peach with melted currant jam. Let it cool, and garnish with whipped cream and mint leaves.

Whole poached peaches are elegant served with their syrup in large red-wine goblets or saucer-shaped champagne glasses. Garnish them with fan-shaped cookies, sticking the cookies into the fruit as you would into a scoop of ice cream.

Pile small poached peaches into a large glass bowl with scoops of lime sherbet. Garnish with green grapes. Or mix whole poached peaches with raspberry sherbet and garnish with blueberries.

Peel a whole poached peach. Cut through the bottom with a paring knife until you can remove the pit. Stuff sweetened ricotta cheese and almonds into the hollow. Set the peach upright in a bowl, with the hole at the top overflowing a bit with the ricotta, and serve it garnished with mint leaves and chopped almonds, as a peach surprise. *(Fig. 217)*

Raw Peaches

Serve raw peaches during those few weeks in midsummer when you get truly local, truly fresh fruit.

Cut them in thin wedges. Arrange them in a pinwheel or fan shape on a plate or on a pool of pureed raspberries. Pour port over them, or heavy cream or yogurt. Add brown sugar and blueberries.

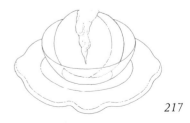

217

193

Pears

There are pears in season for much of the year. They come to the market, one after the other, in a variety of colors and sizes, but with the same distinctive shape. In midsummer we get yellow and red Bartlett pears, juicy and sweet and full of fragrance. Just in time for Thanksgiving come tiny brown Seckel pears that crunch when you bite into them. In winter there are green Anjous, russet Boscs and blushing yellow Comice. (And all year long, of course, we have canned pears: not so much fruit as confection, reliably sweet, cool and pale yellow, the ultimate sickbed food, guaranteed to soothe a sore throat and reduce a fever.)

Raw Pears

When it is ripe, there is nothing as wonderful as a fresh raw pear. Nor is there anything with such an affinity to good cheese. Put three lemon leaves on a plate. Set a whole washed pear on them, with a wedge of Brie or Roquefort cheese.

If the whole pear seems unmanageable, you can cut it in half or in long slices, then lay them on the plate with the cheese. But you're asking for trouble. Pears, like apples, discolor when they are exposed to the air. Lemon juice will help, but why add an unnecessary flavor to the perfect marriage of the pear and cheese?

Raw pears cut into slices and chunks go well in fresh fruit salads and green salads. You don't have to peel them first—pear skins are easy to eat—but if you should want to, just scrape them off with a vegetable peeler.

Cooked Pears

We poach pears, bake them and sauté them. Before you poach pears, you can either remove all the skin with a vegetable peeler, or leave strips of skin on the white flesh, or remove only the top half or the bottom half of the skin.

Pears poached in red wine turn red. That's fine if it's what you

194

had in mind. Done in white wine, or in sugar syrup with lemon juice, they turn slightly brown.

Because pears are so beautifully shaped, the most elegant way to serve one is whole, peeled and poached, standing on its wide bottom in a pool of sauce. On a white plate, pour a circle of thick chocolate sauce. Place a pear on it. The vase shape of the fruit against the round plate creates a design that needs no elaboration or garnish.

Dip the bottom half of a whole poached pear in chocolate sauce, and press a border of chopped nuts around the edge of the coating before you set it on the chocolate pool. Add a dark green mint leaf for garnish. *(Fig. 218)*

Make a pool of thick raspberry or strawberry puree. Set a poached pear on it, and drizzle sauce down the sides of the fruit. Once again add a leaf: either a real one, or a cookie made of almond paste and dark chocolate.

Glaze a poached pear with melted currant jam. This can be done on a whole poached pear, or on two pear halves, placed facedown on a plate.

Try this easy way of dressing up pear halves. Cut a poached pear in half and put one half facedown on a dark plate. Spoon some zabaglione or raspberry sauce on the wide end of the pear without obscuring the outline. Sprinkle the sauce with amoretto crumbs, and garnish the stem with a mint leaf.

Scoop out the pit area of the pear half, and fill the trough with yogurt. Sprinkle with blueberries and set on a bed of mint leaves.

Slice pears vertically in wedges through the stem. Remove the pit section. Then make a pinwheel or fan with the segments, accenting the joining place with cottage cheese, an orange slice or a triangle of yellow Cheddar. Between the pear slices, place a variety of other fruit: a peach segment, some blueberries, half a strawberry.

Lay down a wheel of pear wedges and put crinkled prosciutto between the spokes of the wheel. Place a garnish of watercress at the center point.

Sauté pear segments in butter. Sprinkle with brown sugar and chopped nuts.

Peas

There are three different forms of the vegetable that we call peas: fresh, frozen and canned peas.

In the spring, when they are truly young, buy fresh peas. Choose pods that are bright, smooth and that snap crisply when you open them. Avoid overgrown, yellowing or starchy pods. Tiny fresh peas are delicious and should be served with butter and freshly ground pepper only. Old starchy peas can be made into purees.

To retain the color of fresh-cooked peas, boil them in a pot with the lid on. Or better yet, gently steam them.

Frozen peas are available at a consistent quality all year round. The small ones are especially good: usually better than the fresh peas on the market at that moment. And their familiar Technicolor appeal brightens any plate, adds a touch of green to cold vegetable salads, cold pastas and stir-fried dishes.

Canned peas, the little tiny ones, are a special semi-junk food, pale green and mushy. All people who hate vegetables adore canned peas, and we forgive them their color and texture because of their sweetness.

Most often, you find yourself with a package of frozen peas. What's to be done with them? Mix them with another vegetable.

Carrots are the obvious choice. But instead of the conventional carrot cubes, carve balls of carrot with a small scoop and mix them through the peas. Or make notches down the length of a carrot and slice it crosswise into flat flowers.

Toss the peas with sautéed mushroom caps or whole tiny onions. Mix them with chunks or strips of ham and slivers of lightly sautéed onion. Mix the peas with chopped fennel or crumbled bacon bits.

Instead of mixing in these other foods, surround an accompanying vegetable with a ring of peas. Or make three concentric circles: a mound of peas in the center, then a ring of mushrooms, then an outer border of peas. Parsley or dill placed here and there adds texture.

Peas generally go on the table in a serving bowl. Make a border on a bowl of peas of sautéed frozen artichokes and cherry tomatoes.

Cover a shallow 7-inch bowl with five beautiful leaves of Boston or leaf lettuce, the stems pointing into the center. The ends of the leaves should hang over the edges of the bowl. Make sure that they are freshly washed, with drops of water still sparkling on them. Spoon cooked frozen peas, mixed, if you wish, with lightly steamed celery, into the bowl. *(Fig. 219)*

219

A more expensive version of this presentation employs a wheel of endive spokes radiating from the center of the plate, with frozen peas and cherry tomatoes served over it.

Leftover peas, rinsed clean of butter, are always good sprinkled on salads, wonderful in cold rice salads.

Pea Pods

Or snow peas, or Chinese peas, or mange-tout. These used to be an exotic vegetable, to be found only in Chinese neighborhoods or in limp and waterlogged packages frozen in Taiwan. Now we buy fresh, crisp pea pods at our supermarkets.

Choose them young, bright green and so firm that they snap when you bend them. Avoid pale spotted pods. To prepare the pea pods, break off the blossom end and, if you can, pull away the attached string that runs down the side of the pod.

They're very good served raw in salads, either whole, cut into lengthwise strips or slanted strips across the pod. Or cook them briefly, never long enough to make them lose their crispness. Blanch for 30 seconds, or stir-fry for a minute in garlic-flavored oil.

Lightly cooked cooled pea pods add a linear garnish to arranged salads, one that used to be made by green beans. Now green beans are often tough and overgrown, while pea pods are tender and fresh. Use the pea pods instead on an appetizer plate, three or four fanning out from a spoonful of salmon salad or a scoop of Russian vegetable salad.

Use pea pods with strips of sweet red pepper, with radishes, cherry tomatoes and mushrooms. Use them on aspics, forming the leaves of a flower whose stem is a scallion leaf and whose blossom is made of carved turnips and radishes.

Peppers

Sweet bell peppers are colored green, red and yellow, but the red and yellow peppers are really ripened states of the green. They are a native American vegetable with a firm shiny skin and a sculptured, convoluted shape. Choose peppers without soft or pale spots. Since tomatoes are so pallid nowadays, red peppers are one of the few reliable ways to add a scarlet color to a plate.

(Pimientos are roasted, fully ripened sweet red peppers that have been skinned, seeded and canned in oil. Whole, cut into strips or chopped, they are a pantry-shelf necessity for the foodstylist.)

Because the seeds and membranes of peppers can be irritating, they must be removed before you use them. Slice off the stem end of the pepper, taking with it a big chunk of the membrane. Reach into the cavity with your fingers and remove the seeds. Use a paring knife for the rest of the membranes.

The pepper can be left whole for stuffing. It can be sliced lengthwise in half, in quarters or in strips. To make fairly straight strips, slice off the curved bottom of the pepper.

To make rings and arcs, remove the cap, then slice the pepper crosswise.

Cooked Peppers

Many people find the skin of a cooked pepper tough and inedible. To remove it, hold the pepper over a gas flame on the end of a fork, or put it under the broiler. Cook until the skin chars. Let it cool, and then scrape off the skin with the back of a knife. Peppers peeled this way can be dressed with oil and vinegar and served with anchovies or sliced Bermuda onions.

When these peeled peppers are cooled, they can be stuffed with cold mixtures, such as ham and potato salad, or rice and tuna fish, or corn relish. Or, after the brief cooking, they can be stuffed with creamed corn, macaroni-and-cheese or sausage, and baked in the oven. If they are too floppy to stand upright, bake them in muffin tins. Always stuff peppers with fillings that set off their colors: spinach in

220

red peppers, rice and red beans in green peppers. Soften the edges with plain or Italian parsley.

Whenever you sauté peppers for a cooked dish—as, for example, in a supper dish of peppers, potatoes and Italian sausages—try to have both red and green peppers. There won't be any difference in the taste, but there will be a great difference in looks.

Remember that for a change of shape, besides the round bell peppers, there are the long, slim, light green Italian peppers. To turn these into vegetable flowers, cut each horizontally through the middle with a zigzag cut. *(Fig. 220)*

221

222

Raw Peppers

Raw peppers, chopped, slivered and in rings, go into green salads. They also make nice strong containers for cold relishes and salads to go on buffet platters or on sandwich plates. After you remove the stem end, cut the edge in a zigzag. Then pile high with coleslaw or sweet pickle relish. *(Fig. 223)*

Bits of raw pepper are often used as garnishes for other food. Make a border with arcs of red or green pepper. The arcs can bulge all in one direction, or they can loop back and forth in a wavy pattern. *(Figs. 221, 222)*

Make another chain of rings cut from cross sections of peppers. (This is best done with long narrow Italian peppers, which are more or less the same diameter for their whole length.) If you cut a slit in every other ring, you can pass it through the rings on either side of it. Use one of the chains around the base of a mound of rice, on a plate around a dish of pepper steak or on top of a bowl of tuna salad.

223

199

Pickles

Pickles, like olives, are both food and garnish. They are just as versatile, giving a lift to plain as well as fancy foods. What's a corned beef sandwich without a kosher dill? Or pâté without tiny French cornichons?

Pickling is a method of preserving food by soaking it in salt water and then in brine. Although we are most familiar with pickled cucumbers, we also get pickled carrots and green beans, pickled green tomatoes, tiny onions, beets and cauliflower. Not to forget the sweet-and-sour pickled fruits, such as watermelon rind, crab apples, pears; even pickled figs and kumquats.

If you make your own, make sure that you use wonderfully fresh produce, worthy of being preserved. Trim it carefully. If you buy ready-made pickles, shop for the best around. There are several small companies that put up regional styles of pickles and relishes. Sample different varieties: garlic, dill, sweet pickles, mustard pickles, country-style bread-and-butter pickles, chowchow and piccalilli relishes. At country inns, you are frequently offered a selection of both sweet and sour pickles to nibble with your tomato juice.

As for ordinary cucumber pickles, cut them as you do cucumbers. Cut lengthwise halves or quarters. Cut crosswise rounds or slanted ovals. Leave small pickles whole.

Caterers make pickle fans from small pickled gherkins. They cut three lengthwise slits from one end nearly to the other. Then they spread the slices gently to make an open fan. These may be used as part of a border, alternating with wedges of hard-boiled egg. Or place them on the rim of a plate that holds a crock of pâté and some crackers.

Arrange three or four tiny whole pickles in a fan shape radiating from a dab of horseradish next to a slice of pâté. Set the crock holding the rest of the pickles on the table nearby (pickle-lovers never get enough of them).

Mix pickled cucumbers with other pickled vegetables and with black olives. Or combine them with fresh vegetables, such as cherry tomatoes, radishes, cauliflower flowerets. Cut celery sticks to the same length as the pickle slices.

Serve different pickled vegetables in layers in a clear glass jar.

Pies

American pies—by and large—have top crusts, either whole, crumb or latticed. European tarts and flans—by and large—do not.

We're not talking here about turnovers and Cornish pasties and the tiny ravishing French tartlets that hold one perfect strawberry. These are ideas for finishing off with a flourish an old-fashioned American pie. One with a golden-brown flaky crust domed high over an extravagant amount of fruit filling. With slits cut cleverly to let the steam and the fruit aroma escape. And with neatly crimped edges that shade from pale tan to dark brown.

Top Crust

The top crust of a pie is usually a solid sheet of pastry. But it must have vents cut in it so that the steam made by the boiling fruit juices will have a way to escape.

Pierce the crust with the tines of a fork.

Cut slitted vents in an orderly fashion. Try doing it with a sharp knife. If you find that difficult, you may prefer to use your kitchen shears.

Do three slits in the center of the pie ||| or do five slits around a central hole ⋇ . Cut a hole in the crust with a cookie cutter. For example, a heart cut out of the top crust of a strawberry-rhubarb pie. Or remove a series of sprightly shapes with a truffle cutter in a circle around the edge or the center of the top crust.

Top crusts can also have decorations applied to them, but don't forget to cut steam vents as well. One logical thing to do is to cut crescent shapes out of the crust with a cookie cutter ⌒ , and then stick them elsewhere on the crust.

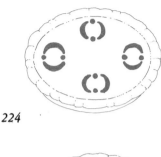

224

225

226

227

Or else bake two pies at the same time. Cut shapes out of the top crust of one, and use the shapes by themselves on the glazed fruit filling of the other. If you're having a big party, serve both pies together, one with a crescent moon and stars cut out of the top crust, the other with nothing but the pastry crescent moon and stars laid over a striking blueberry filling.

Ideas for cutouts can also be silly and slightly corny. Like a Christmas tree on a mince pie, or jack-o'-lantern faces on pumpkin pies. Or even letters: CHERRY or NOEL or BERNIE.

Or they can be sophisticated, for example, a motif of small circles and arcs. Do it once in the middle of a piecrust, thus. Or make four of them at the compass points of the pie. *(Fig. 224)*

Try another design using the cutouts as appliqués. Cut triangles out of the crust. Then cut into the pastry triangles with scissors to make fans, placing the fans all around the edges of the pie, alternating with the triangular vents. *(Fig. 225)*

Cut out two sides of a triangle. Then fold the flap back toward the center of the pie. Six of these will fit nicely around the edge of a pie. *(Fig. 226)*

One ambitious design we've done was a della Robbia sculpture made of pastry. To a piecrust with a circular vent cut in the center, we applied pastry flowers and leaves. We then cut thin ropes of pastry dough from a second sheet of firm pastry to use as stems. Next we cut 1-inch by 2-inch lengths of dough and twisted them into roses. The final arrangement used the flowers, leaves and stems, with balls of dough as a decorative counterpoint. All were stuck to the top crust with water, painted with egg and sprinkled with granulated sugar. *(Fig. 227)*

Lattices

Halfway between closed and open pies are lattice-topped pies. Cut ½-inch to ¾-inch strands of dough with a sharp knife, a pizza wheel or a fluted pastry wheel. Then lay all the verticals down, and cross them with all the horizontals.

For a fancier surface, twist the strands before you lay them down.

If you're feeling somewhat confident, remove the center vertical, and put it into place after all the horizontals have been set down.

If you're feeling very confident, and if it's a dry, cold day, and if your hand with the pastry was inspired, then weave the strands. Here's how you do it. Lay down all the verticals. Then fold back every *other* one, and put the first horizontal in place. Cover that with the folded-back verticals, and fold back the *other* verticals. Put the second horizontal in place. *(Fig. 228)*

(Try it with yarn or paper streamers first, and you'll have a surer hand with the strips of pastry.)

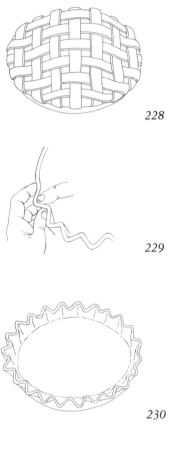

228

229

230

231

Edges

The edge of a pie is its frame. An untidy edge can destroy the finished look of the pie more quickly than anything else.

Essential: don't stretch the dough. It shrinks as it bakes. If you stretch it, you'll get gaps and tears and burned spots.

The simplest edge is made by pressing down with the back of a fork.

The next simplest is the pinched edge, where you pleat the dough between your thumbs in ridges that are 1 inch apart.

For the basic ruffle, you hold your left thumb and index finger an inch apart on the rim of the pastry, and push the dough between them with your right index finger. *(Figs. 229, 230)*

Make a braided edge by cutting three very narrow strips of pastry, braiding them and applying them to the circumference of the pie.

Or make a twist from two ropes of pastry, one very thin and one of medium width. Fasten the twist to the rim of the pie with cold water, and glaze it with beaten egg.

Do a chain of overlapping shapes cut with aspic cutters into diamonds, leaves or circles. *(Fig. 231)*

Another way to finish the edge of a pie is to bring the decoratively cut bottom crust up over the top crust. To do this, trim the bottom crust with pinking shears, or cut it with scissors in scallops or V's. Fold it over the edge of the top crust, trimmed to size. Be careful not to stretch it. Glue it down with water.

Finishing

Don't forget to glaze the piecrust. Use a dorure, or egg wash, a golden finish achieved by painting with egg yolk mixed with milk. Paint with plain milk. And sprinkle the moistened crust with granulated sugar to make a sparkling surface.

Pineapple

Pineapples are available year round, but are best in the spring. They come to us from Hawaii, Mexico and the Caribbean, and although they are never tree-ripened, some are riper than others. Choose a pineapple that is heavy in the hand, showing that it has lots of juice. Pick one with flesh that gives at the bottom end, with a full fragrance and with fronds that can be pulled out easily. Small pineapples give a lower proportion of fruit to skin than large ones, so if you're looking for value, choose a great big heavy pineapple.

In Colonial America, pineapples were a symbol of hospitality. That's the reason one now finds carved pineapples as ornaments on gates or doorways or at the end of stair railings. Even today, a whole pineapple looks almost excessively abundant. It's so flamboyant, so tropical, so bristling with leaves and prickles. You can do anything to it without upstaging it. Fill it with rum, garnish it with orchids, put a candle in it, surround it with basketry.

Whole Pineapples

Use a pineapple as the tall focal point of a fruit centerpiece. Stick whole strawberries and clusters of green grapes among the fronds.

Pierce a whole pineapple with skewers threaded with chunks of ham and fruit.

Cut off the top and bottom of a whole pineapple. With a very sharp knife, slice around the fruit and push it out the bottom of the shell. Slice it lengthwise into fingers, and replace in the shell, which you then set on a bed of greenery.

204

Cut off the top of a whole pineapple. With a very sharp knife, remove the fruit in small pieces. It doesn't matter if you can't do this neatly. Then chop the fruit, mix it with vanilla ice cream or with pineapple or coconut ice, and spoon it back into the shell. Store in the freezer until you are ready to serve the pineapple with its cap of fronds alongside.

Pineapple Halves

Cut a pineapple in half lengthwise and scoop out the meat. Then lay the shells, cut-side down, on a plate, with the fronds at different ends. Stud them with fruit and shrimp threaded onto toothpicks.

Cut a pineapple in half to make pineapple boats. Remove the fruit, cut it into chunks, combine it with watermelon and honeydew balls and refill the containers.

Pineapple Quarters

The quarter pineapple is the standard single serving. Cut the fruit into four lengthwise sections, either cutting the fronds with the base or removing them. Loosen the meat from the shell. Slice it 1 inch thick, and push slices 1, 3 and 5 slightly to the right, and slices 2, 4 and 6 slightly to the left. *(Fig. 232)*

Quarter the pineapple. Remove the fruit from the peel and cut it into slices. Lay them on a plate, the slices overlapping, with the quartered fronds at one end and a line of strawberries echoing the curve of the fruit.

232

Pineapple Slices

Cut off the top and bottom of the pineapple. Remove all the rind with a sharp knife. The eyes or pines will be left in place. Remove them one by one with the point of a paring knife, or else make a careful spiral around the outside of the fruit, which will remove all the eyes. *(Fig. 233)*

Slice the meat horizontally and remove the cores. On each

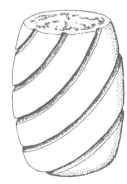

233

205

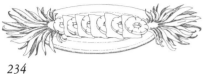

234

dessert plate, lay one large and one small slice, filling the centers with grapes and mint leaves.

On a long platter, lay overlapping pineapple rings with ham slices or melon rings. Decorate both ends of the platter with the pineapple fronds, cut in half. *(Fig. 234)*

Canned Pineapple

It's not as good as fresh, but it's very good. It's the only kind of pineapple you can use with gelatin, since the cooking destroys the enzyme that works against jelling. And its rings and spears and chunks are tidily geometrical, well suited to artificial, perfectly shaped arrangements. Use to make a pattern on a ham, to top a muffin tin full of corned beef hash or, lightly sautéed, to make a ring around a platter of game hens in a fruit sauce.

Plums

Plums are plump, with smooth, brilliantly colored skins. They are in season from July through September, one variety after another, from yellow-fleshed red-skinned Santa Rosas through big blue presidents, green greengages, yellow egg plums, tiny dark Damsons, to the last plums of the season, blueblack Italian prune plums. Buy them soft, heavy in the hand and, if you can, in season. Canned plums are good for baking.

It's very hard to peel and slice a plum. They cling to their skins and, with the exception of freestone prune plums, to their pits. Peel a plum after you poach or bake it. If you must slice them, cut the fruit in half and release the stone with the point of a very sharp paring knife. You can then cut the plum half into slices, but they won't be neat.

Serve plums on light plates, either pale green or white. On a white plate, make an arrangement of the bright red fruit with honeydew melon and green grapes. Combine slices of purple and green plums. Fan the plum wedges around a pile of grapes. Fan honeydew slices around a plum half.

206

Garnish scarlet plums with other reds, with strawberries, peaches or nectarines. Use halves of red plums with vanilla ice cream and vanilla custard. Make a bowl of scarlet plums and tiny green grapes. Set it alongside another bowl of green plums and purple grapes.

Pomegranate

Pomegranates are gorgeous, with their red skins and lovely round shapes. Inside, there is an inedible white matrix holding hundreds of crimson, jewel-like seeds, each with a pit in it. They're a horror to eat, all but inedible. But we go at it anyway, sucking the seeds, spitting out the pits, generally making a mess of ourselves.

(Pomegranate juice is the base of a popular syrup called grenadine.)

Maybe the answer is to think of a pomegranate as part of a work of art. Cut wedges of the crimson fruit and place them around a whole roast chicken or on a platter of browned chicken pieces. Imitate the Dutch painters, and use a single pomegranate with a wedge cut out of it in an arrangement of whole fruit.

If you want to take the trouble, you can collect the seeds from a pomegranate and use them to garnish baba ghanoush, or mix them with a creamy yogurt dressing to serve with fruit salad.

But the best way to eat them is to serve everyone a plate with a quarter of a pomegranate, some grapes and a melon wedge and let the juices go where they may.

Potatoes

Potatoes grow in so many parts of the country—in Idaho, Maine, Oregon, California—that there are always good fresh potatoes in our markets. Choose those with smooth skins, with no sprouting eyes or green spots. Store them in a cool dry place, where air can circulate around them.

Mealy potatoes are best for baking and roasting, while waxy

varieties are best for boiling, steaming and slicing. Both kinds make good fried potatoes. New potatoes are simply waxy potatoes picked before they reach their maturity.

One of the nicest results of the new nutrition is that potatoes are becoming respectable again. No longer do you have to devour them in privacy and guilt. You can come right out and order them in a restaurant, secure that you will be eating a health food, rich in vitamins, low in fat and surprisingly low in calories. It's the added butter or sour cream that does the damage.

Cutting Potatoes

Unless they are to be baked, potatoes are usually cut before we cook them. Smaller chunks cook more quickly than whole potatoes; slices, strips, cubes and shreds provide a lot of surface to hold seasonings and to become crisp and brown.

To keep potatoes from discoloring when they are cut, put them into cold salted water until you are ready to cook them. Grated potatoes, especially, turn an unappealing peachy-brown on exposure to air. Just before they go into the cooking water or butter, drain them, pat them or—in the case of grated potatoes—squeeze them dry.

Different cooking methods demand different shapes. Pommes Anna and potato chips both call for potato disks. To make them, carve a long potato into a cylinder with your paring knife. Then slice it into ¼-inch-thick disks. A waffle-cutting knife makes disks with an interesting surface.

Potatoes that are baked under a roast or in a pan of butter can be trimmed carefully or cut into rough chunks. Make large balls by cutting a potato into quarters, then trimming the quarters with a sharp knife. Make smaller ovals by cutting each quarter of the potato into two or three long pieces, then trimming them into olive shapes. These are traditionally combined with carrots and turnips trimmed to the same shape.

(There will inevitably be a lot of wasted potato when you do fancy trimming. Hold the discarded bits in cold salted water, and use them in vegetable purees.)

Scoop out perfect spheres with a melon baller. Peel the potato, then press down with the tool and scoop out balls. Potatoes cut this way are called Parisienne, and are often combined with carrot balls and mushroom caps.

To make sticks for french frying, peel and slice a long potato, and then cut each slice into sticks. Cut thinner sticks for shoestring and straw potatoes. These can also be cut on a mandoline or with a waffle-cutting knife. A food processor, so perfect for grating potatoes, doesn't make nicely shaped potato sticks.

To make cubes for hash brown potatoes, cut sticks for french frying, and then cut the sticks into cubes. And to grate potatoes, as we said, there is nothing as effective as a food processor. Failing that, you have to settle for a hand grater and, probably, bleeding knuckles.

Baked Potatoes

Scrub a mealy potato and put it in the oven just as it is. Rubbing fat into the surface and wrapping in aluminum foil both interfere with the production of good crisp skins. If you want a very dark, very crisp skin, just bake the potato for half again as long as you need to.

235

After you bake a potato, cut an X on the skin and then pinch it open. Make the X either with the long axis of the potato or else turned 45 degrees.

Cut a baked potato in half along the short axis with zigzag cuts. Take a thin slice off the bottom so that the half can stand upright. It will look like a flower. *(Fig. 235)*

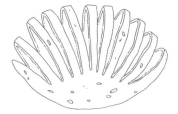

236

Before baking Idahos or new potatoes, make several deep parallel cuts angled toward the center. Drizzle with butter. The cuts will open up as the potatoes bake. Or just take two wedges out of each side for a Deco look. *(Figs. 236, 237)*

Garnish baked potatoes with sour cream, yogurt, guacamole, pimiento, shredded yellow cheese, red caviar, chives, poached eggs, parsley. Garnish baked sweet potatoes with canned chopped pineapple, chopped nuts, apple slices, raisins, yogurt and raisins, mandarin oranges.

Hook a tomato wedge into the slash of an opened baked potato. Stick sprigs of Italian parsley on either side of the tomato.

237

209

Shells

For people who won't believe that potatoes aren't fattening, serve only the boat-shaped shells. Bake potatoes, cut them in half and scoop out the insides. Sliced lengthwise, strips of baked potato shell make a wonderful cocktail nibble with a sour cream dip.

Use baked potato shells as containers for fried potatoes, potato salad. Fill them with corned beef hash, with vegetable purees or mixed vegetables. Fill them with whipped potatoes pressed through a pastry tube into baroque shapes, then brushed with butter and baked again.

Boiled and Steamed Potatoes

Peel, and then carve waxy potatoes into rounds and ovals. Cook until they are just done. (New potatoes should not be peeled before they are boiled.) After cooking you can remove a strip of skin from around the equator of the potato to show the contrast between red skin and white interior. Or cut a wedge from one side and sprinkle the crevice with chopped herbs and butter. Making a second wedge crossing the first works, too. *(Fig. 238)*

After the potatoes are boiled or steamed, drain them and return them to the heat to dry out for a few minutes. Then add butter and chopped green herbs such as parsley, dill or chives.

Potato Salad

Made, of course, with boiled potatoes that have been cooled and then cut into cubes or slices.

Add bright or dark accents, such as green pepper, pimiento, scallions, green and black olives. Garnish with cold mussels, lemon and parsley.

Form potato salad into a mound, and tuck scallion fringes around the base at the compass points. On either side of the scallions, place tomato wedges and black olives. On top of the mound, make a

238

210

star of hard-boiled egg wedges, with a pile of little scallion rings in the center.

Top a mound of potato salad with a bow made from a paper-thin slice cut from the center of a long carrot. *Lots* of dark parsley on either side.

Mashed Potatoes

Which are also, of course, made of boiled potatoes. The classic presentation of mashed potatoes is a scoop of sweet white potato with a pool of yellow butter melting in the center. Tuck fringed scallions and steamed carrot sticks around the base.

Make a pile of mashed potatoes. Press a hollow in the center and fill it with peas or cooked carrot slices. A fringe of watercress goes at the meeting place.

Serve mashed potatoes in a tomato case, in a baked-potato shell or in a zucchini boat. Make zigzag tracings on the top with the tines of a fork. Brush it with butter and stick it under the broiler to brown.

The color and flavor of mashed potatoes will change with the addition of pureed vegetables. Make them green by mixing in pureed peas, spinach or broccoli. Color them yellow by pureeing them with carrots, yams, squash or yellow turnip.

Duchesse potatoes get their yellow color from the addition of egg yolks and butter. These can be made into cakes and other fancy shapes using your hands or a pastry bag. They hold their shapes well and can be used to make a border around a steak or for a fancy presentation on a dinner plate. For example, pat a serving of duchesse potatoes into a flat cake about 4 inches in diameter. With a butter knife, make a crisscross design on top like the grid for a ticktacktoe game. Brush the cake with melted butter and put under the broiler to turn golden brown.

(Remember that most of these suggestions apply just as well to sweet potatoes. Fill a mashed sweet potato mound with cauliflower flowerets sprinkled with finely minced green scallions. Served mashed sweet potatoes inside a baked apple or a tangerine shell.)

Fried Potatoes

Vary the size of french fries. Big fat ones are good with hamburgers and catsup. Thin shoestrings are very French. They're the *frites* that are served in a pile alongside a small steak. Hair-thin strips of potato, cut in a mandoline, get pressed into a special double strainer and deep fried to make potato baskets.

You can fry any shape of potato: cubes, spheres and disks. Add chopped green pepper or sweet red pepper for color. Use diced scallions instead of fried onions, and garnish the plate with tasseled scallions.

To serve a whole platter of fried potatoes, put broiled tomato halves down the center of the platter. Pile french fries at both sides, with watercress at the ends.

Try deep frying chunks of potato with their skins left on. They are delicious and look just right served with breakfast eggs.

Sweet Potatoes

There are two varieties of sweet potato, one somewhat light-colored and dry and the other a deep orange with a very sweet taste. They can be prepared in every way that white potatoes are cut and cooked. Anyone who has not had deep-fried sweet potato slices has missed a treat.

Prosciutto and Fruit

Prosciutto is salted Italian-style ham that is air-cured and served without cooking. It is generally available in Italian groceries, where the berry-red ham with its layer of white fat goes through the machine and falls out in paper-thin slices. We serve it as a first course or luncheon dish with cantaloupe, honeydew and figs. But it can also be served with ripe peaches and pears, with papaya, mango, pineapple and dried prunes.

Cut two thin wedges of cantaloupe. Peel them and set the first one upright on a salad plate. Cut the second slice in half and place it on either side of the first, so that the two seem to intersect at right angles. Drape a slice of prosciutto over the intersection and cross it with a second slice. *(Fig. 239)*

Lay thin slices of prosciutto across a salad plate so that the plate is completely covered. Remove the rind from three thin melon wedges (possibly two cantaloupe wedges and one honeydew wedge). Cut each arc in half across the middle, and turn one half over, so that each slice forms an S. Place the three S's in a row over the ham. *(Fig. 240)*

Make melon balls from cantaloupe, honeydew and watermelon. Fill a wineglass or shallow glass bowl with them and garnish with prosciutto roses. To make the roses, cut a slice of ham in half lengthwise. Wind the slice, keeping one end tight and the fatty border at the looser edge. A second slice goes around the first, becoming looser as you wind. One slice of prosciutto makes a good-sized rose for a small dish of melon balls. A prosciutto rose can also be combined on a plate with melon slices. *(Fig. 241)*

Fresh green or purple figs look good with prosciutto, garnished with lots of mint or basil. Cut a fig in half lengthwise, and place the halves to one side of a salad plate, with two large basil leaves between them. On the other half of the plate, crumple prosciutto slices.

239

240

Purees

Purees are foods—meat, fish, fruit or vegetables—that are cooked, then pressed through a sieve or a food mill or spun in a blender or processor.

Thanks to the food processor, the late 1970s became the Age of Puree. Five seconds too long in the machine, and—whoops—our chopped carrots became carrot puree.

It's a nice change in texture, a good way to serve vegetables. There's something soothing about purees, and people who won't eat turnips or broccoli devour them willingly enough when they come as sophisticated baby food.

The puree must be thick enough to hold its contour on a dinner plate. Those made of watery vegetables, such as zucchini, are thickened by blending with potatoes. If you add too much cream to

241

213

the mixture, or otherwise overdo the blending, you can serve the puree in a food container, putting pureed peas in half a tomato or a baked potato shell.

A visual trick is to serve two purees side by side. They must be in contrasting colors. So: broccoli and carrot, spinach and cauliflower, turnip and beet. Then leave them alone. Don't garnish them, don't sprinkle anything on them, don't decorate the tops with the tines of a fork. Anything put near them will get smudged with the puree, and from elegant you will descend to messy.

Purees are used as parts of garnishes. Pipe them onto hard-boiled eggs, on artichoke bottoms, tomatoes, mushroom caps. Serve chestnut puree on noisettes of lamb. Use stiff purees in canapés.

Radishes

242

Radishes are members of the mustard family. The most familiar variety is the round red radish with a white interior, but you sometimes see long white oriental daikon radishes, or the black radishes used in Eastern European Jewish cooking. Buy firm, brightly colored radishes. Remove and discard the leaves when you get home to increase the life of the vegetable.

243

The French eat radishes and sweet butter for an hors d'oeuvre and have evolved several recipes for cooking them. But by and large these crisp, peppery vegetables are eaten raw, either as part of a salad or as a garnish alongside another food.

They're often carved into fancy shapes. That's because they're firm and hold their shape well. But even more important, a whole radish is merely red, while a carved radish is both red and white.

They're a favorite of caterers, who make them into feathery roses and nosegays. The message is confusing: you see rosebuds but taste pepper.

A little of this can go a long way. We'd rather see radishes cut into simple bold shapes that show off their dramatic color contrast. Mix these with radishes left in their natural form, so that you are always aware of the real food.

244

Start with a bunch of firm, well-shaped radishes, the leaves

214

trimmed off. You need a sharp paring knife and a bowl of ice water. As you finish each radish, drop it into the water so it will stay crisp.

To make a rose, hold the base of the radish in one hand. With the side of the knife held in your other hand make four vertical cuts around the circumference, almost down to the stem. Make a second row of cuts inside the first and, if there's room, a third row inside this. You'll be cutting through some of the original petals. When you're done, there should be no uncarved radish. For a variation on the rose, slice off the outer cuts completely, so that you have a red-tipped white flower. *(Figs. 242, 243)*

245

Make an abstract flower by slicing the radish in half perpendicular to the stem. With the side of your knife blade, crosshatch the exposed white surface. *(Fig. 244)*

246

Make another abstract flower by cutting out four narrow vertical wedges from the four "corners" of the radish. *(Fig. 245)*

Remove one vertical wedge from a side. Then turn the radish 90 degrees and cut another wedge to cross it. *(Fig. 246)*

To make a fan, place an oval radish in a soup spoon. Slice straight down, making cuts ¹⁄₁₆ inch apart perpendicular to the stem. The edges of the spoon will stop you from cutting all the way through. (The Chinese accomplish this by laying the radish between two chopsticks.) When you drop it in ice water, the fan will open up. (In China, they put fan-cut radishes into containers with salt and sugar and no water. In a few hours, they are soft enough to be molded into open fans.) *(Fig. 247)*

247

In *Japanese Garnishes* by Yukiko and Bob Haydock (Holt Rinehart Winston, 1980) we found directions for making jacks and mushrooms from red radishes. The jacks are wonderful alongside a sandwich or on a plate of cold sesame noodles. The mushrooms are set on a nest of alfalfa sprouts and the whole thing becomes a salad garnish.

To make a jack, slice a radish into ⅛-inch rounds. Cut a narrow triangular notch in each round. Then fit two rounds together, notch to notch.

To make mushrooms, cut a line ¼ inch deep around the equator of a radish. One half of the radish becomes a red mushroom cap. Cut into the other half, forming a broad white cylindrical stem. *(Fig. 248)*

248

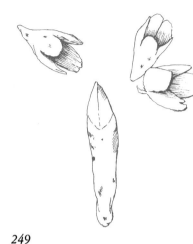

249

You can make white flowers from long icicle radishes. Holding the stem end in one hand, cut four petals with the side of the knife blade. You're trying to make a cup whose base is the pointed end of the radish. After you cut, twist out the radish in your other hand. It will come easily, leaving a cup-shaped flower in your hand. Continue to cut thin flowers from the rest of the radish. *(Fig. 249)*

Using Radishes with Other Foods

For maximum color display with salad greens, cut radishes in half and then in half again, as though you were quartering a melon. Use them with shiny black olives.

The grating disk of the food processor transforms red radishes into a mass of magenta. Sprinkle on salad, or place gently on top of a clear soup. Pile a heap of shredded radish on snowy rice or cottage cheese.

Take one carved radish and place it, way off-center, on an individual salad plate that contains only dark mixed greens.

Add radishes to an arranged salad of grapefruit and pale-green avocado.

Make a centerpiece by filling the bottom of a basket with small apples or new potatoes. Stick leaves of red-tipped lettuce between the apples or potatoes, completely hiding them. When you've created a good bed, arrange groups of five radishes each here and there among the lettuce, mixing carved radishes with whole ones. Tall stalks of endive provide extra height.

Rice

Although for most of the world rice is the staple grain, in America it lags behind bread, noodles and potatoes in popularity. Only in parts of the South is it a staple.

We buy fluffy long-grain rice with separate grains or short-grain rice that sticks together, making the best rice puddings and risottos. (The Japanese *prefer* rice that sticks to itself.) Brown rice is white rice with most of the coating, and most of the nutrition, left on. Wild rice, however, isn't rice at all, but rather the seed of a grass that grows wild in the North Central states.

Rice is cooked in liquid by boiling or baking. It incorporates the liquid in which it cooks, tripling in volume as it cooks. Fried rice, rice croquettes, parched rice and rice salads are all made with leftover cooked rice.

Visually, rice is pretty bland. White rice in a white bowl is not a thrilling picture. We can change its look by mixing cooked rice with colored garnishes, by cooking the rice in colored liquids or by molding the rice into an interesting shape.

Toss cooked white rice with olives, peanuts, walnuts, pignolias, with cooked red lentils, corn kernels, bacon, shredded carrots, chopped red and green peppers, ham, parsley, chives, bits of orange rind.

Cook rice in colored liquids. To make rice brown, cook onion until the sugar in it caramelizes. Then stir in the rice, coat with the butter and add beef broth. To make rice green, cook in water flavored with pureed spinach, parsley or basil. To make it yellow, cook in water seasoned with saffron or turmeric.

For light red rice, cook it in tomato juice or in water to which you have added tomato paste. For pale orange dessert rice, cook in half water and half orange juice.

Rice Molds

Rice has shape as well as color when it is pressed into a mold. Use short-grain rice that is sticky enough to cling together when it is unmolded. Mix the lightly cooked rice with melted butter and pack it into a mold. Let it rest for half an hour, then turn it out onto a platter.

Mix the rice with chopped nuts, apricots and raisins. Then pack into a bowl, turn it out and decorate the base with nut halves and apricot halves.

Pack layers of different-colored rice into a glass bowl. Alternate bands of red-orange rice with thin bands of white. Turn out and garnish with chopped parsley.

Press rice into a ring mold. When it is unmolded, lay blanched

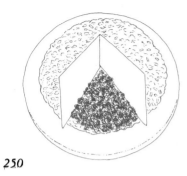

250

strips of leek or scallion over the curve of the ring, and fill the center with bright stir-fried vegetables.

On a mound of molded yellow rice, make a garland using cherry tomatoes, Chinese pea pods and mushroom halves.

Use an ice-cream scoop to make hemispheres and cones of rice. Garnish the top of a rounded scoop with a sautéed mushroom cap and Italian parsley leaves. Sprinkle chopped parsley all over the rice cone.

To decorate a mound of rice, fold a sheet of paper to make an angle. Place it over the top of the rice, the point at the center of the mound. Sprinkle the exposed angle with parsley. Move the paper one third around the mound. This time, sprinkle the exposed area with chopped egg yolk. Put a few cherry tomatoes at the top, where the points meet. *(Fig. 250)*

Roasts

A roast is a large, serious and usually expensive piece of meat—beef, pork, lamb, veal or poultry—that is cooked by dry heat in the oven, on a spit over coals or by moist heat in a braising liquid. It's a saddle of lamb surrounded by oven-browned potatoes and carrots; a plump chicken, its skin crisp and brown; a boned veal breast stuffed with spinach and pignolia nuts; a braised beef brisket in a dark garlicky sauce.

Roast meats vary in taste and appearance, but they have certain elements in common for the foodstylist. They are the large cuts of meat that appear on special occasions: the Easter leg of lamb and the company roast beef. They are usually garnished in a manner consistent with the size of the meat and the importance of the occasion.

There are three ways to bring roast meat to the table: uncarved, partially carved and fully carved.

We can present the whole roast. It sits on a large platter surrounded with watercress and vegetables. Then it is carved by the family carver, who doles out slices of meat and portions of vegetables onto individual plates. This is the ceremonial or Thanksgiving method, used when everyone is already half-stuffed and has the patience to wait and to admire the carver's skill.

The second method is used when the roast is so big that you intend to use half of it another day, or when you want to create a look of splendor and excess, implying that you have much more meat than you need. You carve only half the roast, lay the slices on half the platter and put the uncarved meat alongside it. You often see this kind of platter on a buffet table or sideboard, with forests of watercress filling in the awkward spaces.

Finally, there is the method of presentation where the carving is done in the kitchen before the meal is served. The slices are arranged neatly on a serving platter, garnished with greens, vegetables and stuffing, and the platter is brought to the table. This is the safest method for the insecure carver, for anyone who prefers to work unobserved and for the host who feels the strain of making the guests wait to eat. It's also the method that permits the hiding of badly cut bits underneath all the beautifully regular slices of meat.

No matter which method you choose, you can follow the suggestions in the section on ARRANGEMENT (see pages 1–7). The whole roast is, by necessity, an arrangement made of a large oval surrounded by a border. The half-carved roast logically goes at one end of the platter, with the cut slices laid out on the other half. The fully carved roast becomes slices that have to be laid out as though they were so many slices of tomato or salami or water biscuits.

The meat goes on a round or oval platter of china, silver or earthenware. Heavy china, warmed in a 200°F oven, helps to keep the cut meat warm. Keep the platter in scale for the amount of meat you have; too small is probably better than too large.

Borders for a Whole Roast

A whole roast sits in the middle of a platter. The simplest, most appropriate border for it is made of fresh, beautifully cooked vegetables.

An artless border is made when you arrange vegetables in large areas with no repetitions. Avoid patterning or the use of tiny-delicate elements, and use enough vegetables in each pile so that every diner can get a respectable portion. Use perfect, top-quality vegetables to give the dish a wonderful springlike look. Surround a leg of spring lamb with areas of asparagus, mushrooms, snow peas, cherry tomatoes, green beans, carrots, new potatoes.

To make the border more formal, substitute intricately shaped vegetables for some of the plain ones. Carve the carrots into perfect ovals. Stuff the cherry tomatoes with spinach puree. Make crisscross piles of beans or asparagus. Instead of snow peas, put fresh peas into tomato cups. Instead of oven-browned potatoes, pipe duchesse potatoes in rings. With each vegetable that is replaced by a carved or arranged vegetable, the design becomes more formal.

Arrange the vegetables around the meat in a regular repeating pattern, an *abab* or an *abcba.* For example, do a border of grilled half tomatoes and oven-browned potatoes. Make a border of watercress/carrot/cauliflower/carrot/watercress. Encircle the meat with a border of asparagus spears and cherry tomatoes, and accent the ends of the platter with bushes of parsley. The borders don't have to surround the meat completely. They can be placed along the long sides or at the ends only. *(Fig. 251)*

251

Place a single large decorative element in five places around the roast, and fill in the spaces between with a background vegetable such as duchesse potatoes or sautéed spinach. The decorative element could be a baked apple surrounded with orange wedges, an orange filled with pureed broccoli and dotted with currants or a red onion cut like a flower and baked in foil.

Half-sliced Roast

252

Picture an oval platter, with a half-carved brisket of beef on one end and the meat slices on the other.

Make two or three rows of overlapping slices of meat. Between them, place cooked carrots or potatoes from the pot roast. *(Fig. 252)*

Make a semicircular design. Again, the roast covers one end of the platter. Place lots of greens around its outside edge. On the other half, an arc of overlapping meat slices, a border of potatoes, another arc of meat and one of cherry tomatoes and greens. *(Fig. 253)*

253

Make a fan-shaped design. The roast is at one end of the platter. The lines of sliced meat radiate out from an imaginary point in the middle of its cut edge. Pot vegetables or greens are placed between the lines of meat.

Or do an *abab* design, using sliced vegetables alternating with slices of meat. Surround a pork roast on three sides with slices of pork overlapping slices of sautéed apple. Next to a roast leg of veal, lay carved slices of veal with sautéed eggplant. Break the chain with large vegetables such as flower-shaped baked onions or clumps of cherry tomatoes and green beans.

254

Fully Sliced Roast

You can adapt any of the ideas offered for the half-sliced roast to a fully sliced roast, continuing it along the whole platter. If you like, you can use as a focal point a pile of stuffing or a major garnish in place of the uncarved meat.

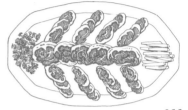

255

Surround a pile of stuffing, vegetables or rice with a circular pattern of overlapping meat slices, with extra meat at the ends of the oval pattern. For example, put sliced chicken around a heap of rice-and-pecan stuffing, with the wings and legs at the ends of the platter.

Lay a pattern of slices radiating from a central puff of greens, with garnishes filling in the empty spaces. Arrange sliced turkey breast in a pinwheel from a mound of parsley or of candied sweet potatoes. *(Fig. 254)*

Make one line of beautifully sliced meat—a fillet of beef, for example—with the small, less-attractive bits at one end and a garnish at the other. Then lay two kinds of vegetables on each side of the meat: a row of french fries and, alongside it, peas and pea pods.

Make three lines of meat. The central line is made of the larger pieces and is set over the stuffing, covering it. In the side rows, smaller slices of meat are set at a slant. Vegetable garnishes go at either end. *(Fig. 255)*

Do an oval pattern of overlapping meat slices covered with sauce. This is a good way to serve meat that is cloaked with a heavy sauce, such as vitello tonnato or sauerbraten. For the veal, you might also sprinkle on capers, garnish the center of the circle with Italian parsley and add cold vegetables vinaigrette here and there around the platter.

Make a wheel arrangement. Lay a pile of meat in the center of the platter—the legs and wings, perhaps—and arrange spokes of sliced meat and vegetables around it.

More Garnishes

The best garnishes for a roast are simple, beautifully cooked vegetables such as browned potatoes, braised leeks, carrots and tomatoes.

An elegant garnish is made by spooning vegetable purees onto flat vegetables such as mushroom caps, artichoke bottoms or tomato halves.

Garnish a large roast for a buffet with skewers of sautéed vegetables or raw fruit.

Wrap whole carrots, roasted in the pan, with garlands of Italian parsley.

For lamb, make bouquets of mint leaves.

Scatter flower-cut carrots and turnips over a bed of fresh raw spinach.

And remember that enough watercress will mask any number of slipups with the carving knife. Most of all, remember that expert carving is the foundation for all meat presentations, and that sharp knives are the foundation of all good carving.

Rolls

Rolls are simply individual loaves of bread, bread dough shaped according to traditional forms and served one to a person. You make a bread dough, let it rise, then punch it down and form the rolls. After a second rising, they are glazed and baked. For glazes, see the section on BREAD (page 58).

Biscuits. Roll out the bread dough about 1 inch thick, and cut it with a round biscuit cutter. For a crusty surface, place the rolls 1 inch apart on a baking sheet. For softer rolls, put them in a cake pan, with their edges touching.

Oval. Roll out the bread dough and cut it with an oval cutter. Then shape the ends of the oval into points. Slash the top lengthwise or snip with scissors several times crosswise.

Parker House rolls. Cut biscuit-shaped rounds. Fold one side over the other, not quite all the way to the other side.

Finger rolls. Pull off small lumps of dough and rol them gently between your palms into cigar shapes.

Twists. Flatten the cigar-shaped finger rolls with your palm or a rolling pin. Then twist each one two times.

Rings and figure eights. Take an unbaked finger roll and make a round doughnut shape like a bagel, using water to help attach the ends. To make a figure eight, twist the doughnut into an eight.

Knots. Again, take an unbaked finger roll. Tie it into a knot. Either tuck the ends underneath, or lay them out decoratively on either side.

Cloverleafs. Pull off small lumps of dough. Roll them into tiny balls and place three balls in every section of a muffin tin.

Brioches. Put a large lump of dough in a muffin tin. Roll a smaller lump between your palms and set one on every large piece.

Crescents. Roll the dough into a ¼-inch-thick circle. Cut it into eight triangular wedges, and roll them up, beginning with the outside of the circle.

Fans. Roll the dough into a ¼-inch-thick rectangle. Cut lengthwise into four equal strips, and make a stack of the strips. Cut the stacks into 2-inch segments, and stand each segment upright in a muffin tin. In cooking, the dough will splay out on the top.

Salads, Composed

A composed salad is one whose ingredients are arranged consciously and artfully on the plate. They are usually small and are served either as a first course or as a main dish at luncheon. They differ from tossed salads both in the care taken in the arrangement and in the fact that the parts don't have to be bite-sized, since they are commonly eaten with a fork and knife. Although some of the elements may be cooked—white beans, for example, or artichoke bottoms—they are still salads, because everything in them is served cold and crisp.

Composed salads can be constructed on individual plates or on large serving platters. The dressing is served alongside, to be spooned on at the last minute. Whether it is made on a large platter or on a salad plate, the salad's design will be the same. The arrangement on

256

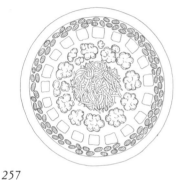

257

258

the salad plate can either be repeated on the platter or else be enlarged. Thus, an individual salad can be made of a half-circle of sliced tomatoes and mozzarella, sprinkled with oil and garnished with basil. The enlarged design can be made either of many such half-circles repeated on the platter or of one large half-circle that covers most of the platter.

Once again, we refer you to the section on ARRANGEMENT (see pages 1–7).

Do a composed salad in stripes. Make a plate of stripes of cucumber rings, sprinkled with chopped radishes, and rows of black olives between the stripes. Do stripes of different vegetables shredded in the food processor: carrot, turnip and green pepper, with, for textural variety, lines of whole radishes, black olives and cauliflower flowerets. *(Fig. 256)*

Do an arrangement in concentric circles. Start with a mound of shredded carrot. Surround it with marinated cauliflower flowerets and a ring of cubed yellow cheese mixed with red kidney beans. Make a circle by putting down a tomato slice, surrounding it by a ring of spinach leaves and black olives. *(Fig. 257)*

Make an off-center radiating pattern on your platter. At one side of the plate place an artichoke. Coming from it are lines of sliced onion, tomato, shredded carrot, green beans and beets, with chopped scallions and tiny olives garnishing the vegetables. *(Fig. 258)*

You may have trouble adapting large circular patterns to individual salad plates. They tend to crowd it. Small plates work better with fan designs or with a segment of a circle. Put the focal point to one side of the plate, and let the other foods come out from it. Make a clump of watercress at one side of a plate. Set spokes of endive coming out from it, and fill them with different vegetables. Place three egg wedges to one side of the plate, sitting on a bed of dill. Around them, arrange an arc of cucumber slices, and then three tomato slices. Garnish with dill. *(Fig. 259)*

A single cold vegetable served on a plate can also be considered a composed salad. Tie cold marinated beans or asparagus with scallions or cover them with pimiento. Lay on the center of a plate and garnish with tomato wedges.

For a buffet table, serve a do-it-yourself salad bar, with each

224

ingredient in its own glass bowl. Or do a large platter of stuffed vegetables. Have red and green bell peppers, endive, cucumber boats, tomato halves, zucchini, all stuffed with chopped salad. The guests help themselves to individual salads in their vegetable containers.

Salads, Layered

Layered salads stand halfway between composed and tossed. They are carefully structured before you serve them, then are mixed on the plate. They are party dishes, nice for a buffet supper.

A clear glass bowl makes an ideal container for a layered salad. You have to be able to see the layers, after all. To prepare the salad, have everything chopped small enough to be eaten without a knife. Think of color contrasts when you make the layers. We made a salad that had layers of zucchini/yellow squash/black olives/carrot/fennel. We decorated the fennel on top with julienne strips of all the other vegetables arranged in a sunburst pattern.

Another time, we did layers of croutons/green peppers/Italian onion/spinach, and topped it off with a thick layer of chopped tomatoes on which we made a design in black olives and parsley.

When the bowl is filled with layers of brightly colored vegetables, stick in a spatula and pull the salad away from the side of the bowl. There, stick in a garnish: stalks of scallion, some cucumber or egg slices, tomatoes sliced vertically.

You might want to try a layered Salade Niçoise. Line the sides of the bowl with half-circles of tomato, with lots of shredded Boston lettuce on the bottom. Add a layer of chopped green pepper and potatoes to the top of the lettuce, then a thick layer of tuna and, on top, a mixture of chopped greens. Over it all, finish with spokes of whole marinated green beans and hard-boiled egg wedges surrounding a heap of tiny black olives.

Salads, Mayonnaise

These are the salads that the English call mayonnaises: tuna mayonnaise, chicken mayonnaise, crab, shrimp, ham, lobster, potato and egg mayonnaise. Visually, they're much alike. They can be very dull, these homogeneous lumps of "something in mayonnaise." You have to help them along by decorating the surface, because the mass is uncompromisingly cold and white.

Serving Bowls and Platters

It's a great help to have a dark-colored bowl or serving plate. Put the salad in a mound in a bowl or plate and surround it with dark greens before you do anything else.

On a bowl of potato salad, place a cross section of hard-boiled egg. Surround it with a ring of chopped parsley, then, working down from the top, sliced radishes, black olives and more parsley.

Or make spokes of scallion spears on the top, surrounding some grated carrots. Cherry tomatoes go between the spears at the base of the mound.

Garnish a platter of tuna salad with shelled mussels. Chop the mussels into the salad, and use the shells with lemon wedges as decorations. Add a bouquet of Italian parsley.

As a finish to a mound of shrimp salad, make a crown of whole shrimp, small leaves of Boston lettuce, cherry tomatoes and a spray of watercress. *(Fig. 260)*

260

Around the edge of a bowl of mayonnaise salad, place a ring of arcs cut from slices of green or red pepper. Then put a bunch of parsley or wheel of tomato wedges in the center of the salad.

For a more contrived decoration on a mayonnaise salad, make a ribbon and bow of carrot. Using a vegetable peeler, make several very thin strips of carrot. Lay down four of them to make a cross, like a ribbon tie. Then using the thinnest strips, fold two of them back on themselves to form equal-sized loops. Place the loops on the crossing of the "ribbon" as you make them, using dabs of mayonnaise as the glue. With a third strip, loop one end and tuck the other into the resulting space, and place it in the center of the bow. *(Fig. 261)*

Use carrot strips to cover the dividing line on a bowl half full of egg salad and half full of chicken salad. Add a carrot bow to one side of the strip.

261

226

Individual Plates

For a very elegant first course, place a small scoop of salmon salad to one side of a salad plate. Then add a fan of cold, stir-fried pea pods, green beans or asparagus coming out from under it.

262

For lunch, place a scoop of tuna salad in the center of a plate. Around it, set out a pattern of parsley/egg/mushroom/tomato repeated three or four times.

Make a Waldorf/tuna salad (tuna, celery, nuts and apples) and garnish with five thin vertically sliced arcs of red apple arched over a scoop of the salad. Soften with Boston lettuce.

Put two scoops on a plate, one of tuna salad and one of cottage cheese. Decorate with arcs of green pepper, making lines that radiate out from the tuna, forming spokes on the cottage cheese. Press thin wedges of tomato into the cheese between the spokes. Flank the mound of cottage cheese with two clumps of alfalfa sprouts. For color top the sprouts with a few sprigs of watercress. *(Fig. 262)*

Place the tuna salad off-center on a plate and surround it with four egg quarters, with tomato wedges on spinach leaves between them. *(Fig. 263)*

263

Serve tuna or chicken salad in tomatoes, on artichoke bottoms, in green pepper cases or cucumber boats.

Salads, Tossed

A tossed salad should look more haphazard than it really is. The care that you can't take in the arrangement can be spent on planning quality and color.

You can't fool around with a green salad. One brown-edged leaf invalidates the whole. Everything should be fresh, clean, colorful and cut to size. No one should have to take a knife to a tossed salad.

Wash and dry your greens ahead of time. One reason that salads turn soggy is that water left on recently washed greens gets combined with the salad dressing and weighs everything down. Instead, wash and spin-dry the greens. Wrap them in paper towels and store them in the refrigerator for at least a few hours.

227

264

Don't drown them in the dressing. Many people prefer to mix in the dressing with their hands (immaculately clean, of course), claim that they can then tell when just enough dressing is on every leaf.

Salads are tossed in wooden or ceramic bowls. They are very nice served on clear glass plates, which give a cleaner, fresher look than individual wooden bowls.

Think of color as well as taste when you gather ingredients for a salad. To a salad composed mainly of pale greens, such as Boston lettuce, add some dark watercress or Italian parsley leaves. To a dark-green salad of romaine or spinach, add a carved radish, two cherry tomatoes and a few pea pods. Slivers of pale endive make the dark green of romaine look even darker.

You can structure a tossed vegetable salad by color. Line a bowl with wholes leaves of romaine. Into this leafy shell, put a salad of sliced sweet red peppers, radishes, tomatoes, Italian onions, cauliflower, mushrooms and white beans. *(Fig. 264)*

An all-white salad is made of cauliflower flowerets, sliced water chestnuts, celery, inch-long bits of endive, half-moons of apple, slices of mushroom. Serve on a black or white porcelain plate.

Make a green salad of lima beans, peas, green pepper rings, spinach, zucchini and parsley. It will be good on white and brilliant on a red plate.

To arrange a large tossed salad for a party, line a bowl with whole leaves of red-tipped or leaf lettuce. Stick the center of the head upright in the middle of the bowl, using a florist's frog for support.

The salad proper, chopped and mixed with dressing, is spooned into the moat between the two. A possible combination would be a mixture of chopped green beans, halved cherry tomatoes, sliced scallions, cubed potatoes and shredded lettuce. To serve the salad, you take one leaf from the lining and spoon a portion of chopped salad onto it. Make sure that the mixed salad contains enough colorful, nongreen vegetables so that the difference between the salad and the greens is apparent.

To save last-minute work at a party, mix the salad dressing in the bottom of the bowl. Then place on it a vegetable that will benefit from marinating, such as mushrooms, sliced onion rings or tomatoes. Then add the greens and put the bowl into the refrigerator. It will be ready to toss at the last minute.

In England they garnish green salads with shredded Cheddar cheese. There are hundreds of foods that can be added discreetly to a salad to increase its visual and nutritional appeal. Don't forget vegetables shredded in the food processor. Consider nuts, chopped hard-boiled eggs, sprouts, sunflower seeds, chopped chives and scallions, green and red peppers, onion slices, shredded beets, marinated artichokes, hearts of palm, avocado, radishes, cucumber, bits of leftover meat and vegetables.

The purest salad is made in the spring with uncut greens, meant to look like wild herbs. Use very pale young leaves and the center of large heads of greens. Instead of cutting them, use the smallest whole pieces available. Choose at least three varieties, such as Boston lettuce, watercress and spinach. Place a few leaves of each on a fragile white or clear glass plate. Add stems of dill and parsley at the edge of the plate, where their stems can be seen. Lay a spray of scallion to one side of the plate and garnish with a thin lemon slice for a natural, gardenlike look.

Sandwiches

Every generalization about sandwiches has its exception. They are portable—except for grilled cheese sandwiches, hot turkey sandwiches. They are informal—except for tea sandwiches and Scandinavian open sandwiches. But most sandwiches are indeed both portable and informal, hearty meals to eat on the run, casual combinations of good bread and appropriate fillings.

The style is determined by the bread. A cheese sandwich or a chicken salad sandwich changes depending on what its casing is. Start with square American white and whole wheat, plain and toasted. Add a third slice (and a layer of bacon and lettuce) and you've got a club sandwich. Change to rye bread (and some mustard) and you've got a deli sandwich. Put the filling in a hero roll for a New Orleans poor boy sandwich or an Italian hero, submarine or grinder. Put it in a hard roll, a hot dog roll or a long thin French baguette. Use English muffins, pita bread or dense, thinly sliced German rye or pumpernickel.

A great sandwich is made of good bread, lots of filling, an orderly arrangement on the plate and, sometimes, a garnish.

But unless you let the world know there's something terrific inside, sandwiches look just like bread. Give an impression of lushness. Let greens extend out between the edges of the roll. If you have cucumber slices covering the cheese, let arcs of cucumber show outside the crusts. It should look as though there is so much filling that the bread casing can scarcely contain it—shredded lettuce spilling out of the opening of a pita, the ends of the lox falling from between the bagel halves, ham salad bursting out of a hollowed-out dinner roll.

Next comes the cutting. Remember how much it mattered when you were a child that a sandwich be cut just so, in proper squares, with the crusts trimmed away? There was then, as there is now, a right way to do it.

Bread that isn't cut in half looks simple, hearty and unsophisticated. This is the standard way of serving hamburgers, heroes, sandwiches on pita and on rolls. It's also all right for a man-sized roast beef on rye.

But ordinary packaged bread can be cut in many different ways. *(Fig. 265.)* Cut it in half, either parallel to the edges or on the diagonal. *(a, b)*

Slice the bread in quarters, either parallel to the edges or on the diagonal. *(c, d)*

Make three rectangles by cutting the bread twice parallel to the edges. *(e)*

Make three triangles by cutting the bread twice. *(f)*

Cut the bread into four pieces. Cut it in half diagonally, and then make two slices parallel to the long cut. *(g)*

Or cut off triangles from opposite ends of the bread, then cut the remaining strip in half. *(h)*

Cut off triangles from all four corners and cut the remaining center square into two triangles. *(i)*

Cut the square into a fan shape, making one diagonal cut, then two others that start from the same corner but go to the centers of the opposite sides. *(j)*

If you're training someone to like whole wheat bread, make a sandwich with one slice of white and one of dark bread. Cut the sandwich into quarters and turn over half the pieces. No one will guess that the checkerboard has anything to do with improved nutrition. *(k, l)*

Garnishes

Once the sandwich is filled and cut, you have to soften the unyielding geometry of the square sandwich and the round plate. One way to do it is to stand all or some of the pieces on end or to tilt them against one another. Another way is to add a garnish.

Tuck a leaf of lettuce under one corner of the sandwich, and the harsh line is broken. Add a tablespoonful of salad or some raw vegetables, such as carrot sticks or string beans, to the leaf. Combine cherry tomatoes and black olives, radishes and raw turnip sticks, carrot sticks and green olives. So long as they are fresh and edible, they will add to the composition.

Use a fruit garnish. Serve a tiny bunch of grapes with a tuna sandwich, pineapple chunks with a ham sandwich, fresh strawberries with a peanut butter sandwich.

If the filling requires extra dressing, such as mayonnaise, mustard or horseradish, serve it in a mushroom cap or a hollow tomato. Served this way, it helps to keep the bread from becoming soggy.

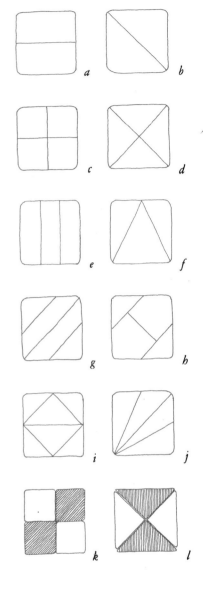

265

231

Sandwiches, Open-faced

Sandwiches are more interesting to look at when you aren't faced with the top slice of bread. Even if you prefer the convenience and heartiness of a closed sandwich, you can serve it open, laying the top slice to the side of the plate or tilted over the filling. Decorate the filling as though it were an open sandwich, and let the diner make his choice of finger-feeding or eating with a knife and fork.

Just remember that whatever garnish you add to a mock-open sandwich must be flat enough to fit easily when the lid goes on. Some suggestions: an open-faced BLT, made with tomato and avocado slices over the lettuce, and sprinkled with crumbled bacon. Or an egg salad sandwich on which you place thin circles of green and red bell peppers.

Hot open-faced sandwiches have a traditional pale and homogeneous look. White bread on the bottom, thinly sliced meat, then lots of pale chicken or beef gravy. If you like them this way, at least add a lot of parsley for contrast, and serve with shoestring fried potatoes instead of the traditional mashed white potatoes.

But give a thought to varying the sandwich by using a more interesting bread. It should still be soft enough to sop up the gravy, of course. English muffins are good. So is a hard roll, split in half, or a thick slice of good rye bread.

Sandwiches, Scandinavian

There is a whole aesthetic in Scandinavia governing the making of open-faced sandwiches.

Begin with dense, regularly shaped bread. Cut the crusts away, so that the bread is perfectly square or rectangular, forming an orderly frame. Apply a thick spread of butter, like the undercoat of a painting. The proper name for these sandwiches, *smørrebrød*, means "smeared bread."

The main ingredient goes on in a flat layer. It can be meat, cheese, fish or salad. It can lie flat, overlap, be folded, placed on the diagonal or straight down the middle of the bread.

Add a second ingredient, such as a sliced vegetable or egg. Finally, apply a garnish for flavor and visual contrast. Try a sprinkle of chopped onion, a sprig of dill, a dab of sour cream or, for height, a standing lemon twist or cucumber slice.

Sometimes a piece of the main ingredient is laid flat, and a second piece is wrapped around the second element. For example, ham is wrapped around a pickle and placed over another slice of ham. Or a salami cornucopia holds a spoonful of vegetable salad topping a flat circle of salami.

(Most canapés, by the way, are miniature sandwiches, and follow the rules for Scandinavian open sandwiches.)

266

When you have mastered the basic scheme, try to vary the ingredients innovatively, adding chopped nuts, seeds, bean and alfalfa sprouts, avocado.

Some examples: bread and butter, thin potato slices, then pieces of herring and a dab of sour cream.

Bread and anchovy butter, a slice of tomato, a round of hard-boiled egg and a puff of parsley.

Bread and butter, chopped egg white on half the bread, chopped egg yolk on the other and, crossing them, anchovy strips.

Bread and mustard butter, sliced pâté, thin-sliced pickles.

Bread and butter, sliced Danish cheese and apple.

Bread and butter, smoked salmon, dill and a lemon twist.

And some more complex compositions:

267

Bread and butter, lettuce, turkey slice, beet salad, orange twist, prune. *(Fig. 266)*

Bread and butter, lettuce, salmon salad, hard-boiled egg and tomato wedges and a small slice of salmon. *(Fig. 267)*

Bread and butter, lettuce, ham salad, apple-and-beet salad, two apple wedges, walnut. *(Fig. 268)*

When you arrange Scandinavian sandwiches on a plate, you lay them in very orderly rows, their sides touching or nearly touching. Everything should be flat. Try to have contrasting sandwiches next to one another. It is very common to see these sandwiches put out on the smorgasbord table on large breadboards.

268

Sandwich Platters

When making sandwich platters, it's a good idea to have the fillings matched with the bread. All the egg salad should be on rye, and all the tuna on white. That way, everyone knows what he is getting without having to peek.

Cut the sandwiches in half on the diagonal, forming triangles. Make stripes across the short axis of a long plate, the sandwiches overlapping, with one stripe of one kind of sandwich going up and the second stripe of the other kind of sandwich going down. (You can alternate sandwiches instead of stripes, but that arrangement gets easily messed up when guests pick up the sandwiches.)

On a round platter, make rings of sandwich halves. Let the inner ring overlap in a clockwise direction, and the next ring overlap going counterclockwise, and so forth. Put greens between the rings and, possibly, olives and cherry tomatoes on the greens.

If you are using dark bread for one sandwich and light bread for the other, arrange a checkerboard of sandwiches on a square or rectangular platter. Make a border of parsley around the outside of the platter.

To a platter of uncut or simply cut sandwiches, add a few in fancy shapes. Cut them with cookie cutters or roll soft sliced bread around fillings. If, for example, you made a checkerboard of uncut squares of black and white bread, you could have a border of overlapping sandwich triangles, made by cutting the bread in four pieces on the diagonal. Dot greens between the points of the triangles.

And, of course, you can serve a do-it-yourself sandwich bar. Have a basket of bread or rolls, with platters of meat and bowls of fillings. Put out smaller bowls of lettuce, sliced tomatoes and cucumber, and several pots of mustard and dishes of mayonnaise.

Sausages

Sausage is seasoned ground pork. Sausages are something else again, more than two hundred mixtures of ground meat—usually, but by no means always, pork—that are formed into links, patties and long tubes.

There are fresh sausages, such as boudin noir, or blood sausage. There are smoked sausages, our familiar frankfurters and bologna, which are processed so that they need not be cooked to be safe to eat (although an uncooked kosher frank is hardly the acme of fine eating). And there are dried sausages such as chorizos, pepperoni and cervelat.

In the days before refrigeration, curing and drying meat made it last throughout the year, from one slaughtering season to another. That's why nearly every country in the world outside of the Orient has some form of sausage. We are lucky to get as many as we do in America.

We get Spanish chorizos, made of ground pork heavily seasoned with paprika. We get dried Italian pepperoni, Genoa salami and cotechino, and fresh Italian sweet and hot sausages. We get spicy Polish kielbasa in lengths or rings, and all the German wursts, like weisswurst and bockwurst, made of veal and seasoned with chopped chives. We get fresh French garlic sausage. We even get English bangers, bland links that the English wrap in pastry to make sausage rolls or cover with Yorkshire pudding batter to make the wonderfully named toad-in-the-hole.

Fresh Sausage

Fresh sausage must be thoroughly cooked before it is eaten. It is boiled, sautéed or broiled. Bulk sausage meat is formed into patties or links, then fried. A dusting of flour before it is fried will give it a good brown coating. Chopped parsley improves all cooked sausage meat.

Breakfast sausages go with scrambled eggs, with french toast and waffles. Serve the links all in a heap, with sprigs of parsley sticking into the heap. Don't try to make a design with the dark little arcs. It's much better to have a pile of sausages in the middle of the plate and tiles of french toast arranged around it.

Fresh sausage is also served with potatoes (especially in England, where everything is served with potatoes), with prunes, sauerkraut and lentils. Use it to stuff baked apples. When you use it to make a sausage dressing for a turkey, drape the turkey with other sausages: a chain of small links, crab apples and watercress.

Broil or grill fresh Italian sweet or hot sausages. Serve them on split hero rolls, garnished with sautéed red and green pepper.

Smoked and Dried Sausages

Serve smoked and dried sausage on a buffet table or as an antipasto platter before an Italian dinner. It should never be sliced before it is used. Put several varieties on a wooden board. Cut one or two thin slices from each sausage, leaving the rest whole. Have dark bread or wheaten crackers, with a pot of imported mustard and a dish of pickles nearby.

Special Dishes

There are several special dishes that use sausage as a major ingredient. One is sausage baked in brioche dough, an elevated version of the aforementioned English sausage rolls. Another is cassoulet, a stew of pork, lamb shoulder, white beans and garlic sausage baked in layers. Paella, the Spanish rice dish; Cuban beef roast stuffed with chorizos, called carne mechada; the grand Italian mixed boiled meat, or bollito misto. Nor should we forget pepperoni pizza.

Many countries have a version of sausage with cabbage or sauerkraut, such as the Italian sausage with red cabbage. Of these, the greatest is probably the Alsatian choucroute garnie, in which spareribs, frankfurters, garlic sausage and bacon are cooked with sauerkraut, then served with boiled potatoes and white wine. The choucroute is usually spooned from the heavy crock in which it bakes. But there is a gala method of presenting it in a warming dish with an open bottle of champagne stuck into the center of the cooked meat and cabbage. As the champagne is heated, it begins to foam, spilling wine all through the choucroute garnie. Not, probably, something you'll be doing at home except on very special occasions.

Scallions

Scallions are white onions that are harvested while they are young. Try to buy scallions before the white part has had time to develop a bulb shape, when the end is thin and the leaves dark green and firm. Wrap them in paper towels and store them in the refrigerator. Before you cook them, trim off the root end, the outer layer of skin and most of the greens.

Scallions can be cooked. They are braised, creamed or simmered in broth and served in a vinaigrette sauce with vegetables a la Grecque. We add them to soups and stews and stir-fries. We fry the white part of chopped scallions with hash brown potatoes, adding the chopped greens for the last minute of cooking to preserve their color. But despite their strong flavor, scallions are primarily used as very edible garnishes.

Chopped Scallions

The Chinese have a trick for mincing scallions. Since the white globe end tends to be slippery, they flatten it with one whack of the cleaver. You can do the same with the side of a chef's knife. Then go chopping down the length of the vegetable.

Raw chopped scallions make a wonderful garnish for salads—especially tomato salads—for cottage cheese and for scrambled eggs. Sprinkle them on soups, especially clear broths, rich red tomato bisque or white cream soup.

Scallion Flowers and Brushes

Choose scallions with well-developed bulbs for making flowers. Make chrysanthemums by cutting 3-inch lengths, cutting off the roots straight across, then slicing into the white end in a checkerboard pattern. Allow the flower to open in ice water. Tuck these between the legs and body of a roast chicken or add them to a vegetable arrangement.

Scallion brushes are made by cutting off the scallion to a 3-inch length, then slicing into both ends several times, making many thin

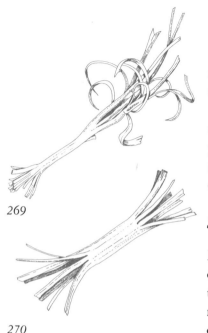

269

270

slivers. Drop them into ice water to curl. The degree of curl depends on the amount of scallion left unfringed in the center. Serve the brushes raw or stir-fry them with other vegetables. To garnish a roast, sauté scallion brushes with cherry tomatoes and mushroom caps, and arrange them around the meat. *(Fig. 269)*

Use 2-inch scallion brushes, frayed on one end, to cover the ends of anything that needs finishing. Since radish leaves wilt instantly, you might want to try cutting off all but ¾-inch stems of whole radishes, then slipping fringed scallion brushes over them to make decorative artificial stems. *(Fig. 270)*

Scallion Greens

In classic French presentation, scallion greens are used like ribbons in decorating. Once they have been blanched to remove their sharp taste, they are quite malleable. Slit them lengthwise to cut them into slim ribbons. Then bend them to form the stems and leaves of a floral design or lay them crisscross down the side of a fish. Use malleable scallion greens to outline the shape of a vegetable mold.

Scallops

In Europe you can buy scallops in their shells. Here, we buy them already shelled, fresh and smelling sweetly of the sea. It's convenient, but we lose both the shells for future cooking and the tiny pink roe, which is considered a delicacy.

Buy tiny pinkish-white bay scallops, which are most tender, or the large white sea scallops, which are firm. However you buy them, cook them quickly, or they will toughen.

Scallops are white and shiny and flat. In addition, they tend to roll all over the plate. Think of contrast when you make up a plate holding scallops. Don't use potato balls, use fried shoestring potatoes. Not lima beans, but broccoli and sliced tomatoes. Not white rice, but rice sparkling with chopped parsley or pimiento. Serve the scallops on a bed of dark-green spinach or on steamed yellow squash. Use lots of parsley, either in bushy bunches or chopped.

Scallops' whiteness and cube shape make them a natural food for skewering. The other foods on the skewer should be brightly colored.

For example, on a skewer of scallops  , use squares of green pepper and cherry tomatoes , and top with a large piece of lemon .

Push the scallops off the skewer onto a bed of yellow rice.

Seviche, the South American method of cooking by marinating in lime juice, is often done with scallops. Once the fish is done—that is, once it has lost its transparency and turned as opaque and white as if it had been steamed—garnish it with sliced lime and chopped chives, or with avocado and chopped pimiento.

Scallop shells are one of the great everlasting designs of nature, one of the few from food that have gone over into architecture and textiles. Since you can't buy them with the scallops, buy scallop shells in a housewares department. Fill them with any kind of fish in a sauce: tuna Provençal, crab Maryland, curried shrimp.

Shortcake

The quintessential American dessert. We all eat strawberry short-cake. But strawberry-and-blueberry shortcake is a red-white-and-blue Fourth of July treat. And, as they come into season, serve raspberry, gooseberry, peach, nectarine shortcakes as well.

Keep it homey: a split biscuit, a heap of sugared strawberries, some cream whipped so that it barely holds its shape. For a real farm look, serve it in a shallow soup bowl, and provide both a fork and a soup spoon. Some add a pitcher of heavy cream.

For a slightly party presentation, cut out the biscuits in two different sizes, 3 inches and 4 inches in diameter. Bake them one on top of the other, then split them apart and fill with the fruit.

A really formal look comes when you place biscuit halves side by side on a pool of pureed fruit. Spoon a blob of firmly whipped cream where the biscuits meet. Then garnish each of the split biscuits with fresh fruit, placing three or four whole berries or arcs of peach on either side of the whipped cream. *(Fig. 272)*

Simple or formal, you can enliven the plate by sprinkling dark blueberries over everything.

Shrimp

Shrimp is the most popular fish food in America. Heated in gumbos, chilled in cocktails, deep fried and sautéed in garlic butter, these small arched shellfish are enjoyed by people who wouldn't eat any other fish.

They come in varying sizes, from tiny Maine and California shrimp to huge prawns that go two or three to a serving. They are gray-green when raw, turn pinky-white when they are cooked.

Buy shrimp from a dealer you know. Buy them firm and dry. They come raw and cooked, in and out of the shell. It makes most sense to buy them raw in the shell. Precooked shrimp is usually rubbery, and shelled shrimp means that you've paid someone else to do a very easy job. Besides, many people believe that shrimp cooked in its shell has more flavor than shrimp cooked nude.

(Frozen shrimp is a definite second best. Canned shrimp is awful.)

To peel and clean shrimp, cut through the arched surface with kitchen shears, and take out the black sand vein. This is not a matter of hygiene but of aesthetics. It won't harm you, but most people prefer the clean look of deveined shrimp.

To keep a shrimp from curling while cooking, run a toothpick lengthwise through its body. *(Fig. 273)*

To butterfly a shrimp for broiling and frying, you have to cut it through what seems like the wrong surface. Peel the shrimp, leaving the tail feathers intact. Then cut through the *inner* curve, not the surface from which you took the sand vein. Leave the two arcs attached for just ½ inch near the tail. Flatten it out into a butterfly shape. Butterflying is best done on very large shrimp. *(Fig. 274)*

Appetizers

If shrimp is our most popular fish, then shrimp cocktail is the most popular way of serving shrimp. You can serve it in the small glass bowls that sit on beds of ice in larger bowls, if you can find them. (You can probably get them from a restaurant-supply house.) But

240

don't worry. As a substitute, take a red-wine or flat champagne glass. Put the cocktail sauce in the bottom of the glass, and hook five shrimp around the rim.

Or use a flat plate. Put the sauce on the plate, or spoon it into half a lemon or lime, into the hollowed end of a cucumber or in a shot glass. Then arrange the plate. Put the sauce in the center or off-center. Place the shrimp around it, tails pointing toward the outer rim of the plate. Use more or fewer shrimp, depending on their size and your budget.

If it's fewer shrimp, fill in the spaces between them with thin strips of zucchini, cucumber or scallions. Cold mussels make an even better contrast.

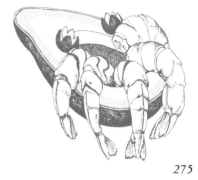

275

Serve cold cooked shrimp cocktail hooked over the edge of a large flat shell, such as a scallop shell, with the sauce pooled in the cup of the shell or served separately in a small glass.

Or make it in half a melon or avocado, with the sauce in the hollow, the shrimp hooked on the meat and radish flowers used as a garnish. *(Fig. 275)*

Other Presentations

Shrimp cooked in sauces should be served on beds of yellow or red rice or of white rice with lots of chopped parsley. Use brightly colored plates.

Serve a large bowl of shrimp boiled in their shells in a peppery broth. Each diner gets a pot of garlic butter, lots of crusty bread and a good-sized napkin. Then he peels and dips his own shrimp.

Prop a few broiled butterflied shrimp on a cucumber cup that you have filled with cold curried mayonnaise. Garnish with carved radishes.

Make a crown of fried shrimp. Around a central core of saffron rice, stand three jumbo fried shrimp, butterflied, with their tails in the air. Garnish with cherry tomatoes.

Prepare huge shrimp on skewers. Combine with bits of broccoli, cubes of parboiled sweet potatoes and red pepper squares, and cook it over charcoal.

Garnishes

Whenever you buy fish, buy a few shrimp to add to them as a garnish. One or two shrimp make a very austere, very Japanese garnish for a large fish. Try one made by fitting two shrimp into one another and holding them in place with a toothpick. Dip them in batter and cook them together. Stick a stem of parsley between them. *(Fig. 276)*

276

Another garnish from the Japanese is a cooked butterflied shrimp, slitted in the center of its meat, with the tail run through the slit. *(Fig. 277)*

On a plate of fish, make a garnish of two boiled shrimp arching away from each other, with a mussel shell in between them. Or put a shrimp on a round crouton and add a tuft of dill. Or add a dried prune to the shrimp and serve with fish and yellow rice.

277

Smoked Salmon

Smoked salmon is sold in thin, thin slices that are pale bright pink with a fresh, slightly sea-like odor. The best comes from Nova Scotia and from Scotland. Lox, which is heavily salted, is served differently from smoked salmon, which is always a very elegant food.

It's expensive. Therefore, by reverse snobbery, it must never look skimpy. You are permitted to serve too few potatoes, but never just a little bit of smoked salmon.

For an individual appetizer serving, use a smallish dessert plate. Cover it to the edges with strips of smoked salmon. Garnish with a lemon half, its edges zigzagged, with capers and a spray of dill. Add triangles of buttered brown bread, and have a pepper mill close at hand.

For dramatic color, decorate a plate of smoked salmon with two shiny black mussels and a lemon wedge.

To make the serving platter of salmon look full to bursting, invert a saucer on it. Cover the saucer with overlapping slices of fish, and it will look like a mound. Sneaky.

Smoked salmon makes beautiful canapés on squares of dense dark bread. Make a checkerboard, using alternating squares of smoked salmon and black caviar.

If you have just a little bit of salmon left over, use it in an omelet, which you should flavor with dill.

Soufflés

Soufflés are mixtures of cream sauce and a sweet or savory food that are miraculously enlarged by the action of beaten egg whites. They come in all varieties, from simple cheese to baroque dessert soufflés like the soufflé Rothschild. They are tall, puffy, golden-brown. And the best-looking soufflé is always the tallest.

The secret of the height is in the egg whites. The higher and firmer they rise, the higher and firmer your soufflé will be. Three rules apply. Have the egg whites at room temperature before you beat them. Make sure that there is not a trace of grease, not a speck of egg yolk in the whites. And finally, as you beat them, add a pinch of cream of tartar to the whites just when they reach the foamy stage. This will help them rise higher and hold their elevation longer.

You can increase the illusion of height by optical tricks. Incise a trench with your forefinger or the tip of a teaspoon 1½ inches in from the outside of the soufflé. Draw this circle on the top just before you put the mixture in the oven. The central plateau will rise higher than the part that surrounds it and will look like the tower on a skyscraper.

Another trick is to cook your mixture in a transparent glass dish. The eye takes in the *whole* height, not just the upper two inches of the soufflé, and it makes a difference.

For a very special look, make a two-layered soufflé in a glass soufflé dish. We did one with cheese on the bottom and spinach over it. It was both beautiful and delicious, although the cheese mixture didn't rise as much as it would have had it been uncovered.

Serving the Soufflé

Every portion should include some of the crust and some of the creamy interior of the soufflé. But a portion of soufflé is shapeless and

243

looks best when it has something hard-edged along with it. Use green pepper rings rather than canned asparagus with cheese soufflés, bacon strips and fried apple rings rather than applesauce with ham soufflés, mussels in their shells with fish soufflés, broccoli flowerets with pale vegetable soufflés.

If you're serving a sauce with the soufflé, remember to put it down on the plate first. First sauce, then soufflé, then garnish. Try chocolate sauce under a Grand Marnier soufflé, with a garnish of chocolate curls. Or tomato sauce under a spinach soufflé, with a garnish of scallion brushes.

Individual soufflés can be made in any container. The French put seafood mixtures on fish fillets or in scallop shells. Try making cheese soufflés in tomato shells and dessert soufflés in half grapefruits. The mixture doesn't rise as high as it might in a straight-sided dish, but you'll still get the required "ah!" of admiration.

Cold Soufflés

They aren't really soufflés at all, just molded desserts and, occasionally, luncheon foods that try to copy the look. You simulate the rising by tying a band of wax paper or foil around the dish, standing two inches above the rim. Pour in the mixture, let it set and remove the collar.

When it's partially chilled, sprinkle the top of the soufflé with finely chopped nuts, chocolate sprinkles, cookie crumbs or thin lemon slices. Or drizzle sauce along the edge and let it run down the sides. Because there's nothing to rise, you won't have to worry about weighing it down.

Soups

Soup rises and falls in popularity. Yesterday, it seemed too filling, too much food for a population living on Perrier water and lime. Now, hot hearty soups are coming back into style as the country learns to live with lowered thermostats.

Soup can be anything from a hearty peasant meal to a highly

elegant refined first course. Visually, they fall into four categories. There are clear soups, opaque soups, lumpy soups and jellied soups. The categories have nothing to do with flavor. You can, for example, have fish soups in all four forms: clear clam broth, creamy pink shrimp bisque, chock-full crab gumbo and jellied tomato-clam aspic.

Clear Soups

Clear soups include chicken, fish and beef consommés, miso and vegetable and mushroom broths. We serve them in cups with handles, set on small plates. Put them in white china to show off their clarity. Even better, put them in black bowls. In a glass bowl, clear broth looks delicate, insubstantial.

Because they are transparent, clear soups are garnished both inside and out. Some things sink to the bottom, while others float on the top. Cross two snow peas on the bottom of a cup of chicken broth. Float a cube of tofu on the top. Or with a flower-shaped aspic cutter, cut out the red skin of a radish and float this in the soup along with a few slivers of the white of the radish and a few chopped scallion greens. Take care not to add so many garnishes that they begin to look like part of the soup. At some point, vegetable garnishes become vegetable soup.

Garnishes for clear soups should stay light. They would include thin lemon slices, minced herbs or herb sprays, bean sprouts, julienned meat and vegetables, finely sliced scallion rings.

Opaque Soups

Opaque soups can be very refined, like crab bisque, or very hearty and simple, like leek and potato soup. They can be served cold as well as hot: a chilled puree of broccoli is a summer opaque soup. Garnish them on the top, or mix two different-colored soups for a marbled effect. Serve them in large flat bowls with wide rims, and garnish them with things that float on the top, such as sausage or egg slices, croutons, sour cream bristling with chopped dill, chunks of ham, nuts or pretzels.

Lumpy Soups

These are chowders and gumbos, minestrone, lentil soup, mushroom-barley and cabbage soup. They can't take too much garnishing, since they're already full of stuff. You could hold back one of the elements of the soup and float it on top, something like a whole shrimp or some tomato slices. Stick a skewer of vegetables into a bowl of vegetable soup. Float a slice of bread sprinkled with cheese on bean soup. Spoon white rice onto black bean soup. Serve lumpy soups in heavy earthenware bowls or in mugs.

Jellied Soups

We serve these in the summer, cool jellied tomato bouillon or beet consommé. If you don't cut them into cubes, they look like dessert. Serve jellied soups in unusual containers: over ice, as you would a shrimp cocktail, in hollowed-out oranges, melon and avocado, in large wineglasses. Garnish them with thin lemon and orange slices, with sprays of dill, mint leaves, and with creamy things like whipped cream, aioli, yogurt or sour cream. A dish of brilliantly red tomato aspic is smashing with a spoonful of black caviar.

Garnishes

There are hundreds of garnishes to choose from once you have the general principles in mind.

Creams	Meat
sour cream, yogurt, crème fraîche, whipped cream	tiny meatballs
(any of these, mixed with horseradish, grated cucumber, caviar, ginger, parsley, dill)	frankfurter or sausage slices
	chopped bacon
	thin strips of ham, tongue, chicken
aioli	diced ham
tofu	skewers of chicken livers

Grains

rice, barley, wheat berries
noodles
thinly sliced crepes
dumplings, matzo balls, spaetzle
gnocchi
popcorn

Greens

dill, mint, watercress, parsley,
    Italian parsley, basil
chives, scallions
sprouts
lemon or toast slices dipped in
    parsley

Nuts

pecan or walnut halves
salted peanuts
chopped blanched almonds
pistachios
coconut
chestnut puree
water chestnuts

Fish

shrimp, whole or chopped
clams, oysters
anchovies on toast
fish dumplings

Fruit

lemon, orange slices
lemon peel shredded or tied into
    knots
avocado
banana on curried soup,
    black bean soup
tomato slices sprinkled with herbs

Bread

toast stars, fingers, triangles
cubed croutons
thick slices of french bread
    sprinkled with cheese
crackers, animal crackers
pretzels

Egg

poached egg
hard-boiled egg slices with herbs
sieved hard-boiled egg
egg drop
thinly sliced omelet
custard cut into cubes

Vegetables, by color

red:
beets, red pepper, pimiento,
    tomato, red cabbage, radishes,
    red onion
green:
asparagus, Brussels sprouts,
    green pepper, shredded lettuce,
    spinach, scallion tops, broccoli,
    peas
white:
celery, onion, mushroom,
    potato, scallions
yellow:
turnip, carrot, yam

Etcetera

cranberries
dabs of jelly
sliced pickle
kumquats
ginger
whole peppercorns
cinnamon sticks

Mixed Vegetable Garnishes

Vegetable garnishes benefit from being combined. Use two or three elements. More than that, and you begin to get vegetable soup.

Mix different-colored vegetables cut in the same fashion, or float one vegetable on another. The garnishes that float best are thin and broad. Use a lettuce leaf rather than a carrot cube. Use them to support a second or third garnish. You may make a mess when you first try to float a garnish on the surface of the soup. Here's how it's done. Put the cucumber slice on a fork. Place it gently on the soup, trying not to break the surface tension. Continue down with the fork, leaving the cucumber floating on top.

Here are some suggestions for mixed vegetable garnishes.

A raft or a disk of yellow squash holding a smaller circle of red pepper. Garnish with four Italian parsley leaves. *(Fig. 278)*

Chop some scallions. Slice radishes thin, cutting notches in the skin so that the slices look like flowers. On a clear soup, float two radish flowers, and sprinkle scallion bits around them.

Cut mushrooms in profile, very thinly. Float them, carrying minute dabs of sour cream, on the surface of an opaque soup.

Make a lettuce fan by cutting a triangle of lettuce nearly as large as the soup bowl. Cut strips from the wide end to the opposite point, leaving the point intact. Lay it very carefully on the soup, and float some tiny peas on it. *(Fig. 279)*

278

To a clear tomato soup, add a skewer of black olive, mushroom and basil.

Self-service Garnishes

Some soups are served with a choice of garnishes that the diner adds by himself. Gazpacho, the cold vegetable soup, comes with chopped onion, green pepper, celery and cucumber.

You can also serve garnishes with curry-flavored soups, such as Mulligatawny or lightly curried vegetable purees. Provide diners with bowls of coconut, peanuts, raisins, chutney and other illegitimate but delicious accompaniments to an Indian dinner.

279

248

Serve black bean soup with bowls of chopped parsley, hard-boiled egg, cooked rice and lemon slices.

Marbling Opaque Soups

Mix thick smooth soups in a marbled design, garnishing a soup with another soup. Make a pattern on thick pea soup with cream of tomato, drizzling a stream of tomato from the tip of a spoon. Try a zigzag pattern, a coil or a flower, with the tip of the spoon barely touching the surface of the soup.

Find a dessert plate that will fit across the diameter of your soup bowl. Stand it on end across the bowl. Pour potato soup on one side and cream of asparagus on the other. Lift out the plate, and float slices of cucumber and chopped red pepper to cover the bordering line.

If you want to bother with three soups, you can make a Mark Rothko painting in a soup bowl. Onto a base of potato soup, pour stripes in two different colors. For example, two of green, with one of red between them. They are easily put into place with a large soup spoon. If you don't want to make different soups, color portions of the potato soup with beet juice or tomato puree, or pureed spinach and parsley.

Spinach

Healthy spinach is a good dark green, a colorful alternative to pale iceberg and Boston lettuces. It is available year-round. Try to buy loose spinach with tender dark-green leaves. The see-through bags of prewashed spinach that are available in supermarkets often contain damaged leaves, and the moisture in them sometimes turns the spinach slimy.

Frozen spinach is a good alternative to fresh. Canned spinach is an emergency ration at best.

Before you serve fresh spinach, wash it well in lukewarm water. Although spinach is now marketed in a cleaner state than in past years, it may still have a lot of grit in the leaves, especially if you buy fresh farmstand spinach. Pull off the larger stems. Dry the greens in a salad spinner or basket, or between paper towels.

249

Spinach Salad

Instead of slicing the mushrooms for a spinach salad, fill the bowl with greens and then stand whole mushrooms on it, to look as though they were growing on the leafy base. Scatter crumbled cooked bacon among them.

Or forget the mushrooms and bacon. Instead, scatter orange sections and chopped radishes on spinach salad.

Or make a composed salad plate. Set a cluster of carved radishes surrounded by a ring of orange slices on a bed of dark-green spinach.

Garnish spinach salad with cauliflower and cherry tomatoes, or with avocado and sections of hard-boiled egg. Line a glass bowl with pale endive or leaf lettuce. Then fill it with shredded spinach leaves.

Cooked Spinach

To retain the dark-green color of fresh spinach, cook it briefly. Steam it in the moisture that clings to its leaves, or sauté it briefly in butter or oil. Spinach decreases dramatically in bulk as it cooks. One moment, you can't get it into the pot, and the next, you have a dark-green layer on the bottom.

Lemon juice bleaches the color of spinach. So does cooking in aluminum utensils. Use stainless steel or enameled steel for spinach.

Florentine, on menus, means cooked with spinach. The many dishes with this name indicate how well the dark green goes with other foods: with fish and eggs, with sliced tomatoes, with cheese sauces and other vegetables.

Line a serving dish with endive. Then spoon cooked spinach into the center, and garnish it with three cherry tomatoes.

Put the spinach in a bowl. Make a border around the edges with hard-boiled egg sections and cherry tomatoes. Or make a pinwheel in the center of avocado and mandarin orange sections.

In the center of a dish of cooked spinach, stand a single orange twist (as on a Danish open-faced sandwich).

Creamed Spinach

Creamed spinach is made by mixing pureed cooked spinach with cream sauce, heavy cream or, sometimes, cheese. It tastes voluptuous and has a rich color, paler than leaf spinach. The problem is how to anchor it. Put creamed spinach in a bowl and top it with a fried crouton: a nicely browned toast star sprinkled with sieved hard-boiled egg yolk or parsley and chopped egg white.

Serve pale creamed spinach in a bowl lined with dark-green leaf spinach.

Serve creamed spinach in a scooped-out tomato or an orange half. Try a small baked potato shell. Spoon the spinach into a red pepper case, then top it with a cherry tomato flower or a black olive.

Use creamed spinach as though it were a sauce, to make a background for another food. Make a layer of creamed spinach on the plate, and over it, spoon lightly cooked carrots or summer squash.

Squash (Summer Squash). *See* ZUCCHINI

Squash, Winter

Winter squash is more interesting visually than gastronomically. Unlike immature, soft-skinned summer squashes such as zucchini, winter squashes have firm hard rinds and strong autumnal colors. Small green acorn is, in fact, acorn shaped. Buttercup or turban squash has a cap on it. Butternut looks like a long tan pear. And big Hubbards come green and gold, with lots of curves, pleats and bulges.

They all taste somewhat alike—bland and sweet—and are cooked by similar methods. Squash is baked or steamed, either in the shell or cut into chunks. Because the shell is so attractive, it is preferable to serve in the shell. A peeled chunk of squash looks not unlike a chunk of potato or turnip. For making purees, of course, peeling and chunking is as good a method as any.

251

280

Small squashes are baked or steamed whole, then served like baked potatoes. Slice off the tops and add some butter when they are done.

Medium-sized squashes can be cut in half horizontally before they are baked. That way, the scalloped shape and bright color will show. They make excellent containers for stuffing. Fill half an acorn squash with cooked apple slices or with hot applesauce. Fill a turban squash with corned beef hash, sausage or creamed chicken. Set the "turban" top nearby. (See illustration, CONTAINERS MADE FROM FOOD, page 102.)

Fill squash with creamed spinach, and garnish with hard-boiled egg wedges. Fill with creamed pearl onions, and garnish with green pepper rings and parsley. Fill a small squash with corn and garnish with tomato wedges.

When you cut the squash in half horizontally, you can decorate its surface. Take a lemon stripper and remove a narrow band of skin from each pleat, starting at the bottom and stopping ½ inch away from the cut edge. *(Fig. 280)*

Large squashes, such as Hubbards, don't go one to a customer. They have to be cut and portioned out into individual servings, either before or after they are cooked.

Cut an uncooked large squash in half horizontally and, then cut down between the scallops to make flower petals. As it bakes, the squash will start to separate. It's nice for a vegetarian main course, with a heap of pilaf and vegetables in the center.

Slice a large squash between the pleats. Bake the wedges separately, and serve them on a platter in a sunburst of arcs. Between the arcs, place peeled orange sections, and in the center of the design, a bunch of purple grapes on a bed of watercress. Or set piles of sausages between the arcs, and a bunch of Italian parsley and nuts in the center of the platter.

Decorate the skin of a wedge of squash. Cut strips in it with the lemon stripper. Lay it on its side and, in the arc, place overlapping slices of tomato or a heap of Brussels sprouts.

Squash as Decoration

Left whole, winter squashes make a strong centerpiece. Arrange them right on the table. Have at least three different varieties—a Hubbard in the middle, flanked with an acorn and turban squash and several slim butternuts—and surround them with grapes, nuts and chrysanthemums.

Use a whole uncooked squash to hold a main course of pilaf or stew. When it's filled, replace the lid, slightly askew. Squash can serve as an original salad bowl. Place a glass bowl in the opening. Then fill with rice salad studded with chunks of cooked squash, tomato and parsley. Or put in a tossed green salad or a dip.

Steaks and Chops

It's the most familiar dinner plate in America: a steak or a chop and "something else." The "something else" can be as simple as a baked potato or as diverse as an assortment of cooked vegetables. It can be braised pork chops with gravy for a hearty midday farm meal or shell steaks and fried onions at a steak house. In any case, it starts with the meat: tender cuts from the rib and loin sections of beef, lamb, veal or pork, that are either broiled, grilled or panfried.

Make a bridge between the meat and the plate by adding a crouton. Trim the crusts from a slice of day-old bread. Then dry it in the oven or sauté it in clarified butter until it is golden. It will catch the juices from the meat.

Or place the meat on the plate on a bed of vegetables or a pool of sauce. Sautéed onions make a logical bed for beef. If you're serving a brown sauce with the steak, lay a film of it on a warm plate. Lay down the meat, and garnish with something of contrasting texture: turnip and carrot ovals, parsley, shredded zucchini.

Arrangement

If you put the meat across the center of the plate, you can garnish it on both sides. Put down a fat veal chop, and, on either flank, arrange

281

282

283

a wedge of tomato with string beans and watercress. *(Fig. 281)*

Balance one garnish with another—put a mound of shredded beets on one side of a steak and pearl onions on the other.

Arrange two rib chops with their long bones forming an X, like crossed swords. The meat should go to the outside of the X. Then fill in the spaces. Put a bunch of watercress between the end bones, a broiled tomato between the eyes of meat and shoestring potatoes to both sides. *(Fig. 282)*

Most often, however, the meat goes on one half of the plate and the "something else" on the other half. If it's just a baked potato, soften the arrangement and make a bridge between them with greens and cherry tomatoes.

Put down the meat and outline its greater curve with a garnish. Do an *abab* pattern with tomatoes and zucchini or with stewed prunes and apples (for pork). Make an *abcabc* pattern alongside a shell steak with turnips, carrots and potatoes carved into the shape of olives.

Make a radiating arrangement of Chinese pea pods and cherry tomatoes to one side of the chop, and to the other, sliced potatoes. *(Fig. 283)*

Do a heap of pilaf or alfalfa sprouts for textural variety. Or an *abab* fan of pear sections and tomato slices, with parsley at each end. Or a pile of Brussels sprouts, every fourth one stuffed with a cherry tomato.

For a strong look, serve crossed skewers alongside the meat. Weave strips of bacon onto the skewers. Cook, then garnish with watercress and cherry tomatoes. Or else do vegetable skewers with mushrooms and zucchini (MZZZ), cherry tomatoes and zucchini (ZTZ) or zucchini and yellow squash (ZYZ). Watercress here and there on the skewer will soften its strictness.

To arrange a platter of chops, set the meat to one side, with their long bones pointing in. On the other half of the platter goes a bed of vegetables and potatoes, with a border of cress down the center.

In the West, they serve steaks and chops on sizzling platters—pewter or aluminum alloy plates on wooden trenchers. The metal plate gets heated in the oven, and the meat should be marked with stripes from the barbecue.

You can broil thin lamb chops in a shallow metal serving pan,

254

then stick triangular croutons around the border of the pan.

Or you could broil a sirloin steak, place it on a wooden carving board and surround it with areas of potatoes, lightly cooked broccoli, sautéed mushrooms and cherry tomatoes. This was once a cliché service for steak, usually involving sculptured borders of duchesse potatoes. But the look is updated when you use areas of beautifully cooked seasonal vegetables that look as though they are truly meant to be eaten.

Stew

There are hundreds of dishes that we call stew, dishes as varied as blanquette de veau, goulash, boeuf Bourguignonne, Irish stew, olla podrida. But to the eye, there is only one dish called a stew, and its main qualities are that it is lumpy and it is one color—usually brown.

You can improve its looks. Is it not brown enough? Sauté some sliced onions in butter until they are nearly black. Pour them into the stew and let the mixture cook for a while (only, of course, if the onion flavor will be compatible). The caramelized sugar in the onions will darken the broth.

Is the broth watery? Make a beurre manié by rubbing together a tablespoon of butter and an equal quantity of flour. Roll the paste into pellets and add them, one at a time, to the simmering liquid in the pot until you have achieved the thickness you want.

Is the color monotonous? Parboil some nicely cut turnips, carrots and celery and add them to the stew for the last five minutes it cooks. The colored vegetables will stand out against the brown background.

We usually bring stew to the table in the pot in which it was cooked. There is a wonderful moment when you lift the lid, and the fragrance escapes. Choose beautiful casseroles. Remember that most stews are brown, so choose a red or yellow enameled-steel pot. Look for earthenware made by potters. It's a wonderful cooking material for slow-cooking stews. There's no excuse for cooking and serving in aluminum when there are so many brilliantly colored casseroles on the market.

But if you do cook in aluminum, you will want to serve the stew

255

on a platter rather than in the pot. It's a good idea to have it rather dry, draining off some of the gravy and serving it on the side in a pitcher or a sauceboat. Frame the stew with a ring of parsley-dotted rice or spaetzle. Make a border with triangular croutons dipped in chopped parsley.

Parsley is the great adornment for stew. Put a border around the edges of the stew in a casserole. Sprinkle it over the stew on a serving platter. Add cherry tomatoes for color, too.

Sugar

There are many kinds of sugar in the markets, most of them made from sugarcane and sugar beets. We are familiar with granulated, powdered, brown and maple sugars. Liquid corn syrup, maple syrup, honey and molasses are still other forms of sugar. Most kitchens, however, contain three common sugars: granulated, for sweetening; powdered, for making icings; and brown, for sweetening with a caramel flavor.

Sugar adds not only sweetness but color to food. It's the sugar in dough that produces a golden-brown crust. Sugar turns brown when it cooks. First it liquefies, then it becomes chewy and, finally, hard. This is the basis for caramel and for most candies. Brown sugar, in fact, is usually granulated sugar with some caramel coloring—that is, cooked sugar—added to it.

Cooked sugar, stored as liquid caramel, can be used to color gravy. The sweetening power is diminished or destroyed entirely by the high heat. Melt a cup of sugar in a pan. Let cool. Then add, very gradually, a cup of water. Stir it over a low flame until the dark-brown sugar becomes a thin liquid. This can be stored in a covered container and added to pale gravies.

Crème brulée is a custard that is coated with brown sugar, then placed under the broiler so that the sugar melts and hardens on the top. You can make the brittle coating right on the chilled custard, or make it on buttered tinfoil. Let it cool, and slide it onto a custard or the top of a layer cake or crumble it on ice cream.

An easy trick for enlivening plain poached fruit is to cook some

256

sugar until it melts and turns light brown. Then drizzle the hot syrup in a spidery pattern over the baked apple or poached pear.

Powdered sugar makes a simple finish on plain cakes and cookies. Sprinkle confectioners' sugar through a strainer onto chocolate icing, or sift it through a doily on a cake. Dust it over waffles or french toast.

Pastry chefs make complicated shapes from sugar, including flowers, baskets and colored ribbons. The prettiest wedding cake we ever saw was topped with a red-and-white-striped ribbon bow that was made, amazingly, of sugar. Before you kick yourself for not being able to do this, you should know that such culinary extravagances generally look much better than they taste.

And what of sugar—plain sugar—the sugar that we spoon into our teacups and sprinkle on our oatmeal? Serve granulated sugar in a bowl. If you have cubes of sugar, be sure to supply tongs. Powdered sugar in a dredger is a nice addition to the breakfast table. In England, they offer Demerara sugar—colored crystals that look like shattered rock candy—with tea. You could serve rock candy instead of granulated sugar with tea or lemonade.

Tarts

A tart is different from a pie. It is made with a shortening-rich "short" dough rather than a flaky piecrust. It often has a layer of crème patissière, then raw or cooked fruit. It is finished with a currant or apricot glaze. And it never has a top crust.

Tarts are made in square, round or rectangular flan rings, inch-high outlines in tin that are placed on cookie sheets. When the tart is baked, you slide it off the cookie sheet onto a serving plate.

An open-faced fruit tart has a two-dimensional pattern whose success rests on the regularity with which the fruit is cut, the neatness of the arrangement and the color of the fruit and glaze. The first rule is to keep the design appropriate to the shape of the frame. A round tart, like a round cake, is most easily arranged with a radiating or concentric design.

For the radiating design, start with a central motif. If you're

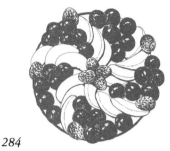

284

285

using sliced pears, then put a pear half, facedown, in the center. If you're using strawberry halves, make a mound of five whole berries in the middle. Then arrange the fruit in spokes coming from the center. For a mixed-fruit tart, make a star of sliced strawberries in the center. Then lay four or five lines of peach slices radiating from these, and fill in the spaces between them with purple grapes. *(Fig. 284)*

For a concentric design using strawberries, peach arcs and purple grapes, again place the berries in the center, circle them with grapes, then with a row of overlapping peach arcs. *(Fig. 285)*

For another concentric design, place half an apricot in the center. Make a ring of grapes around it, then more apricots, more grapes and so forth. At the very outer ring, place sprigs of mint between the grapes.

For a long rectangular apple tart, a bande de pommes, make sure that the fruit is very neatly cut, all the same size, then arrange two rows of fruit down the length of the tart. For a rectangular apricot tart you might put apricot halves down the center of the band, then place apricot wedges on either side, leaning against them.

For a square tart, either arrange several rows of fruit parallel to the sides, or else place the first row on the diagonal, and fill in on either side with rows that are parallel to the edges. Try to use contrasting colors. For example, bananas with apricots, pears with kiwi, apples with plums. Tartlets are best made very small, so that they hold only one or two bits of fruit.

Tea

Tea is so various a beverage that it seems silly to divide it into loose and tea-bag teas.

Better to say that there is green tea, dried right after picking, which becomes the delicate, slightly bitter brew of China and Japan; and also black tea, fermented before it is dried, which makes up the many rich, full-bodied teas that we drink in the West. That there is semi-fermented oolong, smoky Lapsang souchong, perfumed jasmine and blended Irish and English breakfast tea. But the fact remains that

258

for purposes of service and presentation, there are two kinds of tea: loose and in tea bags.

Loose tea should be made in a warmed earthenware or china pot. It should steep for 5 minutes. Then it gets a stir and is poured into the cup through a tea strainer.

As for tea-bag tea, the great concern is what to do with the bag. Before it's used, it has all the charm and style of a paper packet of artificial sweetener. After it's used, it's a formless mess that leaves a brown and stain-producing puddle. If you put the bag in the saucer, you can't lift your cup without getting drips on your lap.

It would be nice (if a bit unrealistic) to avoid the whole problem by insisting that people of culture use only loose tea. The fact is that even in England today you are likely to get tea-bag tea. But there, they solve the problem by putting the bag in the pot. Simplicity, indeed!

Even if you're making only two cups of tea, put the tea bags into a small pot. Pour in boiling water, and hide everything under the lid.

Always serve tea on a tray. Nothing need match—it's pleasant to have a variety of cups or a teapot that's different from the cream pitcher. The tray makes the frame that pulls everything together.

If you want an elegant presentation, use cups that are white inside, so that you can enjoy the color of the tea, from pale straw to green to rich mahogany. It's like serving wine in a clear glass in order to appreciate its color.

But mugs are fine, too. So is tea-in-a-glass, in the Russian tradition. So are handleless Chinese cups, with lids to aid the steeping. But be consistent. Mug tea gets milk and sugar. Tea-in-a-glass gets a bowl of fruit preserves to spoon in the bottom or cubes of sugar to hold in your mouth. Chinese cups get the tea leaves brewed right in the cup.

Serve lemon slices, not wedges, which are too large for the job. Supply a bowl of sugar, rock candy or honey. And don't forget to provide a tea strainer when you use loose tea. You can buy Chinese bamboo strainers for pennies. They look so good that you can even serve them with tea-bag tea!

Tomatoes

When tomatoes are good, they are very very good. The apotheosis of tomato-eating occurs in midsummer, when the lucky home gardener picks a fat, scarlet, perfectly ripe tomato from the vine, rubs it against his shirt to clean it and eats it there, with no salt, and with the sun's warmth still on it.

Unfortunately, the food industry has got to tomatoes, and these days they tend to come in three grades, good, mediocre and lousy. And more often than not they are lousy unless we grow our own or have friends who do. That means that we use canned Italian plum tomatoes for sauces and stews, serve fresh tomatoes only when we know that they are thin-skinned and flavorful, and make do with good looks, sacrificing taste, when we need a touch of red to garnish a plate.

The general rule for skinning tomatoes is yes, for gentility, no, for nutrition. Do it as you would a peach. Drop the tomato in boiling water or hold it over a gas flame for 30 seconds. The skin will peel right off. To seed the fruit—a necessary step for some cooked dishes— cut it in half perpendicular to the stem and squeeze out the seeds and juice.

Sliced Tomatoes

It's mid-July, and you have just picked two ripe tomatoes from the garden. Serve them sliced. Slice them horizontally, in the American style, or vertically, in the French style (which many people think is less likely to leak out juice). Or cut the tomatoes in half through the stem, and slice each half either vertically or horizontally.

Lay the tomato slices on a plate in a circle or lengthwise on a long platter. In between the slices, set thin slices of mozzarella cheese, Italian onion or raw turnip. Sprinkle with chopped chives, scallions, parsley or basil (especially basil), and garnish with one whole leaf of the herb.

For an hors d'oeuvre, cut roundish tomatoes into horizontal slices. Pipe onto each one a stripe of pureed hard-boiled egg, with

260

chopped parsley stripes on either side of it. Then lay four of the tomato slices on a plate, two with its stripes running horizontally, two going vertically. *(Fig. 286)*

Cut the tomato into wedges. Cut six or eight wedges, and add it to a tossed salad just before you serve it. Any sooner, and the juice will leak out and dilute the dressing.

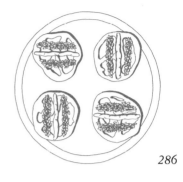

286

Stuffed Tomatoes

Stuffed tomatoes can be served either raw or cooked. When they are raw, they are usually filled with salads and other cold mixtures.

There are many ways to cut a tomato for stuffing. The more complicated cuts work better with raw tomatoes, lose their shape when the tomato is cooked.

Cut the top off straight across and scoop out some of the insides with a spoon.

Cut the top off in a zigzag.

Remove the top, straight or zigzagged, either high up or halfway down the tomato.

Cut the tomato into wheels by slicing it halfway down as though you were going to cut it into wedges. Make eight wedge-shaped petals and scoop out some of the meat to make room for the stuffing.

287

When you cut off the top of a tomato for stuffing, allow an extra 15 minutes so that you can invert it on a rack and let the juices drain out. Fill it with the stuffing, and garnish the top.

Think of color when you stuff a tomato. Fill it with broccoli or spinach puree, saffron rice or egg salad. Use pink shrimp surrounded by greens. Try cold corn relish. Place the tomato on a bed of dark-green spinach or romaine or on a green plate to bring out the red color.

Cap stuffed tomatoes with olive slices, mint leaves, hard-boiled eggs, chopped scallions or chopped Italian onion. Coat the mound of stuffing with mayonnaise and make a flower on it with a radish blossom and scallion leaves. *(Fig. 287)*

288

289

290

Tomato Garnishes

Cut tomatoes into very thin wedges—twelve rather than eight pieces. Use these thin red arcs instead of pimiento for linear garnishes.

Put a half tomato facedown on a plate. Cut three or four parallel slices perpendicular to the plate, nearly all the way to the base. In the slits, put thin slices of unpeeled cucumber, mozzarella or chopped greens. *(Fig. 288)*

There's a reasonably easy way to make neat, round tomatoes to surround a roast. Cut the tomatoes in half after peeling them. Then squeeze out all the seeds. Cut each half in half again. Then put the tomato quarter in a kitchen towel or a clean piece of cheesecloth, the outside of the section against the cloth. Gather the cloth around it and squeeze tightly, so that the pulp is compressed and forms a neat ball. Season it and cook it briefly in butter before placing it alongside a roast or platter of chicken parts.

Try a tomato rose. Peel a tomato in a continuous strip about 1 inch wide. Roll up the skin, skin-side in, in a coil to form a bud. Make leaves of parsley, basil or watercress. *(Fig. 289)*

There's also a "tomato artichoke" garnish. Cut a tomato into six wedges and remove the meat. Assemble the peels as shown in the illustration. *(Fig. 290)*

Use cherry tomatoes as garnish. Starting at the top of a cherry tomato, make cuts at right angles through the skin. Then peel back the skin a bit to form a thistlelike flower. *(Figs. 291, 292)*

Or make three deeper cuts, nearly to the base, remove the center pulp and you have a petaled flower. Sprinkle with chopped greens.

Cooked Tomatoes

For most cooked dishes such as stews and sauces, where the shape of the tomato doesn't matter, you are best off using canned tomatoes. They, at least, were picked ripe. But for fried tomatoes, broiled tomatoes and scallopped tomatoes, you will have to try to get good fresh tomatoes. It's a fallacy to think that it doesn't matter how good the tomato is if you're going to season and cook it.

To broil a tomato, cut off the top in a straight line, squeeze out some of the seeds and drain upside down for 15 minutes. Then broil it with a topping. Most of the stuffings in cooked tomatoes, such as bread crumbs, sausages and mushrooms, turn an uninteresting brown. It helps to garnish them with chopped parsley after they are cooked.

291

Broil the tomato unstuffed. Then cover the top with a layer of warm broccoli or cauliflower puree.

Broil the tomato unstuffed. Cap it with a sautéed mushroom cap. Tuck in sprigs of parsley. *(Fig. 293)*

Thick slices of tomato are often sautéed or fried. The Pennsylvania Dutch fry green tomatoes with some brown sugar and then add cream to the sauce. However you cook tomatoes, they are always improved with garnishes of green—scallions, parsley, watercress or basil—and with settings of green—green peppers, beds of spinach and romaine, dark-green plates and platters. A green plate is an instant cosmetic for even pale midwinter tomatoes.

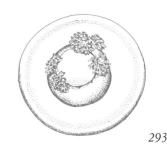

292

Turnips

Turnips are old-fashioned vegetables, back in fashion since someone noticed how good they were eaten raw. Mashed turnips used to be a fixture on the Thanksgiving table. Now they star on platters of crudités, both because of their crisp peppery bite and because they lend themselves so well to being cut into fancy shapes.

There are two kinds of turnips on grocers' shelves more or less all year long, the small white and purple turnips and the large yellow rutabagas.

293

Turnips as Food

Turnips should be peeled before they are eaten to avoid bitterness. Both small and large varieties are boiled, baked under roasts, braised, mashed and sautéed. Really large rutabagas, which tend to be woody, are usually made into purees and often combined with other vegetables.

For the best-looking stews, parboil the turnips and add them to the pot only for the last few minutes of cooking. For a good glaze on sautéed turnips, add some sugar to the butter in which you cook them.

The best way to set off the looks of turnips is to carve them with care. Unless you are going to puree them, any of the methods of carving can be used for any of the cooking techniques. Most of them are also suited to carving raw turnips for a dish of crudités.

Cut a turnip in half, then slice each half into thin semicircles.

Slice a turnip, and cut each slice into long strips.

Cut the strips into cubes.

Cut the turnip into chunks. Then carve the chunks into small or large oval shapes, as you would potatoes.

Cut a turnip with a melon baller.

Shred the turnips in the food processor.

One of the best things to do with turnip is to combine it with another vegetable, cut in the same manner. For example, mix the shredded turnip with three times their measure of carrot shreds.

Mix strips of turnip with strips of julienne-cut broccoli stems and zucchini.

Mix oval-cut turnips with oval-cut carrots and potatoes.

Mix cubes of turnip with mushroom caps and garnish liberally with parsley.

Mashed turnips also mix well with other vegetables. The English mix them with potatoes, the French with chopped mushrooms. Use them with any leftover vegetable you have.

294

Turnips as Garnish

Turnips make excellent garnishes because they are so easy to carve, because they don't turn brown and because they can be eaten raw.

Make turnip cups by peeling egg-sized white turnips and then scooping out the insides with a melon baller. You can zigzag the edge of the cup if you like. Parboil and serve, filled with creamed peas or cubes of carrot with lots of parsley.

Make a flat flower blossom. Cut a turnip into ½-inch slices. Score five radiating lines on the face of the slice. Slice down ¼ inch on each of these lines, and cut slanted wedges from one line down to the

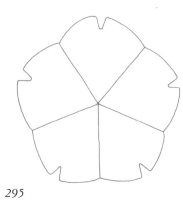

295

¼-inch cut on the next line. Carve the outside of the turnip in curved petals, and notch the middle of each petal. *(Figs. 294, 295)*

Make a big chrysanthemum for a focal point on a platter. Peel a small turnip. Make parallel slices ¼ inch apart across the whole turnip, going nearly all the way to the bottom. Turn the vegetable 90 degrees and make another set of parallel cuts at right angles to the first. Soak it in ice water, and it will spread apart. *(Fig. 296)*

If you have a really big turnip, use it in a centerpiece. First put it in a smallish clay flowerpot, small enough so that the turnip doesn't sink down into it. Then poke holes in it and stick in the slender stalks of bulb flowers such as narcissus. It will look like a huge flower bulb.

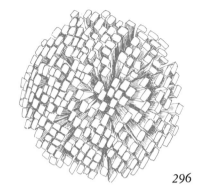

296

Vegetables, Mixed

When we combine vegetables, we deal not only with taste and texture, but also with the dimensions of color, scale and shape. We use color when we add yellow squash to ratatouille, combine cauliflower and broccoli, tomatoes and green peppers. The principles of scale apply when we mix small, medium and large vegetables, combine corn, cherry tomatoes and green pepper rings, or make a centerpiece of tiny Italian peppers, medium-sized zucchini and big eggplants. Shape comes into play when we make a garnish of similarly trimmed carrots, turnips and potatoes, or place a carved radish on a bowl of plain radishes.

There are ways to combine vegetables that are more decorative than frozen peas-and-carrots or frozen mixed varieties.

Stacks

This can be as simple as covering a plate with a large leaf of lettuce, then spooning on a mound of beets. Or as formal as building a tower of tomato, yellow squash and black olives on a slice of eggplant.

Skewers

A skewer is a horizontal stack, a pattern held in place by a stick. Remember to alternate colors and to separate brilliant tones with pale

265

ones or with black olives. Make a skewer of broccoli/mushroom/cherry tomato/mushroom and so forth, or one of tomato/olive/green pepper/olive/tomato.

Garnishes

One vegetable can be used to garnish another. Do it for the contrast in color: put chopped scallions on tomato slices. Or do it for the contrast in shape: put a carved carrot flower on a plate of julienne-cut carrot sticks.

Containers

Using one vegetable as a container for another lets you add height to a flat plate. Look at the section on CONTAINERS MADE FROM FOOD (see pages 100–103) for more ideas than we can give you here. But remember that cold salads go in uncooked cases, and hot vegetables in blanched or precooked cases. Spoon cold shredded carrot and sprigs of dill into a green pepper. Put hot peas and potato cubes in a hollowed-out tomato shell and garnish with parsley. Fill zucchini or yellow squash boats with purees of carrot and spinach. *(Fig. 297)*

297

Arranged Patterns

This means making pictures on a plate. It includes composed salads, vegetable platters for buffets as well as the carefully contrived vegetable side dishes typical of nouvelle cuisine arrangement.

Stand a fat mushroom on its stem in the center of a salad plate, and arrange carrot sticks, scallion greens and yellow squash sticks radiating out from it like spokes in a bicycle wheel. *(Fig. 298)*

298

On an arc of sliced yellow summer squash, set a puff of parsley and a sectioned cherry tomato. *(Fig. 299)*

Surround a barrel of yam with steamed or roasted chestnuts and halved Brussels sprouts.

Make stripes on a serving platter, with white vegetables separating the colored ones. Thus: tomatoes/onions/green beans/cauliflower/carrots/zucchini/broccoli.

299

266

Next to a cold poached chicken breast, put adjoining salads of shredded beets and shredded carrots. Use plenty of parsley to cover the place where they touch and to hide any bleeding from the beets.

Next to strips of teriyaki-marinated steak, make a fan of sautéed pea pods, with a mound of carrot rounds and water-chestnut rings at the joining.

Stand a 3-inch length of cored and cooked zucchini on end. Fill the core with a stick of carrot or yellow squash or with asparagus spears. Add a few sautéed cherry tomatoes at the base. *(Fig. 300)*

Combine peas, pea pods and cherry tomatoes to create a medallion. *(Fig. 301)*

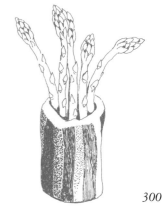

300

Waffles

Waffles are defined by the machine in which you make them. They are something made in a waffle iron. They are usually a quick bread, but old recipes exist for waffles that rise with yeast. And it is not uncommon to dip bread in batter as though you were going to make french toast, and then to press it in a waffle iron.

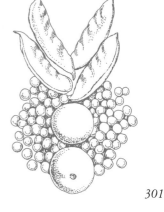

301

Once you have your waffle iron, you're pretty much stuck with the shape of your waffles. When you go shopping, look for an iron with an interesting shape. They come square, rectangular, round and in scalloped circles. Before electricity, irons on long wooden handles were put on top of a wood stove to bake, and you can still find some of the old irons, as well as contemporary imports from Scandinavia, that have ornate and interesting shapes.

We eat waffles at breakfast, with lumps or curls of butter and pitchers of maple syrup, honey or fruit syrup. We add circles of orange to the plate to set off the square shape of the waffles. We lay bacon on top of the uncooked batter in the waffle iron.

We eat them at luncheons and late suppers with sausages and ham or with creamed chicken. In the South, we eat them with whole pecans and honey.

And we eat them for dessert, with ice cream, with stewed figs or apricots, and in Belgian waffles with whipped cream and strawberries.

Plan on using at least two sections to a serving. Place them,

267

overlapping slightly, on a 7-inch dessert plate. The portion will look lush and abundant, instead of like two little tiles adrift on a dinner plate. The garnish—a round slice of orange or a heap of berries and mint leaves—gets tucked underneath the top waffle, peeping out.

Make a sandwich with two waffle sections, making the filling of creamed chicken, ice cream or pureed fruit. Be sure to follow the general sandwich rule, and allow lots of filling to spill out the sides. Have the top waffle tilted over the filling to show it off.

Water

There are two styles of serving water: American and European.

The American style is to fill a big cut-glass pitcher with ice and water and bring it to the table. Farmlike, wholesome.

The European style—now adopted on this continent—is to place a bottle of mineral water on the table. It sometimes gets into complicated snobbery, for the brand must be the right brand of the moment. But many people truly prefer lightly sparkling bottled water to tap water.

Water served as a predinner drink instead of cocktails usually comes with ice cubes and lemon or lime. Siphons of seltzer look sophisticated.

Serve water in tall tumblers, in big wine goblets. In fact, anything goes, and it's just a matter of choosing the style you like.

Watercress

Watercress is more than an alternative to parsley. It is the essence of freshness, with its crisp, dark-green leaves and peppery taste. Buy fresh cress. Cut off the stems and store the leaves, covered with water, in the refrigerator.

Cress is used to flavor and color both vinaigrettes and mayonnaise dressings. It is cooked in chicken soup, much as escarole is. The Chinese stir-fry it with garlic.

Use it in green salads. It does, however, wilt quickly when dressings are added, so that many people prefer to use it on composed salads and reserve it for garnishes.

268

It can take the place of lettuce on a sandwich. And it can be a sandwich filling all its own. It's a tradition of afternoon tea: tiny crustless sandwiches of watercress and mayonnaise, the greens sticking out from between thinly sliced white bread.

But most of all it is an edible garnish, setting off with its dark-green foliage any sort of food it accompanies. Be sure to use it with chicken and fish, with hard-boiled eggs and with tomatoes.

Whipped Cream

Whipped cream is made of heavy whipping cream, which is around 40 percent butterfat. When the cream is whipped, it expands, becoming twice the volume it was when it was liquid.

Help the whipping process by chilling everything in sight. Chill the cream. Chill the bowl and beaters, too. This keeps the globules of fat solid, despite the heat that will be generated in the beating.

(The new ultrapasteurized heavy cream doesn't whip very well, so try to avoid it. If it's all you can get, then follow our directions, chill everything and hope for the best.)

Flavored whipped cream, called chantilly cream, sometimes has egg whites beaten into it. This is supposed to make it whip higher and hold its volume longer.

You can color and flavor whipped cream by adding chocolate, coffee, strawberry or apricot jam, maple sugar or red peppermints. Don't add the flavoring, though, until the cream is approaching the proper consistency, or it may never firm up.

If you're going to serve whipped cream in a bowl, so that guests can spoon it onto food themselves, then whip it to a soft stage, so that it falls in large easy globs. If, however, you plan to pipe the cream through a pastry bag, you should whip it to a firmer stage, so that it almost turns to butter.

To pipe cream in formal designs, spoon it into a canvas or nylon icing bag. When you've used all you need, pipe the leftovers onto wax paper, making cream rosettes. Freeze them. You're sure to find a use for them.

How you put the cream on a dessert depends on both taste and skill. Without the icing bag, you can always spoon a blob of whipped cream on a cup of strawberries, then add a held-back strawberry on top of the cream. If you have a serving bowl of chocolate pudding, spoon small blobs of whipped cream around the edge, pulling up the spoon to form peaks on each one. On an individual dish of custard, drop a small spoonful of cream in the center, and sprinkle it with pistachio nuts.

If you can manage the icing bag, you will be able to manipulate the whipped cream in complicated designs. Make a scalloped border around the edge of a bowl of chocolate mousse. Draw concentric rings on top of a frozen raspberry soufflé. Do a lattice on a slice of chocolate cake.

Always try to garnish the garnish. Put something—chocolate, nuts, mint or glacéed fruit—on top of the cream.

Wine

It isn't snobbery that keeps us faithful to the traditional ways of serving wine. It's simply that the traditions are beautiful, and there are good reasons for most of the rules.

Take the stemmed wineglass. When you drink a good wine, you're supposed to hold the glass by its stem so that the heat of your hand won't warm up the wine. On the other hand, it's quite common in France for *vins ordinaires* to be served in tumblers. And this is just fine, since such wine is drunk rapidly, without ceremony and would not, in any case, be damaged by a little body heat.

Now that we in America are serving jug wines and local wines at family suppers, we should feel comfortable about adopting a more casual style in our wine presentation, never forgetting the traditional manner and the reasons behind it.

Bottle

A wine bottle should stand upright on the table. In fact, it should be upright for hours before it's served, to allow the sediment to fall to the bottom. Place red wine on a flat coaster on the table.

Don't slant it in a wicker basket. You want to be able to see the shape. That's part of the language of wine. We should be able to recognize and distinguish the slender brown bottle of Rhine wine, the round Chianti bottle, the sloping bottle of Burgundy and the necked bottle of Bordeaux.

Champagnes and white wines should be chilled. Champagnes should be served quite cold, white wines at 40°F, rosés at 45°F, and red wines at 65°F—not room temperature by American standards, by the way. (And there are exceptions to these rules. A light Italian red that we serve with fish soup is quite pleasant when slightly chilled.) Bring the white wine to the table in a bucket of ice or stand it on the table in one of the convenient unglazed clay buckets that keeps it chilled.

There is a ritual to the pouring. The host pours a little wine into his own glass. He tastes it, presumably to see if it is good enough to serve to his guests. Then he pours wine into all the glasses at the table, finishing with his own. It is a gracious manner of service, but it implies a host and guest and a good wine. It's not likely to be followed at a family dinner with a jug of local red wine.

Carafe

You use a carafe or decanter with a very great wine or with one that is insignificant.

Great wines are decanted in order to leave behind the sediment they throw off. Cheap wines are decanted so that the host doesn't have to show the label. American jug wines are fashionable right now, but there was a time when they used to come to the best tables disguised in fine crystal decanters.

A pretty finishing touch for a country-style table is to close off the neck of a carafe with a whole fresh lemon.

Glasses

Certain shapes of wineglasses go with certain wines. German hocks are served in long-stemmed bubble glasses, often made of colored glass. Champagne is served in a narrow flute. There are different shapes for Burgundies and Bordeaux in a full set of glasses, but most people would drink both in a 10-ounce bubble-shaped glass. And the same shape, in a smaller glass, is used to serve white wine.

Except for the hock glasses, which were colored because German wines were thought to be off-color, classic wineglasses are supposed to be clear and uncarved.

If you don't have money to spend on different glasses, you can get by with one set of huge red-wine glasses, like brandy snifters on stems. Don't fill them to the brim, though. They hold an astonishing amount. There should, moreover, always be space left in a wineglass so that the aroma can develop.

Yogurt

Yogurt is fermented milk. We buy it plain, mixed with sweetened fruit and frozen. Fruit and frozen yogurts are desserts, while plain yogurt is both a food and, substituting for whipped cream and sour cream, a garnish.

Like ice cream, yogurt goes in glass containers—bowls, wineglasses, champagne flutes. Like ice cream, it is garnished with a fine casual hand.

Flavored Yogurt

Serve coffee yogurt in a white custard dish. Garnish with plain yogurt and canned apricots.

Mix a fruit yogurt with its jam so that the whole container-full is colored. Then make a parfait, alternating pink strawberry yogurt with plain yogurt.

Do the same with blueberry yogurt. Make layers of purple blueberry and plain yogurt, and garnish with cantaloupe balls and fresh blueberries.

You don't have to do these in layers. Fill a glass bowl half full of raspberry yogurt and half full of plain, and garnish the dividing line with blueberries.

Garnish sweetened yogurt for texture as well as color. Add granola, nuts, coconut, raisins, green grapes.

Plain Yogurt

Stir chopped green pepper and radishes into plain yogurt, and serve it in a bowl lined with pepper rings. It's a nice dip for crudités.

Mix cucumber and scallions with yogurt, and serve it in a bowl lined with tomato slices and parsley sprigs.

With curries, serve orange shells filled with cool yogurt.

Fill half a tomato with yogurt, garnish with chives and serve with a diet dinner.

Use yogurt wherever you might use sour cream or whipped cream—on a baked apple, a baked potato or on a bowl of berries.

Zucchini

Zucchini is a summer squash, a tender young vegetable without the hard protective skin of winter squash. (The other common summer squash is yellow—straightneck and crookneck. They are similar in flavor and shape to zucchini—but not in color—and what goes for one in preparation also goes for the other.)

Zucchini looks like cucumber and can be used in all the ways we used to use cucumbers before we had to peel them. The green skin is tender enough to be eaten raw. That means that zucchini can be used to add a touch of green and white to salads, canapés and skewered vegetables.

Buy them as young and small as you can, firm to the touch and heavy for their size. Large zucchini have to be cut in pieces. Tiny zucchini can be eaten whole or in quarters, and need only the briefest cooking. Look for vegetables with smooth bright skins and no dark spots or blemishes. If, however, someone gives you a monstrously huge end-of-summer zucchini, accept it gratefully. It can be stuffed and baked or shredded into a casserole.

Zucchini is eaten raw. It is steamed, baked in casseroles or stuffed, sliced and deep fried, sautéed or stir-fried.

Whole Zucchini

Steam tiny whole zucchini. First score the skins with the tines of a fork or remove patterns with a vegetable zester. Make it simple: two stripes down each side of a zucchini, or a scalloped line around the widest part.

For an hors d'oeuvre borrowed from the cucumber, remove the center and seeds of a large zucchini with a zucchini corer. (Or cut the vegetable in half lengthwise and scoop out the insides.) Stuff it with flavored cheese. (Press the halves back together if you have cut them.) Chill well. Just before serving, cut it across into rings. The stuffing should be colorful: salmon salad or cream cheese with red caviar are both good.

Add whole zucchini to vegetable centerpieces.

Halved Zucchini

Zucchini are among the best vegetables for stuffing. Slice in half lengthwise. Since most of the vegetables are small, you won't be doing a complicated cut. If you have that monstrous end-of-summer zucchini, you may scallop or zigzag the edges. Scoop out some of the meat, shred or cube it and combine it with the rest of the filling. Choose a filling to go with the bright green shell: corn and sweet peppers or rice baked with tomatoes.

Cut the zucchini in half and use it, uncooked, as a container for other foods. A large one can be a serving dish for deep-fried zucchini sticks. Small ones can hold cold vegetable salads and cranberry-orange relish.

Sliced Zucchini

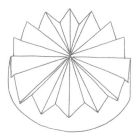

Zucchini is sliced to be braised with other vegetables—as in ratatouille—to be sautéed, stir-fried and deep fried.

Cut straight across to make circles.

Cut across at an angle to make ovals.

Cut the zucchini lengthwise into strips.

302

Shredded Zucchini

Shredded zucchini is a visual revelation. Do it in the food processor. Then combine it with shredded carrot or with orange rind. Use it arranged in a nest, holding a cherry tomato and two mushrooms. Serve it on a bed of thin orange slices and garnish with walnuts. It's good raw, but shredded zucchini can also be cooked briefly or baked in a casserole.

Zucchini Garnishes

Use zucchini rounds with other vegetables in a border—three zucchini slices and then half a cherry tomato. Or make a border of shingled slices. Or alternate with slices of yellow squash. Any of these can be done as well with zucchini whose skin has been scored with a fork or that has had long narrow V-shaped wedges cut out of it with a paring knife.

Make a flat zucchini flower. Cut off the end of the vegetable. Then, using a narrow paring knife, stick the point of the knife into the center of the zucchini at alternating diagonal angles, making a sawtooth cut. Twist out the flower and cut off the next flower by slicing it off ¼ inch down the zucchini. If the center of the flower is messy, place a puff of parsley or a bit of pimiento or a small knot of orange skin there to hide it. *(Fig. 302)*

Make zucchini links in a chain. Slice the zucchini across into rounds. Remove the center of each round. Cut an opening in every other ring, and slip it through an uncut ring, forming a chain.

Here is an easy but decorative way to cut zucchini. It sounds—and looks—more complicated than it is. Cut a 3-inch length from the middle of a zucchini. *(a)* Stick a paring knife through the center, making a cut parallel to the sides of the zucchini. *(b)* Take a second paring knife, and make a diagonal cut in to the first knife. *(c)* Then turn the zucchini over and *(d)* make the same diagonal cut on the other side. *(e)* You can separate the two halves and stand them up on a platter of tomato slices. *(Fig. 303)*

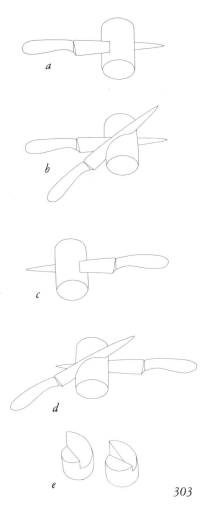

a

b

c

d

e

303

275

3

TABLE STYLING

Buffet

A buffet is more than just an easy way to entertain, although it's certainly that. It's a dramatic presentation of food, where the table becomes a miniature theater. On a buffet table you can get away with decorations that would look extreme on a smaller stage.

The only restriction is that the visual effects should come from planning and foresight. Before you make it beautiful, you have to make it work.

Where do the guests approach the table? That's where you put the plates. Napkins and silverware can wait at the other end of the table. Use oversized dinner plates or serve trays, each one set in advance with a napkin, a plate and stemware. *(Fig. 304)*

Don't provide unnecessary flatware. If the coffee comes later, you don't have to present a teaspoon with the meal. If the guests will be eating off their laps, all the food will be fork food, of course, and you can do without knives. If they will be eating at tables, the silverware will be on the tables.

Present the silverware in rolled napkins, perhaps tied with ribbons. Or roll each napkin into a tidy cone, stick a fork into it, then stand it upright in a vase or basket. Less formally, shake out each napkin, grasp it in its center and stick its tip into a basket, letting the edges flop out. Then insert pine branches or pussy willows on either side. The greenery should stay in place when the napkins are pulled out. Test it.

304

Lay out the food in a logical order. If the rice is to go under the curry, then it should come before it in line. If you offer both ham and turkey, have them next to each other, so that the guest who wants both will know to take less of each.

The buffet table is a stage that can support bold decorations. It's the place for large-scale platters, oversized garnishes, tall skewers, huge roasts. Serve the salad from an enormous shell. Scatter stemless flowers over the table between the platters. Cover the table with a

277

thick bed of dark-green leaves or pine needles and serve the food on clear glass platters. Put low votive candles in among the flowers and leaves. (But keep them toward the back, so that no one's sleeve catches fire when he reaches for the celery in the back.)

Then add some vertical accents. Instead of posies in vases, display a whole branch of flowering peach or apple, or a huge sheaf of forsythia and pussy willows. Create levels with footed bowls and tiered servers. Add height to individual plates by making towers of doughnuts, propping lobsters vertically against one another. Fill a vase with long baguettes of french bread. Fill tumblers with slender Italian grissini.

This is the place for an oversized centerpiece, such as a harvest arrangement of pumpkins, cabbages and gourds. For a punch bowl surrounded by leaves and flowers set in the center of the table.

The lighting can be dramatic. If you can manage it, turn one can of your track lighting around so that the table is spotlighted. We know someone who rented a stand of theatrical lights for a New Year's buffet supper. Buy the tallest candles you can find for your candlesticks, and group all of them at the back of the table.

If you don't have a proper table, look around. You can serve food from a cleared desk, a low bookcase, the top of a drafting table or from the kitchen counter.

If you serve in the kitchen, do it positively. Don't ignore it. Don't act as though your best china is slumming. Instead, serve right from handsome casseroles—low ones are best for easy accessibility—and use large kitchen ladles and spatulas. Line an iron frying pan with a fresh white napkin and fill it with fried zucchini. Decorate the counter with vases of fresh parsley and dill. The cookies can come from cooling racks, the apples and crudités from mushroom baskets. The napkins, of course, will be oversized blue-and-white checks, like dish towels. (Or buy a dozen new dish towels, and use them as napkins.)

Things not to do on a buffet table: don't try to make it look catered. Don't turn pineapples into birds or make ice and chicken-liver sculptures. But on the other hand, don't pretend that this is a formal table. The very fact that your guests are helping themselves should make the decorations easier, more casual, less traditional.

Candleholders

Lucky you, if you have a collection of old brass candlesticks. On the other hand, anything with a hole in it can be a candleholder. Dumb things, like Life Savers and marshmallows, holding tiny birthday and Hanukkah candles. Romantic things, like Chianti bottles waiting to be covered with wax drippings.

We like to use food to hold candles. Keep your eyes open, and you'll be amazed at what is available. Just don't choose anything squishy or obviously perishable. No tomatoes, no bananas. The holder shouldn't rot as the candle melts.

But artichokes look terrific with their middle leaves spread and votive candles wedged into their centers. So do bell peppers, small cabbages and squash. Arrange several of these low vegetables in a flat basket. Get a large red onion, core it and stick in a 5-inch taper. Pull

305

back the onion's skin, so that you see both the matte exterior and the shiny layers within. If you can't get a brilliant Spanish onion, an ordinary yellow one will do. Set this arrangement on a sideboard or buffet table. The odor of the onion may be too much for a dinner-table grouping.

Core an apple or an orange and insert a taper in it. Carve small melons or squash to look like jack-o'-lanterns when they're lit from within by votive candles.

You can get a much more elegant effect without great effort. Buy short votive candles, the kind that burn in glasses. Surround each one with a bunch of grapes, and thread a ribbon in and out among the grapes. Surround a votive candle with flowers or green leaves. In autumn, use a variety of colored leaves.

Centerpieces

A centerpiece is a signal that a meal is a special event. Buffet tables hold huge dramatic centerpieces. But on a dinner table, especially one where the hostess is doing the serving, it's best to keep the centerpiece small so that the table won't become cluttered.

And keep it low, too, so as not to interfere with cross-table conversation. Float flowers in a shallow bowl instead of buying a tall, formal flower arrangement. Set tall candles on the table where they will not be in the eyelines of guests talking across the table. Better still, use votive candles.

Break it up. Instead of a single bowl of autumn squashes, scatter vegetables down the length of the table. Instead of a single flower arrangement, use three pots of flowering plants, or place a bud vase with one or two blossoms at every setting.

Don't feel that you have to stick with flowers and fruit. Lay a branch down the center of the table. In the spring, choose one from a flowering fruit tree, and in the fall, one with colored leaves. Tuck seasonal fruits and flowers in around it. *(Fig. 306)*

Make a centerpiece using a piece of sculpture or ceramic or a potted plant, and surround it with ivy.

280

306

At an informal dinner, tie a sheaf of spaghetti stalks around the middle with a red ribbon, fan the spaghetti and stick the sheaf upright on the table. Make a layered arrangement of different-shaped and colored pastas in a tall glass jar.

Use clay pots with herbs growing in them.

Flatware

When a store offers a place setting of flatware, they mean one dinner fork, one salad fork, one knife, one teaspoon and one soup spoon. That's basic, and, in fact, it's all you really need. The salad fork doubles up for cake, the teaspoon works for custard as well as for coffee, the knife spreads butter in addition to cutting the steak. You may have to wash the knives between courses, but you'll get by.

If you have the money, you can buy extra forks and spoons, as well as some of the more rarefied pieces: round cream-soup spoons, bouillon spoons, luncheon knives and forks, fish forks, butter spreaders and tiny demitasse spoons. But even if you fill in with such exotica as oyster forks and afternoon-tea spoons, you still won't have as many pieces as the nineteenth-century householder. Victorian and Edwardian dinner parties often had twenty courses, with one or two implements provided for each course. On the other hand, the Chinese

10-ounce for red wine

9-ounce all-purpose for wine

8-ounce for white wine

10-ounce for red Burgundies

*8-ounce for Champagnes and
sparkling wines*

307

have been eating since the fourth century B.C. with just two sticks and have never felt the need to improve on them.

There has never been a greater variety of style and materials in flatware than there is now. You can buy sterling silver, silver plate, stainless steel—even brass—with handles made of metal, wood, ceramic, enamel, opaque or clear plastic. If you should buy one of the inexpensive kinds of flatware with handles of a differing material, be sure to ask about cleaning it. Most of them should not be soaked or put in the dishwasher.

Glass

Glass suffers in status from being a native product. Porcelain is associated with the Orient; objects made of metal are often valued beyond their utility or beauty. But glass has been with us at least since the time of the ancient Egyptians and is made of dirt-common materials: sand, soda and lime. These are heated until they melt. The molten liquid is poured into a mold, pressed or blown into shape. After it cools it solidifies, turning into the familiar hard, brittle, transparent product that we call glass.

(Technically, lead crystal is glass containing a minimum of 24 percent lead, but the word *crystal* is used for any high-quality clear and colorless glass.)

Of all the categories of tableware, glass design has changed least over the years, the designs being restricted by the medium as well as by utility. The great development in glassmaking was blowing, which permitted the development of "hollowware." Before that, most people drank from metal or wooden tumblers.

In the nineteenth century, a well-dressed table carried an array of stemware, with a different shape of glass for every drink from Moselle to Sherry. Now we use a minimum of shapes for a maximum of uses. Tumblers, of course, serve water, milk and iced drinks. But many people simply own large bubble-shaped wineglasses and use them for all drinks, as well as for serving ices, puddings and fruit. Choose glassware in shapes that please your eye. Champagne flutes are good for water and beer as well as sparkling wine. Heavy bistro-style tumblers are used for wine in France all the time. If you prefer stemware, the rule of thumb is to see to it that the stem is equal in length to the bowl.

There are a lot of inexpensive glass plates and bowls around. They mix well with other dishes and create a pleasant light look on the table. A glass bread-and-butter plate seems to take up less room than one made of earthenware. A salad served on glass looks fresh, airy, insubstantial.

We used to be told to wash glassware in very hot soapy water, then polish it with a cloth until it shone. If you still wash by hand, add a little white vinegar to the rinse water and watch the glassware sparkle.

Napkins

The easiest and least expensive way to vary the look of a table is by changing the napkins. China is costly, but you can afford to own several sets of napkins and play around with bright colors and trendy patterns without making a lifetime commitment to one decorative scheme.

You can make napkins inexpensively from fabric remnants. (Be sensible, and choose wash-and-wear fabrics.) Measure out generous squares, a good 18 or 20 inches to a side rather than the usual 16 inches. The extra size makes for easy folding and a feeling of luxury. Pull threads to create guidelines for cutting straight edges. Then make hems with a sewing machine or by hand.

Neatly folded in rectangles, napkins go to the left of the fork or on the dinner plate. There is also, however, a tradition of napkin folding that goes back to the Victorian table. We offer several simple and not-so-simple ways to fold a napkin. If you're interested, you will find more instructions on folding napkins in *Folding Table Napkins: A New Look at a Traditional Craft* by Sharon Dlugosch (Brighton Publications, 1977).

Napkin folding is like tying your shoes. Telling someone how to do it makes it sound more difficult than the three-second affair that it really is. To help you visualize the steps, we've named the different parts of an open napkin as shown. *(Fig. 308)*

6-ounce for Rhines, Alsatians and other white wines

5-ounce for Sherry, Port, Madeira

7-ounce for brandies, cordials, liqueurs

307

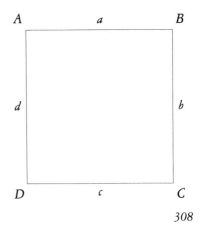

308

To warm up, grip the napkin just off-center. (Makes it look larger.) Shake it into large, open folds. Then stick the point into the water glass, with the edges flopping over the rim. Or set the point under the plate, with the folds flaring out to the left, up to the center of the table or hanging over the table's edge.

A simple, tailored fold. Open the napkin fully. Beginning with side *c,* make 2-inch-wide accordion folds up to side *a.* Tie a trim knot in the center of the napkin. Lay it to the left of the fork or on top of the dinner plate.

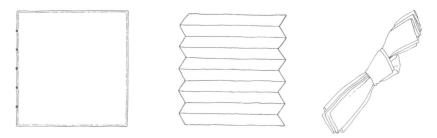

309

A buffet fold. Fold the napkin into quarters. With the open ends pointing away from you, fold the first layer in half, bringing the point down to meet the bottom point. Tuck the second layer under the first, the third layer under the second. Lift the napkin from the table, and fold the bottom point under, and then the two sides under. Tuck flatware into the pockets you have made.

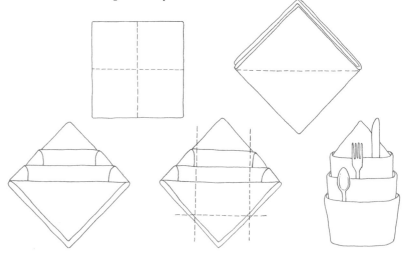

310

284

A simple tower. Open the napkin fully. Bring point *C* up to point *A*. Make a 2-inch cuff at the edge *DB*. Turn the napkin over so that the cuff is underneath the napkin at the edge nearest you. Roll it into a cylinder, beginning from the right side. Tuck the loose end of the cuff into the top of the cuff. Stand the napkin on the plate, flaring the top slightly.

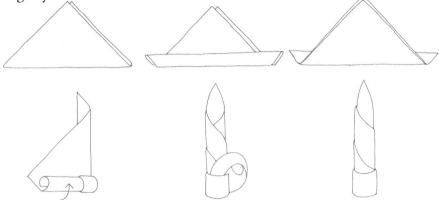

311

A standing ruffled fold. Fold the napkin into quarters. Fold the first two layers down to meet the opposite corner. Pleat the two halves now on top. Fold this in half diagonally. Stand it up, tucking the thinner pointed end into the thicker. To emphasize the loosely falling pleats, use a napkin with a strongly contrasting border.

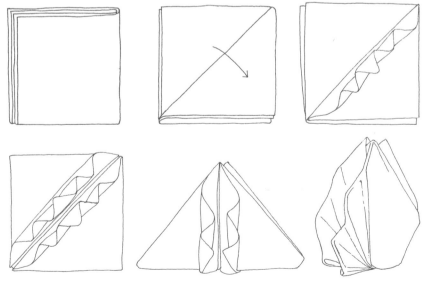

312

285

A hat-shaped cone. Open the napkin fully. Fold side *a* down to side *c*. Roll the napkin into a cone, using the center of the fold as the point of the cone. Turn a deep cuff all around the open end, and stand it up on the plate. For a children's party, stick a lollipop or a whistle into the cuff.

313

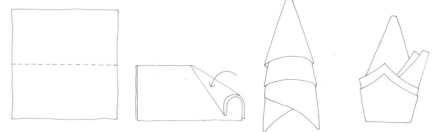

A petal fold. Open the napkin fully. Fold it in quarters, so that the loose edges are at the upper right corner. Take the top level from point *B* and fold it back to point *D*. Fold back the second level to *D*, pressing the crease with your thumbnail. Pleat the loose triangle of this level. Now pleat the third level, so that the pleated panels lie in strips side by side from *A* to *C*. Fold the napkin in half diagonally across the pleated folds, *D* to *B*. Bend the sides back, and tuck the points together so that the napkin will stand up.

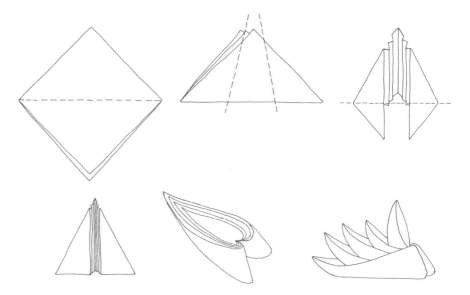

314

A standing fan. Working from an imaginary line drawn through the center of the napkin, divide each half into thirds and pleat these. Now fold the napkin so that the pleats are to the outside. Next, imagine a line drawn through the short axis of the napkin and pleat each half into thirds (steps 2 and 3). Finally, bring the free corners up to touch each other and fold them together, making a diagonal crease. When this fold is complete, the sides are pulled up into a fan.

315

Picnics

A picnic must be portable. Whether you're heading for the beach or up to the roof, you want to keep the food tidy, and you have to keep it at the right temperature.

There's nothing beautiful about the accessories for maintaining the temperature of food. Until designers get to work on improving them, we have to accept the look of vacuum bottles, Styrofoam coolers and lidded plastic bowls wrapped in newspaper.

Tidyness has its own accessories. You can't beat sturdy refrigerator containers. Save margarine cups to fill with individual salads and fruit salads. You can throw them away without a thought after the picnic, while you have to tote the more expensive, store-bought plastic boxes home with you. Bring along a roll of paper towels and some big garbage bags for cleaning up.

Try to think in portions before you take to the road. Stuff shrimp and chicken salads into green peppers or tomato cases, then wrap them in foil. Make hamburger patties ready for grilling. Make skewers of vegetables, sausages or marshmallows. Stuff hard-boiled egg halves, then reassemble them and wrap them in foil.

Use different patterns of gift wrap for covering and coding sandwiches: stripes for ham and cheese, flowers for peanut butter, solid for tuna. It makes for easy identification and eliminates rummaging through the packets at the picnic.

Slice, butter and reassemble a loaf of brown bread. Cut the top from a melon, slice the fruit into chunks and put it back inside with more fruit and a splash of wine. Then replace the top and wrap the whole melon in foil.

Make the most of transparent containers. Layer food of contrasting colors in them. Fill one with potato salad and decorate with tomato slices and scallions wedged between the salad and the sides of the container. Make a star of egg slices on top garnished with parsley and seal the top for transporting.

Once you're at the site, the portable meal will become a feast. Choose a style depending on the location, the food and the mood you want to set.

Supper at an outdoor concert? Bring champagne glasses, linen napkins and a spray of flowers to lay on the blanket. Lunch near a stream? Set a country table, a *déjeuner sur l'herbe,* with checkered cloths, wicker baskets and huge napkins. Take honestly modern stackable plastic dishes and mugs to the beach at midday. At night, lay an Indian tablecloth on the sand and serve skewered lamb from metal plates and beer or sweet tea in mugs. For a children's picnic, arrive with individual brown or colored paper bags, one per child, with his name written on it. Each one should hold a paper plate and cup, a sandwich, fruit and a cookie.

Place Settings

The one act of foodstyling we all do without thinking is setting the table. It's a convention that has developed over the years to give order to the ceremony of eating and to keep people from bumping elbows and crossing knives, a convention that is so ingrained that most people, having picked up flatware and napkins from a buffet table, will lay them out in the usual order when they sit down to eat.

Allow 18 to 24 inches for each place setting. Put the dinner plate in front of each diner, with the silverware to either side of it, one inch from the table edge. Forks are on the left and knives on the right, with their cutting edges turned toward the plate. Spoons are placed to the right of the knives. Dessert forks and spoons should be brought to the table later, with the dessert, or can be placed above the dinner plate, the fork below the spoon, with the fork tines pointing right and the spoon bowl pointing left.

Today's usage, unlike that of Victorian times, sets a limit of three pieces of flatware on either side of the dinner plate. The implement that is used first goes on the outside. Thus, the forks might be—reading from left to right—an oyster fork, a dinner fork and a salad fork.

In Europe, you sometimes find a metal or china knife rest placed to the right of your plate. This is used to prop your fork and knife on when the plates are cleared away. Americans prefer to take away the

316

289

used flatware and supply freshly rinsed forks and knives. You occasionally see a very formal table set with the flatware turned facedown. This was a late-nineteenth-century Parisian affectation, and it works, of course, only when the silver has ornate or beautiful carving on its back.

The napkin is folded and placed to the left of the forks or on the dinner plate. Glasses go above the point of the dinner knife. If you have a variety of things to drink, the glasses for them should read from right to left as follows: white-wine glass, a red-wine glass, champagne glass. The water glass is always farthest left.

Although bread plates are less common than they once were, we think they are convenient, even with family meals. Set to the left of the place setting, a bread plate permits you to take a roll with the soup and enjoy the rest of it with the main course.

Since this book does not presume to include all aspects of current table-setting etiquette, we refer you to *The Amy Vanderbilt Complete Book of Etiquette*, revised and expanded by Letitia Baldridge (Doubleday, 1978).

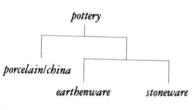

317

Pottery

Unless you use plastic or paper, you probably eat from plates made of pottery. We take this for granted. Yet there was a time when most people ate from pewter or from wooden trenchers. Porcelain plates became widespread in Europe only in the late seventeenth century, along with the craze for tea and coffee drinking.

If you were to make a family tree of fired clay, it would look something like that shown here. *(Fig. 317)*

Porcelain and China

These are both names given to the fine pottery that was developed in China. When the paste is fired, it is transformed into a vitrified or glasslike substance. Then it is given a transparent, colorless glaze, although porcelain is not porous even before it is glazed. The finer grades are thin, translucent, resistant to chipping and, like crystal, ring when they are struck.

290

Show sense when you take care of fine china. Very old or gold-decorated plates should not go into the dishwasher. They should be washed by hand in a sink lined with towels, then dried with a soft cloth and stacked with padding between the plates. Modern china without precious metals can go into the dishwasher, as long as you are careful in the loading.

Earthenware and Stoneware

Earthenware, which is often casually called terra-cotta or pottery, is usually opaque, porous and scratchable. It is also the least durable form of pottery. Unless you are very careful, you will find that chips and chunks fall like magic out of the edges of your earthenware plates. Earthenware is clay-colored in its natural state and is usually glazed to make it nonporous.

Stoneware is fired at a heat far higher than earthenware, which turns it into a very hard glasslike substance. It is nonporous even when it isn't glazed, and it is very durable.

Table Coverings

We think of table coverings as a look, a way to make a table look attractive. But, in fact, they were developed to protect the table surface and to cut down on noise. There used to be a cloth called a silencer that was laid under the tablecloth proper.

During the past twenty years there has been an opening up of the materials considered appropriate for table coverings. No longer are we limited to damask and linen. We now have cloths and place mats in fabrics designed for clothing and upholstery, napkins made of toweling and shirt fabric, place mats made of striped awning canvas, woven reeds and mirrors.

Place mats should be at least 11 by 13 inches in size. Tablecloths come in standard sizes, but they never seem to come quite big enough. The fall, or the part that hangs over the edge of the table, should be at least 12 inches at either end of the table. Thus, a five-feet-long table requires a seven-feet-long cloth. Longer is even better.

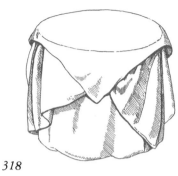

318

319

To vary the look, use layers of cloths. Lay long runners of fabric over the base cloth on a rectangular table. Use place mats over the cloth.

Drop a cloth to the floor on a round or square table, and place a cloth square in a different pattern over it. Gather each point up to the table edge, and hold it in place with a safety pin. For a party, add ribbons and flowers at the gathering point. *(Figs. 318, 319)*

Use three fabrics in the same color range, varying the scale of the pattern. Have one in small checks, another in medium-sized flowers and a bold overall pattern or a solid color for the final cloth.

Takeout Food

Surveys show that Americans are eating one out of three meals away from home. What they don't say is that some of the at-home meals are really ordered in.

Takeout food has its own aesthetic. It comes wrapped in wax paper, white cardboard boxes and barrels, and perhaps it shouldn't ever be served any other way. Sometimes the best way is just to go with the flow, and serve it without embarrassment. But you might want to pay a little amused attention to the way you serve.

Chinese food is the original American takeout. The white carton with its wire handle has become such a classic that one manufacturer has immortalized it in white porcelain. If you're going to serve straight from the cardboard cartons, you can still protect the table with sheets of Chinese newspaper or a bright red paper cloth, red being the color of good luck for the Chinese. Use bright paper napkins, and have a flower vase holding a flare of chopsticks.

If you want to put on a little more show, without quite pretending that supper was stir-fried in your own wok, do some work ahead of time. Make some Chinese garnishes—scallion brushes and radish fans.

When your order arrives at your door, start the water boiling for tea. Transfer the food immediately to warmed patterned Chinese bowls. Personalize each dish with a garnish, a group of persimmon slices, a radish fan or some kumquats.

292

Order lots of fried rice. Pack it into a small mold and turn it out onto a serving plate after a minute. It should hold its shape well. Surround with scallion brushes. On another plate, stack a pyramid of egg rolls and circle it with spareribs. Squeeze out the mustard and duck sauce into handleless Chinese teacups. Then give everyone a colorful rice bowl filled with white rice, and lay a pair of chopsticks on each cloth napkin.

Pizza is the most popular food in America, and we've all been conditioned to salivate at the sight of the flat white box. If you don't want to put the box on the table, however, stick the pizza in its box or remove to a cookie sheet on a warming tray or in a low low oven. Then serve individual slices on warmed earthenware plates. We happen to think that nothing goes with pizza except soda or beer, but if you have to have a complete meal, serve a platter of mixed Italian crudités, an informal antipasto of celery, olives, small hot peppers, marinated carrots, salami curls and chunks of hard cheese.

A recent addition to the standard takeout menu is *Southern fried chicken and ribs.* If you don't want to put the cardboard barrel with its advertising on the table, line two baskets with napkins in country gingham or calico prints. Serve the chicken in one basket, the biscuits in the other. One of the napkins will surely be sacrificed to grease stains, so either use an old one or else a fabric remnant. The ribs go on a warmed platter and the coleslaw in a milk glass bowl. Garnish the chicken with parsley, and set out pitchers of milk or cider.

Then there's *deli,* served on individual trays in front of the Sunday football game or in the flattened wax paper wrappers on the kitchen table. Colorful paper plates are as dressy as you need to get. Transfer the sandwiches to a big flat board (for heroes) or to a basket. Provide a platter of extra sandwich stuffings, such as tomatoes, olives and Spanish onion rings. Add a basket of potato chips or pretzels and beer, either in cans or in a pitcher. Then offer heavy checked napkins and real—not plastic—forks for the potato salad.

Different sections of the country provide different takeout foods, many of which spread nationwide. Look under FISH (see page 137) for the way to serve lox and bagels. In the South, you get barbecue, shredded beef or pork in a spicy sauce. In the Southwest, and fast spreading, you get tacos and tortillas. Big cities have order-in "gourmet" dinners, yard-long hero sandwiches, dial-a-steak. Hamburgers, french fries and milk shakes are universal. Serve them all without pretense and with a sense of humor.

Trays

Trays aren't only for invalids. They're for Sunday breakfast in bed, for supper with the football game and for lunch out of doors. (And, of course, for carrying food to the table and clearing it away.)

Think of a tray as a table for one, a portable place setting. The napkin becomes a tray cloth when you open it and place it with its points hanging over the sides. This napkin and the napkin folded on the tray need not match, but there should be some basis for agreement between their patterns.

Avoid crowding the tray. This is especially true for an invalid, who may not be feeling too hungry to begin with. Use a salad plate rather than a dinner plate. Clear glass gives the impression that it takes up less space than china. Put the silverware to the side in a rolled-up napkin. Serve water or juice in a small wineglass.

4

INTERNATIONAL TABLES

Chinese

Every American has two cuisines, his own and Chinese. We buy it canned and frozen. We eat it out, we order in. Some of us stir-fry green beans, while others hang their own ducks and roll their own dim sum. When we aren't eating hamburgers or pizza, we are more than likely to be eating egg rolls.

How do we make the table suit the meal? A Chinese family sits at a round table. At each place there is a rice bowl and a pair of chopsticks. Everyone takes from the common dishes in the center of the table, reaching with chopsticks for a piece of meat or a broccoli stalk, which is put on the rice and eaten from there.

Without copying the manner of service, you can copy the look of the table. Buy some of the inexpensive, multicolored dishes that are sold in Chinese and Japanese shops. Choose bright rose, turquoise and yellow or classic celadon and oxblood. Buy both plates and rice bowls, which will do double service as dessert dishes.

Give each person a plate. Lay a pair of chopsticks at the right of the plate or above it, with the part that will touch the food pointing left. Chinese chopsticks are made of bamboo, ivory, metal, lacquer, even plastic. They are square at one end and rounded at the other, while Japanese chopsticks are rounded all the way down and pointed at the end that touches the food.

You'll find that footed bowls look very Chinese. Small foods like shrimp toast and dumplings can be presented on steamer trays. And

320

in the store where you bought the inexpensive rice bowls, you should be able to find tiny condiment plates in the shape of butterflies or fish for mustard and sweet sauce.

Cloth and napkins can be either red or white. Red is a symbol of good fortune all over China. It's the color used at birthday parties and weddings. White is, simply, the color we've got used to from Chinese restaurants.

Chinese food, unlike Japanese, is not intricately arranged. It's served in heaps, with the beauty coming from the ingredients themselves, the glistening freshness of well-cut and lightly cooked food.

But there are garnishes that will help make it more appealing.

296

Make a border of one ingredient from the dish. Fried noodles are good, as are briefly cooked greens. Half-slices of sweet red peppers can be joined in a border that looks like the stylized cloud motif in Chinese art.

Cut one ingredient in an eye-catching shape. Do a carrot flower, a scallion brush or a radish fan. These garnishes shouldn't be subtle and restrained, as they would be on a Japanese table. Rather, do huge icicle-radish flowers, clustered with mustard flowers.

Lay egg rolls or spareribs on an oval plate. Decorate each end of the plate with stir-fried pea pods or with scallion brushes.

French

This means, of course, French bistro or French provincial. A formal French table is like a formal table anywhere only more so, because they invented the game.

But if you simply want to create a proper setting for your omelet or your daube Provençale, lay down a red-checked or densely floral cotton tablecloth. Use oversized napkins, printed with more checks or in a different floral print.

The wine goes in a glass carafe in the center of the table. At each place setting there is a heavy glass tumbler. Bread in a long straw basket or, more authentically, right on the table. And the cheese is served on a flat basketry tray.

The plates should be of simple heavy earthenware, either undecorated or else hand-painted with a peasant motif. If you can find it, use the heavy Art Deco café ware with its distinctive red band that is now turning up in housewares stores. Coffee can be served either demitasse or in huge bowl-like café-au-lait cups.

No candles and no flowers. To the French, eating is too serious a business for such frivolous distractions.

Greek

Blue is a good-luck color in Greece. To set a Greek table, use heavy woven linens—cloths, place mats, napkins—of off-white or blue.

For atmosphere, include a bowl of lemons as a centerpiece or a pottery bowl filled with fresh anemones or blazing red and orange poppies.

Avoid candles. Use, instead, bright light, like the pervasive sunlight of Greece.

Plates and dishes should also be heavy. You may be able to find blue-and-white crockery or hand-painted pottery with complicated floral designs. Use crude glass carafes with straight sides, or bottles covered with wickerwork. Wine and ouzo, the strong licorice-flavored liquor, are drunk from tumblers, either clear or colored. Pour the ouzo directly from the bottle.

Serve the food on hand-hammered brass and copper trays. Begin a meal with a huge platter of appetizers including cubes of snowy white feta cheese, salty black olives, tiny green pickled peppers, stuffed grape leaves and quartered red ripe tomatoes. Or serve a plate of feta and black olives. Greek salads should come to the table heaped on platters, never in bowls. Individual portions of taramosalata—creamy Greek caviar—can be served in hollowed lemon shells or scooped-out tomatoes.

Roast lamb or shish kebab can share the platter with a mound of rice. The kebab may come straight from the grill still on the skewers or be piled in the center of the platter, on top of the rice.

Moussaka should be served in a heavy, square pottery casserole.

Many Greek desserts are intensely sweet, so small portions will usually satisfy even the most ferocious sweet tooth. Serve pastries such as baklava cut into small squares or diamonds, on a small serving dish, but be sure to fill the dish to the edges so it won't look skimpy. Kourabiedes (Greek butter cookies) look wonderful on a heavy crockery plate (either white or light brown) dusted with confectioners' sugar. A bowl of pastel Jordan almonds is the perfect accompaniment for the dark bitter coffee.

Indian

The aesthetic in India is different from ours. We like black and white, beige, restraint; they like pink, orange and green, and they like them all together.

298

Think of the colors of turmeric, saffron and coriander, and you'll conjure up the atmosphere of an Indian table, rich with color, the dull glow of brass and lots of flowers.

Buy one of the ubiquitous inexpensive Indian bedspreads to use as a tablecloth. Buy another in a different pattern and cut it up into oversized napkins. Indians don't use knives and forks. They eat with the fingers of their right hand. Your guests won't do the same, but large napkins are a comfort anyway.

Lay flowers flat on the table instead of standing them up in vases. Scatter the stemless blossoms down the center of the table, or make a garland around a serving plate. For a formal dinner, lay out a geometric pattern on a tray in the center of the table using yellow, red and orange flower petals or different shades of dried beans.

Many Indians eat off metal platters, large plates called thalis. We would think of them as trays. The rice goes in the center, in a heap. Different curries and pickles are set around it in small metal cups on on the bare plate. If you can't find round metal trays, use multicolored plates with oriental designs instead. The important part is the arrangement of the food, with all the courses served at once.

321

For lighting, use low votive candles in colored holders, so that the light flickers through red, green or blue glass. Incense candles might be evocative of India, but would interfere with the flavors of the food.

If you have any inexpensive bazaar souvenirs, use them to decorate the table. Painted wooden bracelets with mirror insets make wonderful napkin rings. Don't scorn those bargain-priced stuffed elephants, brass temple bells or carved wooden trivets.

Italian

No matter that contemporary Italian tableware is among the most sophisticated in the world. When we set a table to "look Italian," what we set is a peasant table, a Sicilian table. It's chicken cacciatore for dinner, and out come the earthenware or pottery dishes, the brightly colored tablecloth and napkins, the wicker breadbasket, straw-covered bottles of red wine and dripping candles. *Ecco:* the mood is set.

299

In fact, the true look of Italian food is one of freshness, color and contrast. An assortment of perfect tiny vegetables glistening with oil, each in its own white dish, snowy cauliflower, oily red peppers, black and green olives, white cheese and red-brown sausage. Put each in its own rectangular white pottery dish and let the guests choose their own antipasto.

Nothing should look decorated or added for effect. Set the table with heavy white china. Pour red wine into medium-sized tumblers. Down the center of the table make a line of wine and mineral-water bottles, and glasses full of breadsticks. No flowers. Nothing consciously elegant. (In a family café in Milan we saw peanuts in their shells scattered down the middle of a long table.)

Pasta is the heart of Italian cuisine. It should be served from a heavy ceramic bowl that keeps it hot. Mix sauce and pasta as soon as they come from the pot to be sure that it stays hot. Then portion it into heavy white bowls made just for pasta. If you're lucky, you'll be able to find some without flowers painted on the bottom. They are larger than dessert dishes, smaller than soup bowls—just the right size for a first course.

For dessert, fruit, cheese and small cookies. And tiny cups of dark espresso coffee.

Japanese

When you set a Japanese table, you become part of a long and sophisticated tradition of food presentation. Nothing is done by chance. Every selection is deliberate and conscious, from the position of the chopsticks on the table to the way the fish is skewered to look as though it were still swimming through the water.

The key word is *restraint*. The arrangement of food should be, above all, neat. It's precisely the opposite of the cheerful Chinese jumble of color and shape. The tableware in both cases is similar: rice bowls, chopsticks, handleless teacups, ceramic spoons. But somehow, when it's all put together, the Chinese table looks haphazard and abundant, while there is about the Japanese meal a look of order, restraint and elegance.

Begin with the bare table. On it, if you like, bamboo mats, the sort that are used for making sushi. Or use bamboo trays as place mats.

On the mats, use many small dishes instead of one large one. They can be white, black, brown or pale celadon green. Small laquered bowls for holding dipping sauces or a few slices of cucumber. Raised wooden stands on which you set some shredded horseradish or two cubes of pork. Soup goes into small bowls that have their own covers, like Chinese teacups. The chopsticks are immediately in front of the diner, between him and the food. They are made of wood or laquered wood, and always point to the left, with the tips resting on a proper chopstick pillow of ceramic or wood or, in a restaurant, on the chopsticks' paper wrapping folded into a tidy knot.

At each place setting you put a china saki cup and a bottle holding the rice wine. Service is done from natural-colored earthenware pots, glazed only on the inside, or from heavy iron skillets.

No bouquets of flowers but, possibly, a single branch in a vase. Garnishes drawn from the tradition of *mukimono,* or vegetable carving: either totally abstract or quite realistic.

Above all, a sense of emptiness and space. Nothing should touch anything else. Where we see a half-empty plate, the Japanese see the relationship between the food and its background. Think of the plate, the tray or the table as bodies of water, and then think of the objects on them as islands emerging from the stream, and don't let them touch.

322

Mexican

Mexican cooking is country cooking—peasant food born in a tropical climate. The colors are the pinks and oranges of jungle flowers and the blue-green of the waters off the Yucatán. Use the pale green of avocados, mix shocking pink with orange and yellow. For a quieter table, combine bottle green and amber colored glass.

Mexican tableware is rough, often terra-cotta colored, with painted borders patterned in zigzags, spirals and circles. Sometimes there are stylized floral designs, roughly and irregularly drawn.

Each province has its distinctive style of pottery. In Oaxaca, for

301

323

example, they glaze it in forest green and dark brown. But the secret is that most rough peasant ware can fit on a Mexican-style table.

(Our government stopped the importation of cheap pottery, especially from Mexico, several years ago because the substantial quantities of lead used in the glazes reacted with acid foods and beverages to make a poisonous compound. If you own some that you're not sure of, use it with care. Many people still use such pottery, but only for serving, while others have polyurethaned or otherwise coated the dishes. To be safe, you could use them for display.)

Use roughly woven napkins on bare tables or on thick linen

cloths. Mix in lacy cloths, like the edging on a Mexican blouse. Look for hammered-tin service plates, trays and candelabra. Try gourds as ladles and bowls. Use colored tumblers. Decorate the table with Mexican ceramic fantasy figurines and candleholders, angels and animals painted white, pink and gold and covered with leaves and flowers.

Garnish the food with more food: sprinkles of grated cheese, shredded iceberg lettuce, flowers cut from radishes and carrots, avocado slices, black olives, corn husks and bunches of coriander.

For a festive platter, use real flowers in hot colors. Think about zinnias, marigolds and African daisies on a huge metal tray of orange-colored rice, chicken and sausage. The table should look as hot as the chilies.

Scandinavian

Our image of a Scandinavian table comes mainly from 1950s Danish Modern. Although this is no longer the look of Scandinavian design, it's better than what's happening there now, and it will undoubtedly prove to be an enduring twentieth-century style.

Choose from pale, rough-woven linens in natural tones to cover tables of unbleached oak and teak set with stainless-steel flatware. Serve food in stainless-steel and wooden bowls. Add colored candles in nontraditional shapes: either very fat or pencil thin. Or use masses of different-sized candles all in one color.

Use straight-sided pitchers with clean lines and plain, off-white dishes. Small white plates serve condiments. Provide salt in dark ceramic pots, and use rough-glazed casseroles for main dishes.

Enhance the table with fresh flowers in plain glass or stainless vases. Try to get wild flowers rather than cultivated ones, and add pine branches. Smooth wooden platters and breadboards, open pots of butter, dark bread sliced at the table, baskets of flatbread complete the look.

Mix this twentieth-century classicism with just a little bit of a folk motif, a hand-painted bowl or embroidered napkins.

5

HOLIDAY TABLES

Christmas

Christmas has its own symbols. We think "Christmas" when we see a star, angel, holly leaf, pinecone or the outline of a fir tree. All it takes is a snowflake, a candy cane, candle, bell, bird-and-pear (suggesting partridges in pear trees) or, always, the colors red and green.

Food as Decoration

Because it's a feast of plenty in the middle of the year's most barren season, Christmas is a time for a great display of food, a time when food is used for decoration.

Decorate the door with a mock della Robbia wreath. Buy an ordinary evergreen wreath and tie on clusters of tangerines, lady apples, Seckel pears, kumquats and gilded nuts.

Decorate the tree with food. Tie on Christmas cookies, strings of popcorn and cranberries, oranges and popcorn balls wrapped in colored ribbons and studded with cloves.

On the mantel, stick a fat candle in the top of a pineapple, a traditional sign of hospitality. Put tapers into oranges and shiny candy apples. Make Christmas-cookie place cards for the dinner table with the names written in icing.

You're not going to use all of these ideas at the same time. But you could. Christmas is one time of the year when everything can be decorated, when ordinary restraint is discarded, rather like at a children's party. It's also a time when it doesn't matter if the food looks artificially colored, so long as the colors are red and green. A time when clichés are preferred to innovations. Once decorations look new, they stop looking like Christmas.

Decorating the Dining Room

Modern Christmas gets its look from a fantasy of Victorianism, a period when less was definitely not more. So buy yards and yards of red and green ribbons (blue and white, if you're feeling subtle). Tie ribbon bows onto champagne glasses, on the handles of punch cups, the stems of eggcups, on stems of fruit. Use the ribbons for napkin rings, or to tie cookies onto the tree and wrap oranges into mock pomander balls.

Cover the table with a cloth to the floor and then with an overcloth. Gather the overcloth up to the table edge on each side and in the corners. (See illustration, TABLE COVERINGS, page 292.) Fasten it and accent it with a ribbon bow, holly branches or twisted evergreen garlands.

(Evergreen garlands are a boon for Christmas decorating. They're long ropes of needles attached to wire, available at florists everywhere soon after Thanksgiving. You order it by the yard.)

A miniature evergreen tree makes a striking centerpiece. Choose one about 3 feet tall and attach candleholders and candles to the branches.

Use red napkins with sprigs of holly tucked into the fold. Wrap a white damask napkin in red ribbons, and stick holly into the bow. On a Victorian table, tie up lace napkins with scarlet velvet ribbons, and let the ends trail over the table edge.

For a simpler table, use a length of unbleached natural burlap, simple dishes and a centerpiece of pine boughs and fat candles.

On Christmas morning, have breakfast in the kitchen, which you decorated the night before. Make bouquets of parsley tied with red ribbon. Put stocking presents into small wire or straw baskets lined with colorful napkins, one to a setting. In the center of the table, make a centerpiece out of a wire egg tree filled with lady apples or small Christmas balls and garnished with leaves.

324

Decorating the Food

Christmas garnishes can be as simple as a candy cane stuck into a bowl of diced fruit, as hokey as a peanut butter sandwich tied with a red ribbon to look like a present, as nice as a poached pear floating in a pool of crème de menthe.

Capture a bottle of vodka or aquavit in ice. Set it in an empty milk carton and pour water around it. Shove in evergreen branches and put the carton in the freezer. When you peel off the carton, the bottle will seem to float in a cube of frosty greens, and the drinks will be syrupy and icy-cold.

You can use tree greenery in place of parsley or watercress garnishes. Avoid holly berries, which taste bitter. And for heaven's sake, don't use poinsettia, which is poisonous.

But you can make instant winter on a serving plate by laying pine needles at one end and dusting them with a snowfall of powdered sugar. Arrange Christmas cookies on the rest of the plate, and on the bed of needles, place strawberries that you have dipped in bitter chocolate.

Use tree greens to garnish the turkey. Encircle the platter with long pine needles or an evergreen garland. On it, arrange tangerines, pomegranates, nuts and kumquats. Make orange cups, using one of the cuts we recommend, fill them with cranberry sauce and place them on the garland.

Drape the turkey with evergreen garland. Lay the swag over one thigh, around the breast and back over the other thigh. Attach it with toothpicks and accent with clusters of kumquats and whole cranberries. Then tuck more tufts of greenery under the neck and alongside the legs. Or just cross it with two lengths of strung cranberries.

Easter

When you decorate a table for Easter, you walk a narrow line. To one side lies springtime, to the other, terminal cuteness. The themes are all so damnably adorable: lambs, bunnies, baby chicks, eggs and blossoms. The safest plan is to think spring and concentrate on flowers. Then, if it can't be helped, add some eggs.

Easter is the time to put a clay pot of flowering bulbs in the middle of the table. If you have a really interesting egg—a Russian wooden egg, for example—tuck it between the stems.

Use the colors of early flowers for the cloth and napkins. Violet, pale yellow, green and, with all of them, white.

Put a May basket filled with flowers at every place setting.

At breakfast on Easter morning, use a wire egg holder. Fill it with brown and white eggs, and twist fresh daisy stems around the wires. Place a blue-and-white kitchen bowl of white eggs in the middle of the table.

After this, it's all downhill. Florists sell birds' nests. But what can you do with a fake bird's nest and keep your self-respect?

For Easter decorating in an old tradition, look at the section on EASTER EGGS (see page 122).

Halloween

Although there is no traditional Halloween meal, there is definitely food connected with this holiday. Halloween parties involve bobbing for apples, popping popcorn, foretelling the future in orange and apple skins and dipping into baskets of trick-or-treat candy. And the most emphatic Halloween symbol of all is made of food. It's a jack-o'-lantern.

The jack-o'-lantern goes in the front window to let trick-or-treaters know that there is candy in this house. Or it goes on the sideboard or mantelpiece, surrounded by autumn leaves and Indian corn.

The finished design is up to you. But we cast our vote for Traditional Scary. This is no place for a princess or for Groucho Marx. Better your basic goblin, with creepy cousins such as witch or pirate.

Choose a nicely shaped pumpkin. Before you cut, draw the design with a soft wax pencil.

Cut off the top and scoop out the insides. Carve a circular depression in the bottom, just the size for a votive candle. Or, if you'd rather use a plain candle, a slender nail stuck up through the bottom of the pumpkin will hold it securely.

Use a paring knife to cut out the eyes, nose and mouth. The eyes should be triangles, with or without sections left in place for eyeballs. (Cross-eyed? Why not?) The nose is a triangle, too. The mouth can be smiling or frowning. It should have a few snaggled teeth left in place.

If you're going to draw on the pumpkin with markers instead of cutting it, first rub the area gently with a fine steel-wool pad so that the color will adhere. Outline the features in black.

Now you can add the accessories. A long carrot nose? A fringe of hair made of yarn or licorice whips coming out from under the cap? A moustache made with broomstraws? A witch's hat made of black construction paper rolled into a cone? An eye patch? Tiny marshmallows pinned on with toothpicks for teeth? Just keep it childlike and scary.

If you want to add other Halloween decorations, make an arrangement of oranges and black licorice. Cover the top of a lollipop with white tissue paper, and tie it with black ribbon under the head to make a ghost. Make jack-o'-lantern faces on marshmallows, and place them in a ring, facing out, around an arrangement of apples and nuts.

Thanksgiving

Thanksgiving began, and continues, as a communal feast. You know the story. The early settlers, grateful for their first harvest and confident that they would be able to survive the New England winter, gave a party. They invited the Indians who had shown them how to plant corn, how to hunt the local game and gather mussels and oysters. Yet their Thanksgiving was very much in the tradition of harvest feasts, a tradition that stretches back at least to ancient Greece, and probably beyond that into prehistory.

For most Americans, however, the fantasy of Thanksgiving is dominated by Norman Rockwell. Remember that famous table with its white cloth set with the family's best white china? Remember the covered casserole, the centerpiece made of a tight little mound of fruit, the immense turkey?

Thanksgiving is a time for tradition, not for chic. It's a time for starched white tablecloths, brought out once a year, for complete china sets painted with lots of flowers, for hosts of mismatched serving dishes in painted china, spatterware and silver.

It's the look of middle-class America between the world wars, with memories of peace, prosperity and old-fashioned virtues. If you want to change it, you must become not more up-to-date, but even more old-fashioned.

325

You might even wish to re-create the look of the first Thanksgiving. Use a bare wooden table, with a runner—orange, brown or green—down its length, and on it, a centerpiece of tumbling squash, corn, pumpkins, fruit and nuts. Use wooden and pewter plates and mugs.

Or create a farmhouse Thanksgiving with a cloth of rough white fabric, a second cloth laid over it in checked gingham or an allover floral pattern. Add heavy white plates, spatterware and pewter.

Centerpieces

A harvest centerpiece makes sense on a Thanksgiving table. Start with a basket. Put in the largest vegetable: a pumpkin or turban squash.

Surround it with dried ears of corn in their husks, with zucchini, yellow squash and long red peppers. Fill in with walnuts and purple grapes.

Lay a branch, either bare or with autumn leaves, in the center of the table. Around it, arrange crab apples, Seckel pears, kumquats and nuts. Fill in with more leaves.

Make a circle of small pumpkins and pots of chrysanthemums standing on autumn leaves.

Place votive candles in red peppers, artichokes, small squashes.

Food

With the food, just as with the decorations, there is little need for innovation on the Thanksgiving table. If you must be creative, concentrate on the side dishes. And don't overdo it. Stay in the tradition. Instead of candied sweets, serve chestnut puree. Instead of peas, serve Brussels sprouts. Shape extra stuffing into balls, brown them in butter and bake them under the turkey.

Don't try to give every dish a special garnish. Emphasize the turkey by draping it in strings of cranberries or surrounding it with piles of purple grapes, lady apples and Seckel pears. Carve it at the table. Everything should be traditional, simple and abundant.